BURT'S LETTERS
from the
North of Scotland

BURT'S LETTERS
from the
North of Scotland

as related by
EDMUND BURT

———◆———

Originally published as

LETTERS
from
A Gentleman in the North of Scotland
to
His Friend in London

(S. Birt, London, 1754)

Introduction by
Charles W. J. Withers

Edited by
Andrew Simmons

Birlinn

This edition published in 1998 by
Birlinn Limited
Unit 8
Canongate Venture
5 New Street
Edinburgh EH8 8BH

First published in 1754 by
S. Birt, London

Second edition published in 1876 by
William Paterson, Edinburgh

Reprinted in 1974 by
John Donald Publishers Ltd, Edinburgh

ISBN 1 874744 90 4

British Library Cataloguing-in-Publication Data
A Catalogue record of this book is available from the British Library

The Publisher acknowledges subsidy from the Scottish Arts Council
towards the publication of this volume.

Typeset by Waverley Typesetters, Galashiels
Printed and bound in Finland by Werner Söderström OY

CONTENTS

---◆---

INTRODUCTION

by Charles W. J. Withers

Although not published until 1754, Captain Burt's *LETTERS from A Gentleman in the North of Scotland to His Friend in London* were chiefly written in the late 1720s, with the final one (Letter XXVI) dating from about 1737. This timing is important: the Jacobite defeat at Culloden was nearly twenty years into the future; Highland population was not to reach crisis levels and lead to overseas emigration for another sixty years; and Highland chiefs had not yet been replaced by landlords. Burt's *Letters* are of considerable significance, then, first and foremost as a means to understand and to 'see' the Highlands of Scotland before the 'Improvers' came, before agrarian change, population pressure and migration began to alter irrevocably the relationship of Highlanders to their land and to one another.

Burt notes in his opening letter that 'The Highlands are but little known even to the inhabitants of the low country of Scotland . . . But to the people of England, excepting some few, and those chiefly the soldiery, the Highlands are hardly known at all'. In general terms, his claim then was true: the Highlands were, to most outside observers, as much an unknown 'new world' as the Pacific islands or the African interior. Yet we should not see Burt as a commentator upon a 'traditional' Highlands, a region unaffected by the outside world and populated by peoples living a timeless and unchanging existence. For one thing, Highland people had close contacts with their Lowland neighbours from at least the later seventeenth century: in the movement of cattle, of grainstuffs, and, not least, in the southward migration of Highland labour to Lowland harvest. For another, the Highlands were not a uniform region: to the south and east of the Great Glen running between Inverness and Fort William, mixed farming prevailed, and some parts of the lowland fringes of Inverness-shire and Ross and Cromarty permitted limited grain agriculture. To the north and west, pastoralism was dominant. Burt notes these and other differences within the Highlands. That he does so is, in large measure, because he was a Highland resident. And here is a further reason why he is of value to the modern reader. He is not *of* the region, of course, and, indeed, he makes several comments by way of moral 'judgement' about Highlanders and their customs in terms comparable with later eighteenth-century travellers. But unlike later commentators, he is not a transient visitor, with opinions formed only upon passing acquaintance. His is a detailed eye, almost a local eye, with descriptions born of familiarity, even if he does express surprise and, occasionally, reproof at some of the things he sees. Further, his descriptions are based upon personal encounter. We are invited to accept what he tells us as credible partly because of his own social position – these are, after all, letters from a gentleman – and, partly, because he tells us *he* has seen these things. This is not a tale relayed either from the words of others, or from hearsay, or distilled from earlier accounts without corroboration. There is a real sense, sustained throughout the *Letters*, that we see what he saw and that we do so because his prose accurately conveys the difficulty of moving across the Highland landscape as well as the customs and manners of ordinary people.

Burt's work is not, in the strict sense of the term, a factual account. It does not have the narrative 'thread' of a tour or the ordered structure of an official report. Unlike many later commentators upon the region, he does not attempt understanding through statistical enumeration. He does not cover the whole Highlands: the south-west Highlands are hardly mentioned and he never visited the Outer Isles. Most of his travels are undertaken as trips from Inverness.

Excluding the first two letters which are about Edinburgh and Burt's travels north, about half the book is taken up with descriptions of Inverness and its inhabitants. And in some of his letters, he gets words wrong, putting in a rather curious English what he no doubt first heard in Gaelic and had translated and interpreted to him. Yet it is just these matters of style, of being able almost to hear his voice as he shares his discoveries with his correspondent that also make the work compelling reading as well as historically valuable. To criticise the work for lack of coverage or for a failure to effect an objective rhetoric in enquiry is to ignore the naturalness of Burt's prose and to misunderstand its context.

If, then, Burt's *Letters* are of interest and importance because of *when* they were written, *what* they tell us and *how* he tells us those things – as an engaging, yet partial, personal account of Highland society prior to its transformation – they do not reveal much about *who* Captain Burt was, *why* he wrote what he did and to whom precisely. We know only that Burt was an engineer, most probably contracted in the late 1720s to work on Highland roads and bridges then being built under the overall direction of General Wade. His last letter is revealing in this respect since not only was it written some time after the others – 'It is now about eight years since I sent you the conclusion of my rambling account of the Highlands' – it is also the most technical in language and structure. Under listed headings of the different ground conditions road engineers had to overcome, Burt documents the job of working in the Highlands, interestingly discusses locals' reactions to the new roads and what they were held to signify, and reflects upon his own earlier letters. But neither there nor elsewhere does he reveal much of himself.

Burt's plea to his London friend in Letter I that, for several reasons, the letters should remain private between them and an unnamed third party ought not be taken to suppose that Burt was a spy. His asking that the letters be kept private since 'The contrary might create inconveniences to me in my present situation' may be taken in several senses: the subjects of his enquiries might be less forthcoming if they knew their daily lives were being reported upon; Burt's own reputation as a gentleman officer might suffer; and, not least, his superiors might not be pleased to know that a military engineer had time enough on his hands to undertake such correspondence. After all, as Burt hints at the start of his *Letters* – 'for to tell you the truth, I have at present little else to do' – boredom was a more likely motive than covert military surveillance, removed as he was in Inverness from what was then understood as polite society. Burt's motive is much more likely to have been simple curiosity, a gentlemanly *virtuoso* enquiry mainly rooted in a desire to tell a friend about the novelty of customs and landscape in a part of Britain little known to outsiders, partly because he was an intelligent man with time on his hands in a strange land, and was driven not at all, to judge from what he tells us anyway, by a desire to publish and make money.

Burt had clearly been to Scotland before his duties took him to Inverness, noting in Letter VI how he had been briefly resident near Edinburgh several years before. Even so, the bustle and life of Edinburgh seems unfamiliar to him and he confesses to being confused by the language and geography of the town with its wynds and closes. Yet he also portrays vividly the sights and sounds of the capital's streets: the babble of tavern conversation, of being served food by a cook so dirty that a fellow diner observed that the cook would stick to the wall if thrown against it, and the precautionary cries of his guide calling out 'Hud your haunde' lest city dwellers launch 'the terrible shower' from their chamberpots into the lands below. These capacities – gentle humour, a powerful descriptive sense and a keen ear for local language – are apparent throughout his *Letters*, notably so in those concentrating on Inverness. Passing north, Burt is silent about those parts of Scotland lying between the two towns: 'I was well enough diverted with various prospects in my journey', noting only of the places where he stayed that 'The worst of all was the cookery' and that the livestock seemed to get smaller the further north he progressed.

Inverness is described as a middling size town with stone buildings to the centre but very poor quality dwellings – 'miserably low, dirty hovels' – on the edges of the town, the 'melancholy appearance of objects in the streets'. Local horses ill managed present a 'picture of misery'. Highlanders coming to market are, seemingly, the most pitiful sight of all: 'Good God! You could not conceive there was such misery in this island.'

In one sense, though strongly laced with hyperbole, these are *literal* descriptions of what, for Burt anyway, would have been very unfamiliar upon first encounter. And Burt's rather sensationalist prose clearly owes something to the fact that he was writing to someone both far removed from the facts themselves and never likely to encounter them. This is a rhetorical ploy more common among later eighteenth-century travellers and 'new world' explorers: a style that suggests wonderment and incredulity at the unusual yet, in so doing, tells us about the observer as well as the observed.

Partly, too, Burt is also offering a *moral* description. The lack of 'manufactories', the supposed lack of industriousness as a moral capacity amongst locals and claims that 'natives' were feckless, almost innately incapable of enterprise, are common to many later travellers' descriptions, and not just of the Highlands: these are judgements stemming from urbane society considering how the unknown geographies they encountered *should* be, rather more than how they actually were. If one wanted to maintain that social superiority that birth and social station at this time demanded, one's prose should follow suit: diminish the object of one's enquiry and accord it value only in the terms of the outsider. Burt shows something of these concerns and characteristics: Inverness, like many other places, lacks a local industry of any size – a 'melancholy consequence ... with respect to the common people' – and in Letter VII in particular, he returns to the themes of dirt, dust (on church pews and ladies' dresses), and slovenly cooks. In Letter VIII, dinner with a local Highland chief is memorable more for the competing smells of the diners' socks than for the sophistication of the fare and company. But his comments in such tones are relatively few and, importantly in terms of ourselves as later readers in knowing how to 'interpret' what he tells us, they are hardly apparent at all in later letters. Burt might still have *felt* a certain moral distance from Highlanders and their customs – his own social standing, local purpose and contemporary conventions would have demanded it – but his prose shows an increasing tolerance and understanding of the people amongst whom he lived and worked that make his *Letters* additionally important in respect of later commentators writing upon the changing Highlands. It is a tolerance rooted not in pity at the condition of the Highlander but in sympathy with them, in understanding the ways ordinary life was lived. His sympathy stems, indeed, from a concern neither to glorify Highland people nor to denigrate them, but, essentially, to record what he sees as the hard truths of making a living.

Letters VIII, IX and XI offer interesting descriptions of and commentary upon eighteenth-century church life and practices, in Edinburgh and in Inverness: the standards of oratory; womens' dress codes approved of by the clergy so as not to solicit an inappropriate gaze and stimulate the 'wandering thoughts of young fellows' on the sabbath; remarks upon the kirk sessions' scrutiny of pre-nuptial sexual liaison; and observations upon pre-wedding practices, the wedding ceremony itself, christenings and the nature of funeral processions and Highland funerary rites. This is Burt as social observer upon a Scotland largely long gone. And in Letter X especially, we get closer still to the people and events of the time in Burt's reproduction of a letter from one Donald McPherson, 'a young Highland lad' then abroad in Virginia and writing to his father in Inverness. We are not told if the McPhersons ever knew that their private correspondence had '. . . been lately been handed about this town, as a kind of curiosity' – no doubt to establish its authenticity, to marvel at its existence at all and to learn of kin far away – but through it we can hear and understand something of the experience of Highlanders overseas. It's almost best to read it aloud. 'Teer Lofen Kynt Fater', the letter begins ['Dear loving kind father'], and it goes on to report a wealth of incidental detail often lost in more formal historical narrative: how, amongst other things, there were 60 men on board, that 'Shonie Magwillivray . . . hat ay a Sair Heet' on the crossing [that is, was seasick], that the local planter 'lifes amost as well as de Lairt o Collottin' [the Laird of Culloden], and that the son had had the letter written for him by one 'Shams Macheyne' who 'hes pin unko kyn te mi sin efer I kam te de Quintrie'. Burt, it should be noticed at the end of his letter, offers a brief explanatory note about pronunciation to his London reader. The combined effect is to eavesdrop on the past: as the illiterate Donald McPherson gives voice to his thoughts to his father via his new friend-cum-scribe; as Burt 'translates' them for his distant friend; whilst we, like the folk in Inverness, are both informed and amused.

Burt's attempts to describe Highland landscape are hindered by the sheer scale of the scenes before him and, in contrast to documenting Highland social customs which 'give me little trouble more than the transcribing', he admits to finding topographic description 'my most difficult task'. It may be, of course that Burt spends the time he does upon the difficulties of travel and the nature of the terrain because he saw the landscape through the lens of his own training as a military engineer. What he does give us, however, notably in Letter XV, is of great historical value because it owes much more to earlier intellectual traditions of describing upland environments and an 'unfinished' Nature than it does to eighteenth-century and, thus, to 'modern' sentiments. Investing the Highland hills with notions of romance and sublime grandeur are late eighteenth- and early nineteenth-century practices. For Burt, this is not a landscape of aesthetic majesty. It is one of 'huge naked rocks', of 'monstrous excrescences' and of an all-pervading 'horrid gloom' where even the colours are disagreeable: mountain streams are 'dirty yellowish', the hills 'a dismal gloomy brown drawing upon a dirty purple'. Walking any distance was hard going, crossing fords a dangerous business although Burt, unlike the locals, refused to send his servant first into Highland rivers to test the current 'as is the constant practice of all the natives of Scotland'. Highlanders managed in such a harsh environment because of loyalty to their chiefs and to the clan system, he notes, and in his comments upon such matters (Letters XIX-XXI), Burt offers one of the earliest and most sympathetic accounts of Highland agrarian practices and of the Highland social system as óne founded upon loyalty and mutual deference.

His accounts of the clan system, of the love of Highlanders for their chief and his descriptions of the various retainers and functionaries in a chief's retinue owe nothing to that enduringly influential but false rhetoric of Romanticism and mythology through which Highland clans are usually figured. We should not expect him to have seen them in that way. What we would now see as 'Highlandism' with its tartanised fakery, swirling myths and the cult of Bonnie Prince Charlie had, quite simply, not yet been invented. Burt's tones in describing armed Highlanders, blood feuds between clans, Highlanders lifting cattle in raids to the south are even and unemotive, serving chiefly to describe what he sees and is told in order to relate the scene to his distant friend. These things, he is saying, are what goes on here. The people are not indolent, but proud. The clan system demands an unswerving fealty. Highland life can be, and for many is, a hard grind. And in making us aware of such circumstances, his letters get closer than many commentators to documenting the real social fabric of the historical Highlands.

Letters ends abruptly. Burt's tour of duty may be over. Perhaps the correspondent has tired of asking Burt questions: as he notes in his final letter, 'As my former letters relating to this country were the effects of your choice, I could apologize for them with a tolerable grace'. Burt did not seek justification for his writing them, but he did see a certain value in his having done so. He considered his letters superior 'for information or entertainment' to five other sorts of writing: genealogy; philosophical enquiry; 'Trifling antiquities, hunted out of their mouldy recesses'; 'Tiresome criticisms upon a single word', and, lastly, to 'Dissertations upon butterflies'. This may be so. But their significance now rests less in comparison with other forms of writing and not at all with what the author thought of them. They are, rather, important for what they reveal of social life in the Highlands in the past and for the questions they raise about the ways in which we should approach critical understanding of that past.

EDITORIAL NOTE

THIS edition has been made from that brought out in 1876 by the Edinburgh publisher William Paterson. This is itself a facsimile of the original, together with an Introduction (by R. Jamieson) and a History of Donald the Hammerer (a manuscript 'communicated' to Sir Walter Scott). Both these items are included here.

The underlying editorial principle has been to make Burt's text more accessible to the modern reader, whilst preserving as much as possible of the period flavour. Accordingly, changes have been kept to a minimum: Burt's syntax has not been modified and only minor amendments to punctuation have been made.

The original edition contains a large amount of italicization which has not been retained here. Where Burt draws attention to dialect terms, localised usage of words or attempts a phonetic transcription of dialect, the original italics have been replaced with quotation marks, and spelling has been left unmodernised. Italicization has been retained only for emphasis.

THE EDITOR
TO THE READER

I AM apt to imagine you may be curious to know by what means the following letters came to my hands, after the space of between twenty and thirty years.

The gentleman in whose possession they were, died some time ago, and through losses, unsuccessful lawsuits, and other disappointments, left his family in none of the best of circumstances; and, therefore you will believe I could obtain them no otherwise than by mineral interest.

The person who writ them, has not set his name to any one of them, and, it is very probable, he made use of that caution for reasons given in his introductory letter; but this is not very material, because, if I had known the name, in all likelihood I might have thought myself under an obligation to conceal it.

I cannot but think the writer has kept this promise he made his friend, of writing without prejudice or partiality; and this I the rather believe, because, at my first perusal of these letters, I met with several facts and descriptions, pretty nearly resembling others I had heard from officers of the army, and revenue, who had been in that part of the country; but their stories would have been the same, or very near it, if they had been free from the ludicrous and satirical manner in which they were delivered.

Ill-nature will excite in its unhappy vassals, a malignant satisfaction to find the truth (especially relating to mankind) disguised in an antique dress; and there is nothing more easy than to furnish out the masquerade with ridiculous outward appearances. But neither of our correspondents seems to have been inclined that way; for if the person, to whom these epistles were addressed, had been of that *trempe*, there is no doubt but the writer, who took so much pains for his information, would likewise have gratified him in that particular.

It must be owned, there are some few strokes that savour a little of the satyrical, but they are very few, yet just enough to shew, that if inclination had prompted, humour would not have been wanting; and even those few are only relating to such vices and vanities as might easily be reformed; and, as they are now made public, they may serve as admonitions to such as apply them to themselves.

What shameful portraits have been drawn for a Highlander! I shall only mention one, and that is, in the true-born Englishman.

His description is much more shocking than entertaining to any one who has the least humanity. But the owner of a chaste mind might have been well pleased to see the unknown face divested of the odious vizor.

It may be said —, that poem is a profest satyr, but I even deny it to be one; for a true satyrist is too delicate to lash with a flail.

There be some who have made a reproach of unavoidable poverty, and of customs and methods of acting, which (I now find), according to the nature of the country, and circumstances of the inhabitants, could not be changed for others to be more reasonable and commodious. But, far otherwise, the writer of these letters. He seems to have catched at all opportunities for excuse, and even commendation, and has not spared his own country, or countrymen, when the one deserved his animadversion, or the other required an acknowledgment; so far has he been from invidious comparisons.

I must own he has likewise kept his word in observing little order or method, for it plainly appears he took no pains about either; but then that very neglect has been the cause of more sudden variety (to use his correspondent's phrase), and the little stories that are scattered here and there (I think not much known in England), serve now and then to break, as the painter says, a too-long continued line of description.

I shall say no more in relation to his style, than that a nicety is seldom much regarded in familiar epistles from friend to friend, especially in long relations of facts, or other narrations; besides, he says himself, it would have taken up too much of his time to smooth his periods; and we all know that words and phrases will not dance into elegant order at the sound of a fiddle.

It may possibly be said, by some of the northern people, that the writer has borne too hard upon a part of the then inhabitants of Inverness. Of that I cannot pretend to make myself a judge, only that, as a reader, it does not seem to me to be so by the tenor of his other letters, and particularly by his appeal to the officers of the army who had been in those quarters; and surely this he would not have done (when he might have been so easily disproved) if he was conscious of untruths, and had the least regard to his friend's opinion of his veracity.

To conclude: If the facts, circumstances, and descriptions, contained in the following letters, are allowed to be just and genuine (as I really believe they are) may they not be given in evidence, against such as are fond of showing the wantonness of invention and drollery, upon objects altogether improper for that purpose and might not any one reasonably conclude, that such jokers believe all mankind to be ridiculous, who have not an affluence of fortune, or that entertain a garb, or customs different from their own, and were not born in the same parish? And, if so, I think they themselves are the fittest subjects of ridicule.

I am,
The impartial reader's
Obedient humble servant,
THE EDITOR

INTRODUCTION

THE author of the following letters (the genuineness of which has never been questioned in the country where the accuracy of his delineations may best be appreciated) is commonly understood to have been Captain Burt, an officer of engineers, who, about 1730, was sent into Scotland as a contractor, etc. The character of the work is long since decided by the general approbation of those who are most masters of the subject; so that it will be here only necessary to add such notices and remarks as may tend to illustrate the subject in general, as well as to prepare the reader for what is to follow.

And first, it may be expected that somewhat should be said of the antiquity of the Highlanders, and the unmixed purity of their Celtic blood and language, of which they are more proud than of other more valuable distinctions to which they have a less questionable claim.

Whence the first inhabitants of our mountains came, or who they were, it would now be idle to inquire. They have no written annals of their own; and the few scattered notices respecting them that remain, are to be gathered from strangers, who cannot be supposed to have had any accurate knowledge of their traditions concerning themselves. That a large portion of their population once was Celtic, cannot be doubted; but of this distinction, there seems to be less understood than the learned have commonly supposed. The traditions, superstitions, and earliest impressions of all the nations of the west, of whom in a less cultivated state, we have any knowledge seem to point to the east, the great cradle of mankind, as the land of their fathers; and we consider the Goths and Celts as deriving their origin as well as their language from the same source; the Celts having been the earlier, and the Goths the later wanderers westward. Although their complexion, language, religion, and habits, formed under different skies, and in different circumstances, exhibited in the end different appearances; yet the further back that we are able to trace them, the stronger the marks of identity are found to be; and presumptive evidence must be admitted, where positive proof is not to be expected. Of this kind of evidence, a very curious example is to be found in the end of the seventh book of *Temora*, where the following striking apostrophe occurs:

> *Ullin, a Charuill, a Raoinne,*
> *Guthan aimsir a dh' a om o shean,*
> *Cluinneam sibh an dorchadas Shelma,*
> *Agus mosglaibhse anam nan dàn.*
> *Ni' n cluinneam sibh, shil nam fonn:*
> *Cia an talla do neoil bheil ur suain?*
> *Na thribhuail sibh clarsach nach trom,*
> *An truscan ceò maidne is gruaim,*
> *Far an eirich gu fuimear a' ghrian*
> *O stuaidh nan ceann glas?*

Literally thus in English:

> O Ullin, Carruil, and Rouno,
> Voices of the time that has given way of old,
> Let me hear you in the darkness of Selma,
> And awaken the spirit of songs.
> I hear you not, children of melody:
> [In] what hall of clouds is your [rest] slumber?
> Strike ye the harp that is not heavy,
> In the gloomy robes of the mist of the morning,
> Where the sun rises very sonorous
> From the grey-headed waves?

Now, we know that all nations, having no light but that of nature to guide them, especially when in difficult circumstances, look with fond aspirations towards the land of their fathers, to which they believe and hope that their souls after death will return. This was the belief of the Goths in their state of probation in Scandinavia, and hall of Odin was in Asgard; and here we find the Caledonian bard, in the true spirit of the ancient and original belief of his country-men, supposing the hall of the rest of his departed friends to be in the east, where the sun rises.[1]

But whoever the first settlers were, their state was so precarious, that the same districts were continually changing their masters, sometimes in possession of one tribe, sometimes of another, some-times of Goths, sometimes of Celts, and finally, of a mixed race composed of both. In the earliest periods of which history or tradition have preserved any memorials, the characters and habits of life of the inhabitants of the Scottish Highlands and Isles, and of the northern men, with whom they had constant intercourse, so nearly resembled each other, that what is said of one, may be with equal justice applied to the other; and even their languages bear the nearer resemblance to each other, the further back that they are traced. Almost all the great Highland clans know not only whence they came to their present settlements, where from Ireland, Norway, or the Scottish Lowlands, but many of them know the precise time of their emigration. Of those who came from Ireland, the Celtic origin may well be doubted. We know that the Goths had established themselves in that island as early as the third century, and that Cork, Dublin, Waterford, Limerick, etc., were built by them.[2] As the descendants of these colonists were mariners and pirates, like their fathers, they kept to the sea coast, and were therefore more likely than uplanders to remove in the case of distress, discontent, or want of room at home, to the Scottish Highlands and Isles. That many of these isles

[1] This is only one of many passages in the poems ascribed to Ossian, which cannot reasonably be suspected because they refer to things which the compilers had no means of knowing; the beauty of the poetry has preserved it; but it is in direct opposition to all their own idle theories, and therefore all the commentators have passed it over in silence.

[2] In the Irish legend of Gadelus and Scota, their language is brought from Scythia, to which in the lax sense in which that appellation was commonly used, we see no great objection; and Gadelus is called the son of Niull, a name which has from time immemorial been peculiar to the Goths of the north and their descendants; so long ago was all distinction between Gothic and Celtic lost among the Irish! The Irish dictionary of O'Reilly (so creditable to the zeal and industry of the compiler) is a curious proof of this confusion of identity, as it contains, at least, ten Norse and Anglo-Saxon words, for one that is decidedly Celtic.

were inhabited by Goths from Scandinavia, at a very early period, is evident from the traditions, poetry, and tales, of the Highlanders. Indeed with respect to some of them, no traces remain of their having ever had any other permanent inhabitants.[3] With the history of the more recent arrival of the northern men in Orkney, Shetland, Caithness, Sutherland, etc., we are better acquainted from the Icelandic historians; and of the Hebrideans and Highlanders, properly so called, the great clans of McLeod, McLean, McNeil, Sutherland, McIver, Graham (*Gram*), Bruce (*Bris*), etc., are confessedly from the same quarter; if the McDonalds and McKenzies (to the latter of whom we attach the McRras) came immediately from Ireland their designations nevertheless show that they were not originally Celtic; the Frazers (*de Fresale*), and the Chisholms (whose real name is *Cecil*) went from the Lowlands, as did the Gordons, and the Stewarts of Appin and Atholl; the Kennedeys (one of the last reclaimed of all the clans) were from Carrick and its neighbourhood; the Campbells (*de campo bello*) are allowed to be Normans; the Murrays, as well as the McIntoshes, McPhersons, and other branches of the *Clan Chattan*,[4] are generally understood to have come from the interior of Germany; and, in short, with the exception of the Macgregors, their descendants the Macnabs, the [Irish?] Macarthurs, and a few others of inferior note, there seem to be none of the ancient Celtic race remaining.

How the men were thus changed, while the language continued, is easily accounted for. The frequent appeals made to the king by chiefs at war among themselves, sometimes drew upon them the chastisement of the Scottish government, which was fond enough of

---

[3] The oldest appellation by which the Hebrides are known to have been designated was *Innse nan Gall*, 'the Isles of the Strangers'. The ancient kingdom of Galway in Ireland had its denomination from the same circumstance; and the wild Scot of Galloway in Scotland can hardly be presumed to have been a Celt.

[4] The name of Cameron (Lat. *Camerarius*) seems to have been at first a title of office, such as could not have originated in the Highlands. It answers to the Scottish and English Chalmers, Chaumers, Chambers, Chamberlain, etc. McKay is spelt at least a dozen different ways; but, as it is uniformly pronounced by the Highlanders, it seems to mean the son of Guy. But the three oldest worthies in the genealogical tree of the Reay family stand thus: Morgan, Mac, Magnus, Vic, Alaster (Alexander); a delectable jumble of British, Gothic, and Greek names, for the foundation of an hypothesis!

seizing such opportunities of extending its own influence. Expeditions were fitted out, encouragement was given to the neighbours of the devoted party to join their array, and wherever the army went, submission and order were produced for the time; but the state of the country remained the same as before. The possessions of the parties against whom the vengeance of the invaders was directed, were given, partly to new settlers from the Lowlands, and partly to their more powerful or more politic neighbours, as a bribe to ensure their favour to the new arrangements. These colonists, being mostly young male adventurers consulted their own interest and security by marrying women of the country, and the children of such marriages, being left in childhood entirely to the care of their mothers, grew up perfect Highlanders in language, habits, and ideas, and were no wise to be distinguished from their neighbours, except that, perhaps, they were less civilized, being strangers to the cultivation peculiar to the country of their fathers, without having acquired in its full virtue that of the country in which they were born.

The Scandinavians, who overran a great part of the isles and adjacent districts of the mainland, brought few women from their own country, and their descendants were naturalized in the same manner; and the best dialect of the Gaelic is now spoken by those clans whose Gothic extraction has never been disputed. Their tales, poetry, and traditions, continued with the language in which they had always been delivered down from one generation to another.[5]

[5] 'How shall we sing the Lord's song in a strange land?' is an exclamation, the pathos of which can never be fully appreciated by him who has never quitted the land of his fathers. The bodies and understandings of men are more easily transferred from one region to another, than their spirit, particularly that spirit which is the source, soul, and essence of poetry; and we know of no colonists, properly so called, that have produced any good original poetry. The Greek colonies ceased to be poetical as soon as their identity with the parent states ceased; the Goths, Lombards, Burgundians, Franks, Normans, Anglo-Saxons, and Danes, had plenty of mythic, heroic, and romantic poetry in their own country, which continued to be the delight of the generations that emigrated, while their original impressions remained; but they produced nothing of the kind in their new settlements. It was the same with the Scandinavians, who settled in the Highlands and Isles; and we are of opinion, that, of all the fine national poetry of the old school, preserved till a late period among our mountaineers, none was composed after the arrival of these strangers among them. The Goths lost their own poetry, with their language; and although locality, with the prejudices and enthusiasm thence arising, added to the astonishing

From the accounts to be found in various parts of this work, particularly in the Gartmore MS, it will be seen that, from the manner in which the lands, the superiority of which belonged to the chief of a clan, were portioned out by division and subdivision, according to proximity of blood, to the cadets of great families, the aboriginal inhabitants of the country must in the end have been actually shouldered out of existence, because no means were left for their support, and consequently they could not marry and be productive. These men, attached by habit, language, and prejudice, to their native country, upon which they had little claim but for benevolence, became sorners and sturdy beggars, and were tolerated, and supported, as the lazzaroni were in Naples, and as Abraham-men, and sturdy beggars of all sorts, were in England, after the suppression of the monasteries, and before there was any regular parochial provision for the poor. From this system it arose, that each Highland clan at last actually became what they boasted themselves to be – one family, descended from the same founder, and all related to their chief, and to each other.

If the chiefs of so many such clans were Goths, how is it possible that the pure Celtic blood should have continued its current, unpolluted, among them, till the present day? The Celtic form of their language has been sufficiently accounted for; and its identity with the Irish proves nothing more than what we know to have been the case, that both dialects, having passed through nearly the same alembic, have come out of nearly the same form, with much more purity than could well have been expected, and much less than their admirers have generally claimed for them.

For the illustration of the characters and manners of our mountaineers, such as they were in the days of our author, it will not be necessary to go further back in time than the period when

---

retentiveness of memory, produced by constant habit and exercise (which disappears upon the introduction of letters), preserved among their descendants the Gaelic strains which they found in the country, with the language in which they were clothed; the spirit, feeling, and irresistible impulse which first inspired them died away, and nothing new of the same kind was afterwards attempted with any success. If these observations are allowed to be just, they will serve to throw considerable light upon a subject which has hitherto given rise to much unreasonable and ill-judged cavilling.

their condition began to differ from that of their neighbours, and submission and tribute were required of them by the kings of Scotland, to whom they owed no homage, and whose general enmity was less to be feared than their partial protection. Their liberty, their arms, and the barren fastnesses of their country, were almost all that they could call their own; a warlike race of men, under such circumstances, are not likely to give up their all with good will; and those who had not enough for themselves, must have been little disposed to contribute anything for the support of a power which it was certainly not their interest to strengthen.

Emigrants from Ireland, or from Scandinavia (most of whom had withdrawn from the usurpations of a sovereignty in their own country, to which their proud spirits could not submit),[6] whether they obtained their settlements by conquest or by compact, as they had been accustomed to consider their swords as the sole arbiters of their rights, were not likely to put their acquisitions at the mercy of a king to whom they owed no allegiance, so long as they had the means of asserting their independence. Of the state of our own mountaineers when these strangers first arrived among them, we know very little; but the Irish, with whom they had constant inter-course, and who inhabited a much finer country,[7] must have been in a very rude state indeed, when they suffered themselves to be conquered by a handful of Englishmen. But whatever the previous state of the country was, such an accession of ambitious and adventurous pirates and freebooters to their population, was not likely to contribute to the tranquillity of the neighbourhood; and after the establishment of the English in Ireland the constant intercourse between the Highlanders and Irish afforded the English an opportunity of making alliances with the Highland chiefs, whom they engaged to make diversions in their favour by attacking the Scots, as the French stirred up the Scots against the English.

[6] See Snorro's *Keimskringla, Orkneyigagasa,* the *History of the Kings of Man and the Isles,* Torfœus, etc.

[7] It is probable that the poverty of the Scoto-Gael of that day was in their favour, and that they were in many respects superior to the Irish, because they were altogether free from the debasement of character produced by the clergy of that age, in every country where they acquired such influence as they then had in Ireland, the island of saints.

The attempts made from time to time to civilize the country, by partial colonization from the Lowlands, had very little effect, as the colonists uniformly adopted the spirit and habits of the natives, it being more agreeable and easy to lay aside the restraints imposed by an artificial state of society, than to adopt them; but some better results attended the policy of obliging the refractory chiefs to attend the court, or surrender themselves to some man of rank, under whose surveillance they were to remain till pardoned; after which they were to present themselves annually, either in Edinburgh or elsewhere, to renew their assurances of good behaviour. This produced at least a more intimate acquaintance, and consequent connection, between the gentry of the Highlands and Lowlands, and made the former ambitious of acquiring those accomplishments, which might justify their pretensions to a distinction and consideration, which they had no other means of supporting, beyond the range of their own mountains. Limited as the diffusion of book learning certainly was among them, one thing is nevertheless unquestionable, that history, poetry, and music, were the favourite recreations of their leisure, among the lowest vulgar; and their clergy and physicians, who were all gentlemen, read and wrote, both in their mother tongue, and in Latin. From the Privy Council record, at the beginning of the seventeenth century, it appears that the gentlemen of note, although they understood English, commonly signed their names in a bold distinct Irish character (as it is called), which shows that they were accustomed to writing in their own language, and probably were, partly at least, educated in Ireland, to which country all who adopted either poetry or music as a profession, were uniformly sent to finish their education, till within the memory of persons still living.

The disturbances in the reign of Charles I, opened a new era in the history of the Highlanders; but it is much to be regretted, that, for a long period after, having no historians of their own, their friends durst not speak the truth of them, and their characters have therefore been entirely at the mercy of their bitterest enemies, who knew them only to hate them, in proportion as they feared them. Of all their virtues, courage was the only respectable quality conceded to them, and this out of compliment to the best disciplined troops of the day, whom, with less than equal numbers, they had so often routed; but even their courage was disparaged, being represented as mere ferocity, arising from ignorance, and a blind and slavish submission to their chiefs. To speak of them otherwise, beyond the precincts of their own glens, was so unsafe, that in 1744 and 45, all the measures adopted and recommended by President Forbes, were near being frustrated, and he himself persecuted as a Jacobite, because he spoke and wrote of them like a gentleman and a man of discernment, being almost the only man of his party that had the liberal spirit and good sense to do so.[8]

In one great and radical mistake, all our historians agree. They represent the attachment of the clans to the house of Stewart, as cherishing the ferocious habits, and retarding the civilization of the Highlanders; whereas the very reverse of this was the case. The real friends of the house of Stewart, in England, and more particularly in Scotland, were distinguished by a refined education, high breeding, elevated sentiments, a chivalrous love of fame, a noble and dis-interested devotion to a cause which they believed to be good, and a social, warm-hearted, conviviality and frankness of character, totally different from the sour, intolerant, and acrimonious spirit of Presbyterian bigotry in the north,[9] and the heartless and selfish saving knowledge of the south—

> When the very dogs at the English court
> Did bark and howl in German.[10]

[8] It is no small recommendation of the report of Marshal Wade, that appears from internal evidence, as well as from other circumstances, to have been drawn up in concert with President Forbes (one of the first men of his time), if not by him. Indeed a sketch of such a report has lately been discovered among the Culloden papers, a copy of which Colonel Stuart of Garth, with his usual politeness and liberality, very kindly offered to communicate to the present writer; and it has not been made use of, only because it does not differ materially from the revised copy presented to Government.

[9] This is said of a century ago; to which we are happy to add, that among the Presbyterians of the Establishment in Scotland, acrimonious bigotry is now about as rare as enlightened liberality then was.

[10] It is much to be regretted, that Captain Burt was, by his situation in Scotland, precluded from all intercourse with those who were suspected of attachment to the house of Stewart, and obliged to depend for his information and experience, entirely upon the opposite party. If he had dared to associate with the Cavaliers, his opinion of the manners and spirit of the Scots, even in those times of common suffering, restless impatience, and general animosity (political and religious, as well as national),

From the state of their country, the political bias of the Highlanders, and the éclat which they had acquired under Montrose and Dundee, the eyes of all Europe were turned towards them as the only hope of the house of Stewart. Their chiefs were courted by, and had frequent personal intercourse with the friends of that family who were of most note, both in Scotland, England, and Ireland, and on the continent. Studying to accomplish themselves for the part they had to act, and always received with the greatest distinction in the best society, they became statesmen, warriors, and fine gentlemen. Their sons, after passing through the usual routine in the schools and universities of Scotland, were sent to France to finish their education. As the policy of the Whig governments was to crush and destroy, not to conciliate, and they found neither countenance nor employment at home, they entered into the French or Spanish service, and in those countries were, from political views, treated with a distinction suitable, not to their pecuniary circumstances, but to their importance in their own country. Great numbers of the more promising of the youth of their clans joined them; and, in order that the luxurious indulgencies of a more favoured climate might not render them unfit or unwilling to settle in their own country, at the end of two or three years they returned for a time to their relations, with all their accomplishments in knowledge and manners, and, with their relish for early habits still unimpaired, resumed the quilted plaid and bonnet, and were replaced in their regiments abroad by another set of young adventurers of the same description. Thus among the gentry, the urbanity and knowledge of the most polished countries in Europe were added to a certain moral and mental civilization, good in its kind, and peculiar to themselves. At home, they conversed with the lower classes, in the most kindly and cordial manner, on all

---

would have been very different. Of the kind of information to be derived from Whigs of that day, an excellent specimen will be found in Graham of Gartmore's MS, where, although the sentiments often savour of party spirit and personal dislike, the particular statements are very curious and valuable, and being drawn up with considerable ability, make that article an important historical document. It will be remarked, that in the *Letters upon the Highlands*, where our author depends chiefly upon his own observation, which was shrewd and discriminating, and upon his understanding, which was enlightened and liberal, there is little to be objected to.

occasions, and gratified their laudable and active curiosity, in communicating all they knew. This advantage of conversing freely with their superiors, the peasantry of no other country in Europe enjoyed, and the consequence was, that in 1745 the Scottish Highlanders, of all descriptions, had more of that polish of mind and sentiment, which constitutes real civilization, than in general the inhabitants of any other country we know of, not even excepting Iceland. This a stranger, who, not understanding their language, could see only the outside of things, could never be sensible of. Book learning, it is true, was confined to the gentry, because in a country so thinly peopled, schools would have been useless; they were too poor to have private instructors; and they had good reasons for looking with no favourable eye upon anything that was Saxon. But most of the gentlemen spoke Gaelic, English, Latin,[11] and French, and many of them Spanish, having access to all the information of which these languages were the vehicles. The lower classes were, each according to his gift of natural intellect, well acquainted with the topography of their own country, and with its history, particular as well as general, for at least three centuries back; they repeated and listened to, with all the enthusiastic delight of a thorough feeling and perfect intelligence, many thousand lines of poetry of the very highest kind[12] (for such they really had among them in abundance, notwithstanding the doubts which the dishonesty of MacPherson and his associates has raised on that subject); and their music (which, as it speaks the

[11] Such of the foreign officers stationed in the Highlands, in 1746, as could not speak French, found themselves at no loss among the gentlemen of the country, who conversed with them in Latin; an accomplishment which, we fear, very few of their grandsons can boast of.

[12] My very learned and excellent friend Mr Ewen McLauchlan, now engaged in preparing a dictionary of the Gaelic Language, a few years ago translated the first four books of Homer's *Iliad* into Gaelic verse. This translation he read, in the neighbourhood of Fort William to groups of men and women of the very lowest class, shepherds and mechanics, who had never learnt the power of letters. They listened to him with such enthusiasm as showed that the beauties of the composition had their full effect, and made such remarks as would have put to shame the comments of better instructed critics. We should like to see an Englishman make a similar experiment upon a party of clowns, even of comfortable citizens, of his own country. Book learning is sometimes overrated. A Highlander now learns from books to despise the lore of his fathers, whose minds were much more cultivated than his own; and this is almost all that he does learn.

language of nature, not of nations, is more intelligible to a stranger) is allowed, when performed con amore, to be the production of a people among whom the better sympathies of our nature must have been cultivated to a great extent. These facts indicate a very high degree of intellectual refinement, entirely independent of the fashion of their lower garments,[13] from the sight of which, and the sound of a language which they did not understand, their neighbours were fully satisfied of their barbarity, and inquired no further.

In justification of this account of their character in 1745, in addition to the information procured in the country, as well as in the Lowlands and in England, we can with confidence appeal to the letters of their chiefs, and to the public documents and periodical publications of the time, although these last were written by their bitterest enemies, with a view to influence the public against them. From all the information we have been able to collect, it appears that in their whole progress to and from Derby, their conduct, all circumstances considered, was not only orderly and proper, but, in innumerable instances, in the highest degree humane and magnanimous.[14] In England, the courtly elegance, in manners and conversation, of the Highland gentleman, their dignified deportment,

[13] Delicacy, like civilization, is a relative, and not an absolute term. A gentleman who, in the days of Henry VII of England, had appeared in tight breeches or pantaloons, without a *brayette*, would have been punished for an indecent exposure of his person. A Russian boor wears his shirt *over* his pantaloons, and considers our fashion as impudently indelicate. Who is right?

[14] Inconvenience from the presence of so many strange guests was unavoidable. They wanted horses and arms, which they received from their friends, and took from their unfriends, but with the assurance of indemnification as soon as King James was established on the throne. The common men, also, when not under the eye of their officers, sometimes took shoes which they did not always pay for; but he that looked at their feet, and felt their purses, would have been more disposed to pity the necessity than complain of the outrage. If outrages did take place, it was not from the clansmen, who were too jealous of the honour of their name, to do anything that was discountenanced by their superiors. But in all cases of civil war, there are found in every country great numbers of loose and disorderly persons, who are always ready to take shelter under the standard of insurrection, from the vengeance of the laws which their crimes have provoked. Many such, chiefly from the Lowlands, accompanied the army of Charles, under circumstances that rendered the keeping up good discipline, with respect to them, absolutely impossible. There were still greater numbers of these outlaws and broken men out in 1715, who, after the failure

the discipline they preserved among their men, but, above all, the kind-hearted, sensible, and considerate good nature and indulgence which they everywhere manifested towards women and children (a strong feature in the Highland character, and the best proof of true civilization), which was so different from what the English had been led to expect, made so favourable an impression, and formed such a contrast to the insolent brutality of the king's troops, officers and men, who marched down after them, that in many instances, which we know from the parties concerned, the women (for the men durst not speak out) could not help telling the latter, 'When the rebels, as they are called, were here, they behaved very differently – *they* behaved like gentlemen – quite like gentlemen – God help them!' Such reproaches, so justly provoked, and so often repeated, produced only aggravation of insult and abuse, and (such was the spirit of the time) ladies of the greatest respectability were, by officers of rank, damned for Jacobite b—s, and told that they were all rebels together, if they durst avow it, and deserved to have their houses burnt over their heads![15]

With the exception of Mrs Grant's admirable essays, and those of the Rev Dr Graham of Aberfoyle, almost all the accounts of the Highlanders have been written either by enemies, with all the virulence of party spirit, or by strangers, from partial information; and, consequently, hardly anything has been said of them but to their disadvantage. Hence the vague and idle declamations about deadly feuds between clan and clan, bloody conflicts, desperate encounters, depredations, robberies, murders, assassinations, 'and

---

of the Earl of Mar, found sympathy and shelter among the Jacobite clans; and it was of such vagabonds that the rabble was composed who, in 1719, joined the 300 Spaniards, and were concerned in the skirmish at Glenshiel, of which the government made a handle for exercising all manner of tyranny and oppression upon those who had no concern in it.

[15] One young widow lady in Cheshire, from whose daughter we had the anecdote, told a party of officers on such an occasion, 'If I am not a Jacobite, it certainly is not your fault – Ye have done all ye could to make me one!' An observation, the truth of which would have been sensibly felt by the king's troops, had the Highland army been in a condition once more to enter England, and avail themselves of the favour which their own good conduct and the insolence of their enemies had procured them in that country.

all manner of licentiousness'. In answer to all which, we shall only observe, that every clan was a little community by itself, under circumstances by no means favourable to quiet life among a poor, free, bold, and hardy race of men; and ask the dispassionate reader, what all the great and polished nations of the earth were doing, while the mountaineers of Scotland were thus murdering one another? Amid the proud triumphs of that civilization under which we are now supposed to live, it is mortifying to reflect, that in the course of twenty years, during the last war, there was twice as much Highland blood split (upwards of 13,000 have been enlisted into one single regiment!) as was shed by Highlanders on their own account, in any way whatsoever, during the three centuries that preceded the abolition of the feudal system among them in 1748![16]

That they lifted cattle is true – and this was so common, that the poor beasts, like their fellow denizens of the wilderness, the deer and roe, seldom knew to what glen they belonged – but these things were managed in a way peculiar to themselves, and so seldom occasioned bloodshed, that with all their 'herships', 'riefs', 'hot-trods', and rescues, we may venture to affirm, that ten Yorkshiremen lost their lives for horse-stealing, for one Highlander that died in a case of cattle-lifting.

Private robbery, murder, and petty theft were hardly known among them. It has been said that there was nothing to steal; but there was comparative wealth and poverty in their country, as well as elsewhere; and the poorer the people were, the stronger was the temptation, and the stronger must the principle have been that enabled them to resist it. And here, for the sake of illustration, it

[16] This is a melancholy truth, not a political reflection. We are sensible that the war in which they were engaged could not have been avoided, without giving up all that ought to be dear to a brave and free people; and that the unshaken firmness with which it was prosecuted, under the most discouraging circumstances, has been the means of saving Europe from the last state of political and moral degradation, in which the voice of nature, truth, and honour, would have been utterly stifled, and no example of freedom left for the regeneration of mankind. At the breaking out of the French revolution, France was called the most civilized country in the world, and this insulting jargon still continues in the mouth of a party; but surely Rob Roy and the clan Gregor, at a time when their neighbours hunted them down with bloodhounds, were humane and gallant fellows, when compared with Bonaparte, Massena, Suchet, Davoust, and Vandamme!

may not be out of place to say somewhat of the heavy accusations brought against the clan Gregor, particularly in Graham of Gartmore's MS. As there is no end to the clamours which have been echoed from one generation to another, against this disorderly tribe, we shall state a few simple facts, to show the nature of their irregularities. They had long been deprived of their lands, their name, their political existence, and the protection of the laws, and left to provide for, and protect themselves as best they might. Their lands had been appropriated by their more powerful and politic neighbours, particularly the predecessors of the Duke of Montrose. This, and that nobleman's new-fangled Whig politics,[17] had exposed him particularly to their indignation, which he shared with Graham of Gartmore, and other gentlemen of the clan, who, having adopted the same principles, were regarded as recreant Grahams. When they lifted the Duke's cattle, took his rents from his steward, or emptied his girnel of the farm meal after it had been paid in, they considered themselves as only taking what ought to have been their own. The manner in which this was commonly done, shows how unjustly they were accused of general cruelty and oppression to their neighbours. On one occasion, Rob Roy, with only one attendant, went to the house in which the Duke's tenants had been convened to pay their rents; took the money from the steward in their presence; gave them certificates that all had been duly paid before he seized it, which exonerated them from all further claim; treated them liberally with whisky; made them swear upon his dirk, that not one of them would stir out of the house, till three hours after he was gone; took a good-humoured leave of them; and deliberately returned to the braes. Those who know the spirit of the Grahams of that day, will be satisfied that this could never have taken place had the tenants not been very well pleased to see their money come into Rob's hands. When called out by the Duke to hunt down Rob and his followers, they always contrived to give him timely warning, or to mislead the scent, so that the expedition came to nothing. When the Duke once armed them for defence, they sent notice to Rob's nephew, Glengyle, to come round with such a force as would be a decent excuse for

[17] See the character of the first Whig Marquis of Montrose, in Lockhart of Carnwath's *Memoirs of Scotland*, published in 1714.

their submission, and collect the arms, which they considered as a disagreeable and dangerous deposit; and when the McGregors took the field in 1715, the cavalier spirit of the Grahams rose, and many of the Duke's dependents, scorning their superior and his politics, followed their standard. This showed that they did not consider the braes of Balquhidder as a bad neighbourhood.

In all the thinly-peopled districts by which the McGregors were surrounded, the whole property of the tenants was constantly at the mercy of thieves, if there had been such in the country. The doors of their houses were closed by a latch, or wooden bolt; and a man with a clasp-knife might in a few minutes have cut open the door, or even the wicker walls of the house. Detached from the dwelling-house, from fear of fire, was a small wicker barn, or storehouse, still less carefully secured, in which they kept their whole stock of hams, butter, cheese (for they then had such things), corn, meal, blankets, webs, yarn, wool, etc. These houses and barns were often left un-protected for days together, when the people were abroad cutting and winning turf, making hay or reaping for their superior, or tend-ing their cattle in distant pastures This was the case all over the Highlands; yet nothing was ever stolen or disturbed – of what civilized country, in the best of times, can as much be said?

A spirit of revenge has too often been attributed to them, as a distinguishing feature of character; and the ancient prejudice on this subject remains, long after the habits in which it originated have disappeared.[18] In a certain state of society, in all countries, revenge has been not only accounted manly and honourable, but has been bequeathed as a sacred trust, from father to son, through ages, to be wreaked as an indispensable duty of piety. This was particularly the

---

[18] Campbell of Glenlyon lived to a good old age, and died a natural death, in the midst of the relations and friends of the McDonalds of Glencoe, whose massacre he had acted such an infamous part. In 1745, when the Highland army was encamped in the neighbourhood of the house of the Earl of Stair, whose father had been the chief author and orderer of that massacre, and who himself commanded a regiment in the king's service, Prince Charles, apprehensive of some outrage from the Glencoe men, sent a guard to protect the Earl's house; on which the McDonalds immediately quitted the camp; and although at that time utter ruin must have been the certain consequence of a separation from the army, they were with great difficulty prevailed upon to return, so strong was their virtuous indignation at being thought capable of a cowardly revenge, and visiting the iniquities of the father upon the children.

case among the Scandinavians, from whom many of the Highlanders are descended; and as they remained longer than their neighbours in a state in which they had no laws to appeal to, there can be no doubt that many things were done in the way of retaliation, which would now be considered as lawless and violent; but, as the sum of infliction from wilful resentment among them bore no proportion to the sum of infliction from outraged laws in other countries, the balance in favour of humanity and forbearance, even in the most turbulent times we are acquainted with, will be found to be considerably in their favour. A man killed at his own fireside by him whom he had injured, was talked of for ages, while five hundred such persons hanged at Tyburn were forgotten as soon as cut down![19]

Men of strong and lively feelings are generally earnest in their likings and dislikings; but notwithstanding the constant provocations they have been receiving, during the last thirty years, from their landlords, land-stewards (generally English or Lowland attornies!), Lowland tacksmen, farm appraisers, and farm jobbers, who live among them, or occasionally visit them, like the pestilence, with oppression, insult, and misery in their train,

Destruction before them, and sorrow behind;

in the midst of these grievous and daily wrongs, wilful fire-raising, houghing of cattle, and assassination, so common among their neighbours, are unheard of among them!

On the subject of drunkenness, of which they have been so often accused, we refer the reader with confidence to Mrs Grant's essays,

[19] If a robbery, murder, or assassination did take place, they showed their horror of the deed by raising a cairn of memorial on the spot, to point a salutary moral to all succeeding generations. The deep and lasting impression made by such occurrences showed how rare they were; but when the delinquencies of many centuries were (for want of other news) related to a stranger, in the course of a single evening, with as much minuteness of detail as if they had occurred but yesterday, neither his own feelings, nor his report to others, were likely to be favourable to a people among whom he had heard of so many enormities. But who would look for the character of the English nation in the Newgate Calendar? Captain Burt saw a murderer hanged at Inverness: the hangman was eighty years old, and had not yet learned his trade, from want of practice! In the populous county of Moray, in which the present writer was born, there have been only two executions in his time, being a space of forty-six years.

which are written in the true spirit of candour and of truth, and from an intimate and thorough knowledge of her subject. Donald is a lively, warmhearted, companionable fellow: likes whisky when he wants it, as others learn to do who visit his country; and is no enemy to a hearty jollification upon occasion; but we never knew in the Highlands an habitual drunkard, who had learnt that vice in his own country, if we except such, about Fort William and Fort Augustus, as had been corrupted by the foreign soldiers resident among them. This was the case about thirty years ago, but a melancholy change has since taken place. At that time, the privilege of distilling at Farrintosh had not been withdrawn from the Culloden family, and good whisky was so cheap (about ten pence an English quart), that there was no temptation to illicit distillation. At present, the poor distressed and degraded peasants (who would still do well if they could, and cling to their native glens, the land of their fathers, to the last) are compelled, by hard necessity, to have recourse to smuggling, in order to raise money to gratify the insane avarice of their misguided and degenerate landlords, who, with a view to immediate gain, connive at their proceedings, without considering that their own ruin must be the consequence of the demoralization of their tenants. Illicit stills are to be found everywhere: encouraging drunkenness is encouraging trade; and the result is such as might be expected. But that the Highlander, when he has fair means of showing himself, is still averse to such profligacy, is proved by the conduct of the Highland regiments,[20] which, amid the contagion of bad examples, and all the licences peculiar to camps and a military life, have always been distinguished above all others wherever they have been stationed, for their sobriety, honesty, and kindly good nature and good humour.

[20] Of these regiments, from their first establishment, it is to be hoped that a very complete account will soon appear, which will throw much light on the past, as well as present state and character of the Highlanders; as Colonel Stewart of Garth has for several years been collecting materials for that purpose. The present writer is much indebted to that gentleman's communicative frankness, liberality, and politeness; and with confidence appeals to his extensive collection of unquestionable facts, for the confirmation of such theories and statements, however novel they may sometimes appear, as are found in the Introduction and Notes to this work.

It is almost peculiar to this people, that the greatest beauties in their character have commonly been considered as blemishes. Among these, the most prominent are family pride, the love of kindred, even to the exclusion of justice, and attachment to a country which seems to have so few charms to the inhabitants of more favoured regions. A family consisting of four or five thousand souls, all known to, connected with, and depending upon, each other, is certainly something that a man may be justified in considering as of some importance; and if a Highlander could neither be induced by threats nor promises to appear in a criminal court against a kinsman, or give him up to the vengeance of the law,[21] as is so common elsewhere, we may admire and pity, but can hardly in our hearts blame him. Who that has done such things ever did any good afterwards?[22]

The Highlander loves his country, because he loves heartily well everything that has ever been interesting to him, and this his own country was before he knew any other. Wherever he goes, he finds the external face of nature, or the institutions, language, and manners of the people, so different from what was dear to him in his youth, that he is everywhere else a stranger, and naturally sighs for home, with all its disadvantages, which, however formidable they may appear to others, are with him connected with such habits and recollections, that he would not remove them, if a wish could do it.

Some of the usages mentioned in the following work, may give rise to misapprehension. To strangers, the children of the gentry appeared to be totally neglected, till they were of an age to go to school; and this, in some measure, continued even to our own times; but it was the wisdom and affection of their parents that put them in such situations. Aware of the sacredness of their trust, those with whom they were placed never lost sight of their future destiny; and as they were better acquainted with the condition of their superiors than persons of the same rank in life had means of being in other countries, no habits of meanness or vulgarity were contracted from

[21] The Lowland laws were always held in abhorrence by the Highlanders, whom their vengeance often reached, but their protection never.

[22] Let those applaud the stoical sternness of Roman justice and Roman virtue, who admire it; to us, it has, in general, appeared a cold-blooded parade of theatrical ostentation, with which nature and truth had no connection.

such an education. Delicacy, with respect to food, clothing, and accommodation, would have been the greatest curse that could be entailed upon them: from early association, they learnt to feel an interest in all that concerned those among whom they had spent those years to which all look back with fond regret; and this intimate practical acquaintance with the condition, habits, and feelings of their dependants, produced afterwards a bond of union and endearment in the highest degree beneficial to all parties; at the same time that they could, with less inconvenience, encounter such difficulties and privations as the future vicissitudes of life mighty expose them to.

The ostentatiousness of the public, and beggarliness of the private economy of their chiefs, has been ridiculed. If they stinted themselves, in order to entertain their guests the better, they surely deserved a more grateful return. They lived in a poor country, where good fare could not be found for every day; and after half a dozen servants had waited at table, while the chief and his family were making a private meal of hasty-pudding and milk, crowdy (gradden meal and whipped cream), curds and cream, bread and cheese, fish, or what they might chance to have, those servants retired to the kitchen, cheerful and contented to their homely dinner, without any of those heart burnings produced by the sight of luxuries in which they could have no share. Their fare might be hard, but their superiors were contented with it, and so were they. Such self-denial in the chiefs reconciled their dependants to disadvantages which they had no means of surmounting, and was equally humane and considerate.

Their submission to their chiefs has been called slavish; and too many of the chiefs of the present day are willing enough to have this believed, because they wish to impute their own want of influence to any cause rather than the true one; but the lowest clansman felt his own individual importance as much as his chief, whom he considered as such only *ad vitam aut ad culpam*; and although there was certainly a strong feeling in favour of the lineal descendant of the steam-father of their race, which prevented them from being rash, harsh, or unjust to him, there was also a strong feeling of honour and independence, which prevented them from being unjust to themselves.[23] When a chief proved unworthy of his rank, he was degraded from it, and (to avoid jealousy and strife) the next in order was constituted in his room – but never a low-born man or a stranger; as it was a salutary rule among them, as in other military establishments, not to put one officer over the head of another. But it was not with a Highland chief as with other rulers; 'When *he* fell, he fell like Lucifer, never to rise again'; his degradation was complete, because he owed it to a common feeling of reprobation, not to the caprice, malice, or ambition of a faction; for every one was thoroughly acquainted with the merits of the cause, and while there was any thing to be said in his favour, his people had too much respect for themselves to show public disrespect to him. The same dignified feeling prevented their resentment from being bloody; he was still their kinsman, however unworthy; and having none among them to take his part, was no longer dangerous.[24]

Their affection of gentry (if such a term may be allowed) has been treated with endless ridicule, because it did not (much to the credit of their liberality) include the idea of wealth; but we believe few gentlemen in the Highlands, however poor, would have been flattered by being classed, as to civilization, with the gentleman, our author's friend, who attempted to ride into the rainbow.

The humane, indulgent, and delicate attention of people of fortune in the Highlands to their poor relations was one of the finest features in their character, and might furnish a very edifying example to the inhabitants of more favoured regions; and, to an honourable mind, there are surely considerations of higher importance than fine clothes and good eating. It has been imputed to their pride and stupidity, that they did not flee from the poverty of their own country, and try their fortunes, as labourers and mechanics, among strangers, where

[23] We believe the Highlands of Scotland to be the only country in Europe where the very name of slavery was unknown, and where the lowest retainer of a feudal baron enjoyed, in his place, the importance of a member of the community to which he belonged. The Gaelic language has no word synonymous to 'slave', for *tràill* is Norse (*trael*, in English, 'thrall'); and the thralls whom the Norwegians brought with them soon had their chains decomposed by the free air of our mountains.

[24] In one instance, it is true, a deposed chief was killed in battle by his clan, but it was in an attempt to force himself upon them by the assistance of a neighbouring tribe to which he was allied by marriage.

they might, in time, have obtained better food and accommodation; but to give up their rank in society, with all the endearing
offices and sympathies of friendship and affection to which they had
been accustomed at home, and which were so soothing and so
flattering to their feelings, and to go where they were sure to be
degraded beneath the lowest of the low, and continually exposed to
contempt, ridicule, and insult, for their ignorance of the arts and
habitudes of those among whom they lived – in short, to sell their
birth right for a mess of pottage – would have argued a beggarliness
of soul and spirit, which, happily, their worst enemies do not accuse
them of.

The foregoing remarks, which seemed necessary for illustrating
the characters of a very singular and interesting people, have already
extended this preface to a much greater length than was at first
intended, which will be the less regretted, if the honest wish by which
these details were prompted has been in any degree fulfilled. Of undue
partiality, it is hoped the writer will not be rashly accused, for he is
not a Highlander; and, having gone to the mountains, at the age of
fifteen, from the Laigh of Moray ('whence every man had a right to
drive a prey'; and where, of course, the character of their neighbours
was not very popular), he carried among them prejudices which
nothing but the conviction arising from observation and experience
could have removed. Of what he then heard, saw, and felt, he has
since had sufficient leisure to form a cool and dispassionate estimate,
during a residence of many years in various parts of England, Wales,
the north of Europe, and the Lowlands of Scotland. As he had no
Celtic enthusiasm to struggle with, and his deductions have all been
made from facts, it is hoped they may be received by strangers with
suitable confidence. To what good purpose he has availed himself
of the advantages he enjoyed, in fitting himself for his present task,
every reader will judge for himself; but when he makes it known
that it was first recommended to him by Mr Scott (to whom both he
and this publication, as well as the world in general, are so much
indebted), his vanity will readily be pardoned, as, even if it should
be found that that gentleman's kindness for the man has overstepped
his discretion as to the writer, the general conclusion will not be
dishonourable to either party.

As a close affinity in manners, habits, and character, between the ancient as well as present mountaineers of Norway and Scotland has frequently been alluded to, these prolusions may be closed, not unaptly, with a fragment of Highland biography, which may be regarded as a great curiosity, particularly by such as are acquainted with the Icelandic and Norse sagas, which it so strongly resembles. Of Hammer Donald, we shall only observe, that although the circumstances of his early life made him (like Viga Glum, and other celebrated kemps and homicides of the north) a very unmanageable and dangerous neighbour, there were then varieties of character in the Highlands as well as elsewhere. Donald's clan had been but lately introduced into the country; his father, although a brave man, was denominated 'the Peaceful'; and his son narrowly escaped being murdered in the very act of teaching his servants how to cultivate the ground.

THE HISTORY OF DONALD THE HAMMERER

From an authentic account of the family of Invernahyle.
(MS communicated by Walter Scott, Esq.)

———◆———

ALEXANDER, the first Invernahyle, commonly called
Saoileach, or 'the Peaceful', was son of Allan Stewart, third
laird of Appin. He married Margaret McDonald, daughter of Donald
McDonald of Moidart, commonly called Donald an Lochan, or
'Donald of the Lakes'; but a deadly feud arose between Invernahyle
and the family of Dunstaffnage, which, in the first instance, caused
the overthrow of both.

Alexander walked out early in a summer morning from Island
Stalker, and stepped over to Isle-nan-gall, where he laid himself down
on the grass, with his Lochaber axe beside him, a weapon, at that
period, more used in the Highlands than the broadsword. Whilst he
there reposed, apprehensive of no danger, the celebrated Cailen
Uaine, or 'Green Colin', arrived at the island in his barge, with a
number of men, whom he had brought from Dunstaffnage to assist
him in destroying his brother's enemy. Upon being observed by
Alexander, he advanced in the most friendly manner, and was about

to salute him, when, seeing the axe lying on the ground, he grasped it, and said, 'This is a good axe, Alexander, if there were peace enough in it.' To which Alexander quickly replied, 'Do you think there is not that in it?' and laid hold of the axe likewise, being fully sensible of the spirit of Colin's remark. During the struggle, Colin's men surrounded Alexander, and basely murdered him. They then proceeded to Island Stalker, and after killing every one of Alexander's friends that they could find, took possession of Invernahyle and all his other property.

Not one person escaped the fury of Green Colin and his men, except the nurse, who happened to be out walking in the fields with Alexander's only child in her arms, who had been named Donald, from his mother's father. The nurse was the blacksmith's wife of Moidart, and being an old acquaintance of Alexander's wife, was brought by her into Appin. Upon hearing what had happened to the family in which she was engaged, and that diligent search was made for her by Green Colin and his gang, in order to put the child to death, she fled home to her own country; and, upon discovering to her husband what had happened to the family of Invernahyle, they agreed to bring up the child as one of their own.[1]

When young Donald had acquired some strength, he was called to assist his supposed father in carrying on his trade; and so uncommon was his strength, that when only eighteen years of age, he could wield a large forehammer in each hand, for the length of the longest day, without the least seeming difficulty or fatigue.

At last the blacksmith and his wife resolved to discover to Donald the secret they had so long kept, not only from him, but from the world. After relating the mournful tale of his parents' death, the smith brought a sword of his own making, and put it into Donald's hand, saying, 'I trust the blood that runs in your veins, and the spirit of your fathers, will guide your actions; and that this sword will be the means of clearing the difficulties that lie in the way of your

---

[1] It is said, the woman, being pursued in her flight, and knowing the infant's life was aimed at, hid it in a cave, having first tied a piece of lard round its neck. The nurse was made prisoner, and detained for several days. On her release, she went to the cave, expecting only to find the relics of her charge; but the infant was alive and well, the lard being reduced to the size of a hazelnut. W.S.

recovering your paternal estate.' Donald heard with surprise the story of his birth and early misfortune; but vowed never to put the sword into a scabbard until he had swept the murderers of his parents from the earth.[2] His mother's father, who still lived in Moidart, upon being satisfied that Donald was his grandson, and seeing his determination of recovering his father's property, gave him a few men, with whom he proceeded to Appin.

Upon arriving at Island Stalker, Donald declared himself the son of the late Invernahyle, and sent Green Colin a challenge to fight him singly; but, instead of complying with the challenge, Colin gathered all his retainers, and advanced with them in the order of battle; but Donald and his men commenced the attack, and, after a desperate engagement, succeeded in killing not only Green Colin, but nearly the whole of his men, by which Invernahyle became his property without any further trouble.

Donald's history being now made public, he got the appellation of Donul nan Ord, or 'Donald the Hammerer', by which he was ever after known. Resolving to revenge the wrongs his father had suffered from the family of Dunstaffnage, Donald mustered all his fighting men, and attacked the Campbells wherever he could find any of that name. Argyle came at last to be interested in the distress that Donald was bringing on his clan, and employed several parties to cut him off, but in vain. Donald, seeing Argyle's intention, instead of being intimidated, penetrated, with his trusty band, into the heart of Argyle's country, spoiled his tenants, and carried away a considerable booty from the side of Lochow, which at that time gave a title to the chief of the clan. There is handed down a little roundlet which narrates this transaction:

> Donul nan Ord, dallta Ghobhain,
> Ailleagan nan Luireach leathar,
> Thog a Creach 'o thaobh Loch A; i.e.

> Donald the Hammerer, the smith's foster-son,
> the ornament of the leathern apron,
> lifted a prey from the side of Lochow.

---

[2] The blacksmith also presented Donald with his sons to aid him in recovering his natural rights. W.S.

Argyle, much enraged at this transaction, began to think seriously of revenge, by raising his whole clan, and following to destroy him; but wisely seeing that this could not be done without much noise in the country, and aware that Donald might be supported by the Camerons, and other powerful clans with whom Argyle was at war, set on foot a negotiation with the laird of Appin, to try and get Donald to make restitution, and to be peaceful. The result was, that Appin and his other friends insisted with Donald, that unless he came to terms with Argyle, they would leave him to his own fate. Donald, unwilling to split with his friends, and thinking that he had just done enough to revenge the death of his parents, actually went to Inverary, with a single attendant, to hold a conference with Argyle at his own place. Argyle had too much honour to take advantage of this bold step of Donald; but conceived, from his rusticity, that he might soon get him into a scrape that might prove fatal to him. Upon arriving at Inverary, Donald met Argyle in the fields, and is said to have accosted him thus:

> *A mic Cailen ghriomaich ghlais,*
> *Is beg an hachd a thaead dhiom;*
> *'S nan a philleach mi air mi ais,*
> *Ma's a ma th'again dhiot,*[3]

> Son of sallow, sulky Colin,
>   Small's the grace will go from me;
> And if I get but back again,
>   'Tis all the boon I want from thee.

In the course of some indifferent conversation, Donald frequently indulged in a loud horse laugh (a habit which some of his descendants are noted for as far down as the eighth generation); to rally Donald a little on this, Argyle desired him to look at a rock on a hill above Ardkinglas, then in their view, which resembles a man's face reclined backwards, with the mouth widely expanded, and asked him if he knew the name of that rock? Donald answered in the negative. Argyle then told him, it was Gaire Grannda ('Ugly Laugh'). Donald

---

[3] This is given in the orthography in which we found it, as are all the other scraps of Gaelic.

perceiving the allusion, and, with his other qualifications, being a good poet, replied off-hand:

> *Gaire Grannda s' ainm do'n chreig;*
> *'S fanaudh i mirr sin do ghna;*
> *Gheibhead tu lethid aged fein,*
> *Na n sealladh tu 'n euden do mhna;*

> 'Ugly Laugh' is the name of the rock;
>   An ugly mocker 'twill ever be;
> But if you will look on your own wife's face,
>   As ugly a sight you at home may see.

When at length they came to talk of business, the terms upon which Argyle offered peace were, that Donald should raise a hership (plundering) in Moidart, and another in Atholl, thinking probably that Donald would be cut off in some of these attempts, or, if successful against such powerful people, his own disgrace would be less in what was done to his own lands. Donald readily agreed to the terms, and set out instantly for Moidart to inform his uncle of the engagement he had come under, and asked his advice. His uncle told him, the people of certain farms had offended him much; and if Donald would attack them, he, to save the appearance of being in the plot, would assist them in striving to recover the spoil, but would not be in such haste that Donald would run any risk of being overtaken. Donald soon gathered his men, and set fire to nearly all the farmhouses in Moidart, and got clear off with the spoil. This affair made great noise in the country. He went next to Atholl, and carried desolation through that country with equal success; which intimidated Argyle so much, that he made peace with Donald on the terms proposed by the latter.

Not content with plundering the Highlands from one end to the other, Donald often descended into the low country. One time, as returning from Stirlingshire, on passing through Monteith, his party called at a house where a wedding dinner was preparing for a party, at which the Earl of Monteith was to be present; but, not caring for this, they stepped in and ate up the whole that was intended for the wedding party. Upon the Earl's arriving with the marriage people, he was so enraged at the affront put upon his clan, that he instantly pursued Donald, and soon came up with him. One of the Earl's men called out ironically,

> *Stewartich chui nan t Apan,*
> *A cheiradhich glass air a chal.*

One of Donald's men, with great coolness, drawing an arrow out of his quiver, replied,

> *Ma the 'n t Apan againn mar dhucha,*
> *'S du dhuinn gun tarruin sin farsid;* i.e.

> If Appin is our country, we would draw thee
> (thy neck), wert thou there;

and with this took his aim at the Monteith man and shot him through the heart. A bloody engagement then ensued, in which the earl and nearly the whole of his followers were killed, and Donald the Hammerer escaped with only a single attendant, through the night coming on.[4]

Donald married a daughter of John Stewart Ban Rannoch, alias, Jan Mac Roibeart, by whom he had four sons, first Jan More, who died at Taymouth when young; second, Duncan, who succeeded him; third, Allan, of whom the present Ballechelish; fourth, James nan Gleann, who had the lands of Lettershuna. Donald the Hammerer had only one daughter, who was married to Archibald Campbell called Gillisbuegdie, of whom the present Achalladair. During Donald's lifetime, the feud that subsisted between him and the family of Dunstaffnage did not entirely subside; but it was prudently concluded, in order to put a final end to it, that Duncan should pay his addresses to Helena, a daughter of Dunstaffnage, which he did with success. This was carried on unknown to Donald; and when the marriage took place, he was in very bad blood with his son; and Duncan, not having anything to support himself and his young wife, went to live with the smith's wife of Moidart, who had nursed his

---

[4] This skirmish took place betwixt Loch Katrine and the Loch of Monteith. (See Dr Graham, on the scenery of these districts.) As the quarrel began on account of the poultry devoured by the Highlanders, which they plundered from the Earl's offices, situated on the side of the port of Monteith, to accommodate his castle in the adjacent island, the name of Gramoch an gerig, or 'Grames of the hens', was fixed on the family of the Grames of Monteith. W.S.

father, upon the farm of Inverfalla, which her husband had received
from Donul nan Ord as a grateful recompense for his former kindness
but, the smith being dead, the old woman now lived by herself.

Being more inclined to live by cultivating the arts of peace than
by plundering his neighbours, Duncan spent much of his time in
improving the farm of Inverfalla, which his father, considering as
far below the dignity of a Highland gentleman, could not brook to
see.

Once, as Donald was walking upon the green of Invernahyle, he
looked across the river, and saw several men working upon the farm
of Inverfalla. In the meantime Duncan came out, and took a spade
from one of the men, seemingly to let him see how he should perform
the work in which he was employed. This was too much for the old
gentleman to bear. He launched the currach (a wicker boat covered
with hides) with his own hand, and rowed it across to Inverfalla. As
he approached, Duncan, being struck with the fury of his countenance, fled from the impending storm into the house; but the old man
followed him with a naked sword in his hand. Upon entering a room
that was somewhat dark, Donald, thinking his degenerate son had
concealed himself under the bedclothes, made a deadly stab at his
supposed son; but instead of killing him his sword went through the
heart of his old nurse, who was then near eighty years of age.

After this unfortunate accident Donald became very religious; he
resigned all his lands to his sons, and went to live at Columkill,
where he at last died at the age of eighty-seven.

LETTERS

FROM

A Gentleman in the North of *Scotland*

TO

His FRIEND in *London* ;

CONTAINING

The Defcription of a Capital Town in that
Northern Country ;

WITH

An Account of fome uncommon Cuftoms
of the Inhabitants :

LIKEWISE

An Account of the HIGHLANDS, with the
Cuftoms and *Manners* of the HIGHLANDERS.

To which is added,

A LETTER relating to the MILITARY WAYS
among the Mountains, began in the Year 1726.

The Whole interfpers'd with *Facts* and *Circumftances*
intirely New to the Generality of People in *England*,
and little known in the Southern Parts of *Scotland*.

In TWO VOLUMES.

VOL. I.

LONDON:
Printed for S. BIRT, in *Ave-Maria-Lane*.

MDCCLIV.

LETTER I

INTRODUCTION—Familiarity the basis of this correspondence—To be shown
to one friend only—Reasons for this stipulation—Genius of a people known
only by their native manners—Folly of being offended at descriptions of
one's country—Highlanders little known to the low country, still less to
the English—Scantiness of written information respecting the Highlands—
Lowlands have been misrepresented—Notice of a work called *A Journey
through Scotland*—Old seats in Scotland—Plan of this correspondence—
The descriptions mostly from personal knowledge—Danger of letters being
intercepted—Egotism excused

IN the course of evidence, or other examination, one slight
accidental hint may be the cause of a long and intricate enquiry;
and thus the bare mention I lately made of a few notes I had taken,
relating to these parts and to the Highlands, will be the occasion of
some employment for me; but I am far from making a merit of any
trouble I can take to gratify your curiosity; and more especially in
this; for to tell you the truth, I have at present little else to do; my
only fear is, my endeavour will not answer your expectation.

Our friendship is as old as our acquaintance, which you know is
of no inconsiderable standing, and complimental speeches between
us were, by consent, banished from the beginning, as being unsuitable
to that sincerity which a strict friendship requires. But I may say,
with great truth, there is but one other in the world could prevail
with me to communicate, in writing, such circumstances as I perfectly
foresee will make up great part of this correspondence; and therefore

I must stipulate, even with you, that none of my future letters, on this subject, may be shown to any other than our common friend — in whom you know we can confide.

I have several reasons for this precaution, which I make no doubt you will approve.

First, the contrary might create inconveniences to me in my present situation.

It might furnish matter for disobliging comparisons, to which some of our countrymen are but too much addicted.

This again might give offence, especially to such who are so national as not to consider, that a man's native country is not of his own making, or his being born in it the effect of his choice.

And lastly, it would do me no great honour to be known to have made a collection of incidents, mostly low, and sometimes disagreeable. Yet even in this I have a common observation on my side, which is, that the genuine character of any particular person may be best discovered, when he appears in his domestic capacity; when he is free from all restraint by fear of foreign observation and censure; and, by a parity of reason, the genius of a whole people may be better known by their actions and inclinations in their native country, than it can be from remarks made upon any numbers of them, when they are dispersed in other parts of the world.

In public, all mankind act more or less in disguise.

If I were to confine myself to the customs of the country and the manners of the people, I think it would need but little apology to the most national; for the several members of every community think themselves sufficiently furnished with arguments, whereby to justify their general conduct; but in speaking of the country, I have met with some, who, in hearing the most modest description of any part of it, have been suddenly acted upon by an unruly passion, complicated of jealousy, pity, and anger: this, I have often compared in my mind to the yearnings of a fond mother for a misshapen child, when she thinks anyone too prying into its deformity.

If I shall take notice of anything amiss, either here or in the mountains, which they know to be wrong, and it is in their power to amend, I shall apply, in my own justification, what is said by Spenser upon a like occasion:

The best (said he) that I can you advise,
Is to avoid the occasion of the ill:
For, when the cause whence evil doth arise
Removed is, the effect surceaseth still.

The Highlands are but little known even to the inhabitants of the low country of Scotland, for they have ever dreaded the difficulties and dangers of travelling among the mountains; and when some extraordinary occasion has obliged any one of them to such a progress, he has, generally speaking, made his testament before he set out, as though he were entering upon a long and dangerous sea voyage, wherein it was very doubtful if he should ever return. But to the people of England, excepting some few, and those chiefly the soldiery, the Highlands are hardly known at all: for there has been less, that I know of, written upon the subject, than of either of the Indies; and even that little which has been said, conveys no idea of what a traveller almost continually sees and meets with in passing among the mountains; nor does it communicate any notion of the temper of the natives, while they remain in their own country.

The verbal misrepresentations that have been made of the Lowlands are very extraordinary; and though good part of it be greatly superior in the quality of the soil to the north of England, and in some parts equal to the best of the south, yet there are some among our countrymen who are so prejudiced, that they will not allow (or not own) there is anything good on this side of the Tweed. On the other hand, some flattering accounts that have been published, what with commendation, and what with concealment, might induce a stranger to both parts of the island, to conclude, that Scotland in general is the better country of the two; and I wish it were so (as we are become one people) for the benefit of the whole.

About a week ago, I borrowed a book called *A Journey through Scotland*, published in the year 1723; and having dipped into it in many places, I think it might with more propriety be called, *A Journey to the Heralds Office, and the Seats of the Nobility and Gentry of North Britain*.

He calls almost all their houses palaces. He makes no less than five in one street, part of the suburbs of Edinburgh, besides the real Palace of Holyrood House; but if you were to see them with that pompous title, you would be surprised, though you would think some of them good houses when mentioned with modesty.

But I think every one of the five would greatly suffer by the comparison, if they stood near Marlborough House in St James's Park; and yet nobody ever thought of erecting that building into a palace.

It would be contrary to my inclination, and even ridiculous to deny, that there is a great number of noble and spacious old seats in Scotland, besides those that were kings' palaces, of both which some are built in a better taste than most of the old seats in England that I have seen: These I am told were built after the models of Sir William Bruce, who was their Inigo Jones; but many of them are now in a ruinous condition. And it must be confessed there are some very stately modern buildings: but our itinerant author gives such magnificent descriptions of some of his palaces, as carry with them nothing but disappointment to the eye of the travelling spectator.

He labours the plantations about the country seats so much, that he shows thereby what a rarity trees are in Scotland; and indeed it has been often remarked, that here are but few birds except such as build their nests upon the ground, so scarce are hedges and trees.

The post house at Haddington, a wretched inn, by comparison, he says, is inferior to none on the London Road.

In this town he says there are coffee-houses and taverns as in England – who would not thence infer, there are spacious rooms, many waiters, plentiful larders, etc.? And as to the only coffee-room we have, I shall say something of it in its proper place.

But the writer is held greatly in esteem by the people here, for calling this the 'pretty town of Inverness'. How often have I heard those words quoted with pleasure!

Here I am about to premise something in relation to the sheets which are to follow: And first, I intend to send you one of these letters every fortnight, and oftener if I find it convenient, till I have, as I may say, writ myself quite out. In doing this, I shall not confine myself to order or method, but take my paragraphs just as they come to hand, except where one fact or observation naturally arises from another. Nor shall I be solicitous about the elegancy of style, but content myself with an endeavour only to be understood; for both or either of those niceties would deprive me of some other amusements, and that, I am sure, you do not expect, nor would you suffer it if you could help it.

There will be little said that can be applicable to Scotland in general; but if anything of that nature should occur, I shall note it to be so.

All parts of the Highlands are not exactly alike, either in the height of the country or the customs and manners of the natives, of whom some are more civilized than others.

Nothing will be set down but what I have personally known, or received from such whose information I had no reason to suspect; and all without prejudice or partiality. And lastly, I shall be very sparing of the names of particular persons (especially when no honour can be dispensed by the mention of them), not only as they are unknown to you, but, to tell you the truth, in prudence to myself; for, as our letters are carried to Edinburgh the hill way, by a foot post, there is one who makes no scruple to intrude, by means of his emissaries, into the affairs and sentiments of others, especially if he fancies there is anything relating to himself; so jealous and inquisitive is guilt. And therefore I shall neglect no opportunity of sending them to Edinburgh by private hands. But if you should be curious at any time to know the name of some particular person; in that case, a hint, and the date of my letter, will enable me to give you that satisfaction.

But I must add, that the frequent egotisms which I foresee I shall be obliged to use in passages merely relating to myself, incline me to wish that our language would sometimes (like the French) admit of the third person, only to vary the eternal I.

This is all I have to say by way of preface: what apologies I may have occasion to make in my progress, I do not know; but I promise that as they are dry, so shall they be as few as possible.

LETTER II

———◆———

Manner in which the introductory part of these letters originated—
Passage of the Tweed at Kelso—The inn and its accommodations—
Innkeeper a 'gentleman'—Potted pigeons—Disgusted, and quit the inn—
First impressions—A specimen of cookery—Miserable bedding—Excellent
linen—Edinburgh—Height of houses there—Tavern—Description of the
cook—City drum—A guide for protection in passing the streets—Public
nuisance—Number of families in a house—Site for a new city—Rejected,
and why—Tedious mode of directing strangers—The cawdies and their
constable—Leave Edinburgh—Glasgow, its uniformity and neatness—
Church at Linlithgow—Formerly a cathedral—Its neglected state—A curious
remark—Leave Glasgow—Road—Contradictory information—Romantic
appearance of the mountains—Poverty of the towns—Singular custom of
quitting houses when old—Disagreeable smell of fishing towns—Cattle
smaller towards the north of Scotland

ABOUT a twelvemonth after I first came to this town, and had
been twice to Edinburgh by the way of the hills, I received a
letter from an old acquaintance, desiring me to give him an account
of my first journey hither, the same to commence from the Borders
of Scotland.

I could not, you may imagine, conceive the meaning of a request
so extraordinary; but however I complied implicitly. Sometime
afterwards, by a letter of thanks, I was given to understand, it was
an expedient, agreed upon between him and another, whereby to
decide a dispute.

7

Now all this preface is only to introduce my request to you, that you will absolve me from the promise I made you last week, and in lieu of what you might demand, accept of a copy of that letter.

I should not have waved my promised design, but for an affair which something related to myself, and required my attention, and therefore I could not find time to tack together so many memorandums, as such letters, as I intend to send you, require; for if they are not pretty long, I shall be self-condemned, since you know I used to say, by way of complaint against —, that letters from one friend to another should be of a length proportioned to the distance between them.

After some compliments, my letter was as follows:

'According to your desire, I shall begin my account with the entertainment I met with after passing the Tweed at Kelso, but shall not trouble you with the exaction and intolerable insolence of the ferryman, because I think you can match their impudence at our own horseferry: I shall only say, that I could obtain no redress, although I complained of them to the principal magistrate of the town.

'Having done with them, my horses were led to the stable, and myself conducted up one pair of stairs, where I was soon attended by a handsome genteel man, well dressed, who gave me a kindly welcome to the house.

'This induced me to ask him what I could have to eat: to which he civilly answered, the "good wife" will be careful nothing shall be wanting; but that he never concerned himself about anything relating to the "public" (as he called it): that is, he would have me know he was a "gentleman", and did not employ himself in anything so low as attendance, but left it to his wife. Thus he took his leave of me: and soon after came up my landlady, whose dress and appearance seemed to me to be so unfit for the wife of that gentleman, that I could hardly believe she was any other than a servant; but she soon took care, in her turn, by some airs she gave herself, to let me know she was mistress of the house.

'I asked what was to be had, and she told me potted pigeons; and nothing, I thought, could be more agreeable, as requiring no waiting, after a fatiguing day's journey in which I had eaten nothing.

'The cloth was laid, but I was too unwilling to grease my fingers to touch it; and presently after, the pot of pigeons was set on the table.

'When I came to examine my cates, there were two or three of the pigeons lay mangled in the pot, and behind were the furrows, in the butter, of those fingers that had raked them out of it, and the butter itself needed no close application to discover its quality.

'My disgust at this sight was so great, and being a brand-new traveller in this country, I ate a crust of bread, and drank about a pint of good claret; and although the night was approaching, I called for my horses, and marched off, thinking to meet with something better, but I was benighted on a rough moor, and met with yet worse entertainment at a little house which was my next quarters.

'At my first entrance I perceived some things like shadows moving about before the fire, which was made with peats; and going nearer to them, I could discern, and that was all, two small children in motion, stark naked, and a very old man sitting by the fireside.

'I soon went out, under pretence of care for my horses, but in reality to relieve my lungs and eyes of the smoke. At my return I could perceive the old man's fingers to be in a very bad condition, and immediately I was seized with an apprehension that I should be put into his bed.

'Here I was told I might have a breast of mutton done upon the "brander" (or gridiron): but when it was brought me, it appeared to have been smoked and dried in the chimney corner; and it looked like the glue that hangs up in an ironmonger's shop: This, you may believe, was very disgusting to the eye; and for the smell, it had no other, that I could perceive, than that of the butter wherewith it was greased in the dressing; but, for my relief, there were some new-laid eggs, which were my regale. And now methinks I hear one of this country say, "—, a true Englishman! He is already talking of eating."

'When I had been conducted to my lodging room, I found the curtains of my bed were very foul by being handled by the dirty wenches; and the old man's fingers being present with me, I sat down by the fire, and asked myself, for which of my sins I was sent into this country; but I have been something reconciled to it since then, for we have here our pleasures and diversions, though not in such plenty and variety, as you have in London.

'But to proceed. Being tired and sleepy, at last I came to a resolution to see how my bed looked withinside, and to my joy I found exceeding good linen, white, well aired and hardened, and I think as good as in our best inns in England, so I slept very comfortably.

'And here I must take notice of what I have since found almost every where, but chiefly in the low country, that is, good linen; for the spinning descends from mother to daughter by succession, till the stock becomes considerable; insomuch that even the ordinary people are generally much better furnished in that particular, than those of the same rank in England – I am speaking chiefly of sheeting and table linen.

'There happened nothing extraordinary between this place and Edinburgh, where I made no long stay.

'When I first came into the High Street of that city, I thought I had not seen anything of the kind more magnificent: the extreme height of the houses, which are, for the most part, built with stone, and well sashed; the breadth and length of the street, and (it being dry weather) a cleanness made by the high winds, I was extremely pleased to find everything look so unlike the descriptions of that town which had been given me by some of my countrymen.

'Being a stranger, I was invited to sup at a tavern. The cook was too filthy an object to be described; only another English gentleman whispered me and said, he believed, if the fellow was to be thrown against the wall, he would stick to it.

'Twisting round and round his hand a greasy towel, he stood waiting to know what we would have for supper, and mentioned several things himself; among the rest, a "duke", a "fool", or a "meerfool". This was nearly according to his pronunciation; but he meant a duck, a fowl, or a moorfowl, or grouse.

'We supped very plentifully, and drank good French claret, and were very merry till the clock struck ten, the hour when everybody is at liberty, by beat of the city drum, to throw their filth out at the windows. Then the company began to light pieces of paper, and throw them upon the table to smoke the room, and, as I thought, to mix one bad smell with another.

'Being in my retreat to pass through a long narrow "wynde" or alley, to go to my new lodgings, a guide was assigned me, who went before me to prevent my disgrace, crying out all the way, with a loud voice, "Hud your haunde." The throwing up of a sash, or otherwise opening a window, made me tremble, while behind and before me, at some little distance, fell the terrible shower.

'Well, I escaped all the danger, and arrived, not only safe and sound, but sweet and clean, at my new quarters; but when I was in bed I was forced to hide my head between the sheets; for the smell of the filth, thrown out by the neighbours on the backside of the house, came pouring into the room to such a degree, I was almost poisoned with the stench.'

I shall here add to my letter, as I am making a copy of it, a few observations.

When I was last in Edinburgh I set myself to consider of this great annoyance, and, in conclusion, found it remediless.

'The city, it seems, was built upon that rock for protection, by the castle, in dangerous times; but the space was too narrow to contain a sufficient number of inhabitants, otherwise than by very high buildings, crowded close together, insomuch that there are hardly any backyards.

'Eight, ten, and even twelve storeys have each a particular family, and perhaps a separate proprietor; and therefore anything so expensive as a conveyance down from the uppermost floor could never be agreed on; or could there be made, within the building, any receiver suitable to such numbers of people.

'There is indeed between the city and the sea a large flat space of land, with a rivulet running through it, which would be very commodious for a city: but great part of it has been made the property of the corporation; and the magistrates for the time being will not suffer any houses to be built on it; for if they did, the old city would soon be deserted, which would bring a very great loss upon some, and total ruin upon others, of the proprietors in those buildings.'

I have said thus much upon this uncleanly subject, only, as you may have heard some maliciously, or at best inconsiderately, say, that this evil proceeds from (what one would think no body could believe) a love of nastiness, and not necessity. I shall only add, as it falls in my way, that the main street is cleaned by scavengers every morning early, except Sunday, which therefore is the most uncleanly day.

But to return. Having occasion the next morning after my arrival to enquire for a person with whom I had some concerns, I was amazed at the length and gibberish of a direction given me where to find him.

I was told that I must go down the street, and on the north side, over against such a place, turn down such a 'wynde'; and, on the west side of the wynde, inquire for such a 'launde' (or building), where the gentleman 'stayd', at the 'thrid stair', that is, three storeys high.

This direction in a language I hardly understood, and by points of the compass which I then knew nothing of, as they related to the town, put me to a good deal of difficulty.

At length I found out the subject of my enquiry, who was greatly diverted when I told him (with as much humour as I was master of) what had been my perplexity. Yet in my narration I concealed the nauseous inconvenience of going down the steep narrow wynde, and ascending to his lodging.

I then had no knowledge of the 'cawdies', a very useful blackguard, who attend the coffee-houses and public places to go of errands; and though they are wretches, that in rags lie upon the stairs, and in the streets at night, yet are they often considerably trusted, and, as I have been told, have seldom or never proved unfaithful.

These boys know every body in the town who is of any kind of note, so that one of them would have been a ready guide to the place I wanted to find; and I afterwards wondered that one of them was not recommended to me by my new landlady.

This corps has a kind of captain or magistrate presiding over them, whom they call the constable of the cawdies, and in case of neglect or other misdemeanour he punishes the delinquents, mostly by fines of ale and brandy, but sometimes corporally.

They have for the most part an uncommon acuteness, are very ready at proper answers, and execute suddenly and well whatever employment is assigned them.

Whether it be true or not I cannot say, but I have been told by several, that one of the judges formerly abandoned two of his sons for a time to this way of life, as believing it would create in them a sharpness which might be of use to them in the future course of their lives.

This is all that I knew about Edinburgh at that time, by reason of the shortness of my stay: the day following, my affairs called me to begin my journey to Glasgow.

Glasgow is, to outward appearance, the prettiest and most uniform town that I ever saw; and I believe there is nothing like it in Britain.

It has a spacious carrifour, where stands the cross; and going round it, you have, by turns, the view of four streets, that in regular angles proceed from thence. The houses of these streets are faced with ashler stone, they are well sashed, all of one model, and piazzas run through them on either side, which give a good air to the buildings.

There are some other handsome streets, but the extreme parts of the town are mean and disagreeable to the eye.

There was nothing remarkable in my way to Glasgow, that I took notice of, being in haste, but the church at Linlithgow, a noble old Gothic building, formerly a cathedral, now much in ruins, chiefly from the usual rage that attends reformation.

It is really provoking to see how the populace have broke and defaced the statues and other ornaments, under the notion of their being relics of popery.

As this town was our baiting-place, a gentleman (the son of a celebrated Scots bishop) who was with me, proposed, that while dinner was getting ready we should go and view the inside of the structure; and as we took notice that great part of the floor was broken up, and that the pews were immoderately dusty, the pre-centor, or clerk, who attended, us took occasion to say, he did not apprehend that cleanliness was essential to devotion; upon which, my friend turned hastily upon him, and said very angrily,

'What! This church was never intended for your slovenly worship.' This epithet, pronounced with so much ardour, immediately after his censure of the Presbyterian zeal, was to me some matter of speculation.

My stay at Glasgow was very short as it had been at Edinburgh, to which last, in five days, I returned, in order to proceed to this town.

Upon consulting some gentlemen, which of the two ways was most eligible for me to take, i.e. whether through the Highlands, or by the sea coast, I found they were divided; one giving a dreadful account of the roughness and danger of the mountains, another commending the shortness of the cut over the hills. One told me it was a hundred and fifty miles by the coast, another that it was but ninety miles the other way; but I decided the matter myself upon the strength of the old proverb, that 'the farthest way about is the nearest way home'. Not but that I sometimes met with roads which, at that time, I thought pretty rough; but after passing through the Highlands, they were all smoothed in my imagination, into bowling-greens.

As the country near the coast has, here and there, little rising hills, which overlook the sea, and discover towns at a considerable distance, I was well enough diverted with various prospects in my journey, and wanted nothing but trees, enclosures, and smoother roads, to make it very agreeable.

The Lowlands, between the sea and the high country, to the left, are generally narrow; and the rugged romantic appearance of the mountains was to me, at that time, no bad prospect; but since that, I have been taught to think otherwise, by the sufferings I have met with among them.

I had little reason to complain of my entertainment at the several houses where I set up, because I never wanted what was proper for the support of life, either for myself or my horses: I mention them, because, in a journey, they are as it were a part of one's self. The worst of all was the cookery.

One thing I observed of almost all the towns that I saw at a distance, which was, that they seemed to be very large, and made a handsome appearance; but when I passed through them, there appeared a meanness which discovered the condition of the inhabitants: and all the outskirts, which served to increase the extent of them at a distance, were nothing but the ruins of little houses, and those in pretty great numbers.

Of this I asked the reason, and was told, that when one of those houses was grown old and decayed, they often did not repair it, but, taking out the timber, they let the walls stand as a fit enclosure for a 'kaleyard' (i.e. a little garden for coleworts), and that they built anew upon another spot. By this you may conclude that stone and ground-rents in those towns are not very valuable. But the little fishing towns were generally disagreeable to pass, from the strong smell of the haddocks and whitings that were hung up to dry on lines along the sides of the houses from one end of the village to the other: and such numbers of half-naked children, but fresh-coloured, strong, and healthy, I think are not to be met with in the inland towns. Some will have their numbers and strength to be the effects of shellfish.

I have one thing more to observe to you, which is, that still as I went northward, the cattle and the carts grew less and less. The sheep likewise diminished in their size by degrees as I advanced; and their wool grew coarser, till at length, upon a transient view, they seemed to be clothed with hair. This I think proceeds less from the quality of the soil than the excessive cold of the hills in the winter season, because the mutton is exceedingly good.

Thus I have acquainted you how I came hither, and I hope it will not now be very long before I have a greater pleasure in telling you, by word of mouth, in what manner I got home; yet must I soon return.

LETTER III

I AM now about to enter upon the performance of my promise, and shall begin with a description of this town, which, however obscure it may be thought with you, yet is of no inconsiderable account in these remote regions. And it is often said to be the most like to an English town of any at this end of the island.

But I have a further view than barely to make you acquainted with these parts without your having the inconveniences, fatigue, and hazards of a northern journey of five hundred miles; and that design is, to show you, by example, the melancholy consequence of the want of manufactories and foreign trade, and most especially with respect to the common people, whom it affects even to the want of necessaries; not to mention the morals of the next degree. It is here, indeed, their happiness, that they do not so sensibly feel the want of these advantages, as they would do if they had known the loss of them.

And notwithstanding the natural fertility of the south, I am, by observation, taught to conclude, that without these important profits, which enable the higher orders of men to spare a part of their income to employ others in ornamental and other works not absolutely necessary; I say, in that case, the ordinary people with you would be, perhaps, not quite, but nearly as wretched as these, whose circumstances almost continually excite in me the painful passion of pity, as the objects of it are seldom out of my sight.

I shall not make any remarks how much it is incumbent on the rulers of kingdoms and states (who are to the people what a father is to his helpless family) to watch over this source of human convenience and happiness, because this has been your favourite topic, and indeed the contrary would be in me (as the common phrase is) 'like carrying coals to Newcastle'.

If wit were my talent, or even a genteel ridicule, which is but a faint resemblance of wit (if it may be said to be anything like it) – I say, if both or either of these were my gift, you would not expect to be entertained that way upon this account; for you perfectly know that poverty, simply as such, and unattended by sloth, pride, and (let me say) other unsuitable vices, was never thought by the judicious to be a proper subject for wit or raillery. But I cannot forbear to observe, *en passant*, that those pretenders to wit that deal in odious hyperboles create distaste to ingenuous minds.

I shall give you only two examples of such insipid jests. The first was, in describing the country cabins in the north of Ireland, by saying, one might put one's arm down the chimney and unlatch the door. This regarded all of that country; but the other was personal to one who, perhaps, had carried his economy a little too far.

'Sir,' says the joker to me, who was a stranger to the other, 'this gentleman is a very generous man – I made him a visit the other day, and the bars of his grate were the wires of a birdcage, and he threw on his coals with an Ockamy spoon.'

It is true, the laughing part of the company were diverted with the sarcasm; but it was so much at the expense of the old gentleman, that I thought he would run mad with resentment.

It would be needless to describe the situation of this town, as it relates to the island in general, because a map of Britain will, at one view, afford you a better idea of it than any words I can put together for that purpose; I shall therefore content myself with saying only, that the Moray Firth is navigable within less than half a mile of the town, and that the rest of the navigation to it is supplied by the River Ness.

Inverness is one of the royal boroughs of Scotland, and jointly with Nairn, Forres, and Channery, sends a member to Parliament.

The town has a military governor, and the corporation a provost and four bailies, a kind of magistrates little differing from our mayors and aldermen: besides whom, there is a dean of guild who presides in matters of trade; and other borough officers, as in the rest of the corporate towns of this country.

It is not only the head borough or county town of the shire of Inverness, which is of large extent, but generally esteemed to be the capital of the Highlands: but the natives do not call themselves Highlanders, not so much on account of their low situation, as because they speak English.

This rule whereby to denominate themselves, they borrow from the Kirk, which, in all its acts and ordinances distinguishes the Lowlands from the Highlands by the language generally spoken by the inhabitants, whether the parish or district lies in the high or low country.

Yet although they speak English, there are scarce any who do not understand the Irish tongue; and it is necessary they should do so, to carry on their dealings with the neighbouring country people; for within less than a mile of the town, there are few who speak any English at all.

What I am saying must be understood only of the ordinary people; for the gentry, for the most part, speak our language in the remotest parts of Scotland.

The town principally consists of four streets, of which three centre at the cross, and the other is something irregular.

The castle stands upon a little steep hill closely adjoining to the town, on the south side, built with unhewn stone; it was lately in ruins, but is now completely repaired, to serve as a part of the citadel of Fort George, whereof the first foundation stone was laid in summer 1726, and is to consist of barracks for six companies. This castle, whereof the Duke of Gordon is hereditary keeper, was formerly a royal palace, where Mary, the mother of our King James I, resided, at such times when she thought it her interest to oblige the Highlanders with her presence and expense, or that her safety required it.

You will think it was a very scanty palace, when I have told you, that before it was repaired, it consisted of only six lodging-rooms, the offices below, and the gallery above; which last being taken down, and the rooms divided each into two, there are now twelve apartments for officers' lodgings.

While this building was in repairing, three soldiers who were employed in digging up a piece of ground very near the door, discovered a dead body, which was supposed to be the corpse of a man; I say supposed, because a part of it was defaced before they were aware.

This was believed to have lain there a great number of years, because when it was touched it fell to dust. At this unexpected sight, the soldiers most valiantly ran away, and the accident, you will believe, soon brought a good number of spectators to the place.

As I was talking with one of the townsmen, and took notice how strange it was that a body should be buried so near the door of the house; ''Troth,' says he, 'I dinno doubt but this was ane of Mary's lovers.'

I verily believe this man had been afterwards rebuked for this unguarded expression to me, an Englishman; because, when I happened to meet him in the street the day following, he officiously endeavoured to give his words another turn, which made the impression I had received, much stronger than it had been before.

But this I have observed of many (myself not excepted), who, by endeavouring to excuse a blunder, like a spirited horse in one of our

The S.W. Prospect of the Castle at *Inverness*.

The N.W. Prospect.

F. Gordon Sculp.

bogs, the more he struggles to get out, the deeper he plunges himself in the mire.

Upon the whole, this hint at the policy of her amours, from a native of this town, induced me to believe there is some received tradition among the people concerning her, not much to the advantage of her memory. I had often heard something to this purpose in London, but could not easily believe it; and rather thought it might have arisen originally from complaisance to one, who, if we may believe some Scots memoirs, was as jealous of the praises of her fine person, as apprehensive of a much more dangerous competition.

Before I have done with the castle, I must acquaint you with an odd accident that had like to have happened to it, not many days after the above mentioned discovery. And first I must tell you, that one end of the building extends to the edge of a very steep descent to the river, and that slope is composed of a very loose gravel.

The workmen had ignorantly dug away some little part of the foot of the declivity, to make a passage something wider between that and the water. This was done in the evening, and pretty early in the night we were alarmed with a dreadful noise of running about, and calling upon a great number of names, insomuch that I concluded the town was on fire. This brought me suddenly to my window, and there I was informed that the gravel was running, and followed by continual successions; and that the castle would be down before morning.

However, it was prevented; for the town masons and soldiers soon run up a dry wall against the foot of the hill (for stones are everywhere at hand in this country), which furnished them with the hasty means to prevent its fall.

The bridge is about eighty yards over, and a piece of good workmanship, consisting of seven arches, built with stone, and maintained by a toll of a 'bodle', or the sixth part of a penny for each foot-passenger with goods; a penny for a loaded horse, etc.

And here I cannot forbear to give you an instance of the extreme indigence of some of the country people, by assuring you, I have seen women with heavy loads, at a distance from the bridge (the water being low), wade over the large stones, which are made slippery by the sulphur, almost up to the middle, at the hazard of their lives, being desirous to save, or unable to pay, one single bodle.

From the bridge we have often the diversion to see the seals pursue the salmon as they come up the river: they are sometimes within fifty yards of us; and one of them came so near the shore that a salmon leaped out of the water for its safety, and the seal, being shot at, dived; but before anybody could come near, the fish had thrown itself back again into the river.

As this amphibious creature, though familiar to us, may be to you a kind of curiosity, perhaps you may expect some description of it.

The head at some distance resembles that of a dog, with his ears cut close; but when near, you see it has a long thick snout, a wide mouth, and the eyes sunk within the head; and altogether it has a most horrid look, insomuch that if any one were to paint a Gorgon's head, I think he could not find a more frightful model.

As they swim, the head, which is high above water, is continually moving from side to side to discover danger.

The body is horizontally flattish, and covered with a hairy skin, often finely varied with spots, as you may see by trunks that are made to keep out wet. The female has breasts like a woman, that sometimes appear above water, which makes some to think it occasioned the fiction of a mermaid; and, if so the mermaid of the ancients must have been wondrous handsome! The breast of the male is likewise so resembling to that of a man, that an officer, seeing one of them in cutting up, went away, telling me, it was so like that part of a human body, he could not 'stand it', for that was his expression.

Beneath the skin is a deep spongy fat, something like that of the skinny part of a leg of mutton: from this they chiefly draw the oil.

The fins or feet are very near the body, webbed like a duck, about twelve inches wide, but in shape very much like the hand of a man: when they feed as they swim, they stoop the head down to the forefoot, as I once saw when one of them had a piece of salmon (I may say) in its hand, as I was crossing Cromarty Bay.

When they dive, they swim under water, I think I may say, a quarter of a mile together; and they dart after their prey with a surprising velocity, considering their bulk and the element they divide.

The fishermen take them by intercepting them in their return to the water, when they have been sleeping or basking in the sun upon the shore, and there they knock them down with their clubs. They tell me, that every grown seal is worth to them about forty shillings sterling, which arises from the skin and the oil.

When you happen to be within musket shot of them, they are so quick with the eye, that, at the flash in the pan, they plunge so suddenly, they are under water before the ball can reach them.

I have seen ten or fifteen of them, young; and old, in an arm of the sea among the mountains, which, upon the discovery of our boat, flounced into the water all at once, from a little rocky island, near the turn of a point, and raised a surprising surge round about them.

But as to their being dangerous to the fishermen, in throwing stones behind them when they are pursued, it does well enough for the volume of a travelling author, who if he did not create wonders, or steal them from others, might have little to say; but in their scrambling flight over a beach of loose stones, it is impossible but some of them must be removed and thrown behind them; and this, no doubt, has given a hint for the romance. These writers, for the better sale of their books, depend on the reader's love of admiration, the great assistant to credulity.

But, in particular, that those animals, with their short fins or feet, can wound at a distance, must certainly be concluded from this false principle, viz. that a stone may be sent from a sling of four inches long, with equal force, to another of as many feet.

Before I leave the bridge, I shall take notice of one thing more, which is commonly to be seen by the sides of the river (and not only here, but in all the parts of Scotland where I have been), that is, women with their coats tucked up, stamping, in tubs, upon linen by this way of washing; and not only in summer, but in the hardest frosty weather, when their legs and feet are almost literally as red as blood with the cold; and often two of these wenches stamp in one tub, supporting themselves by their arms thrown over each other's shoulders.

But what seems to me yet stranger is, as I have been assured by an English gentlewoman, that they have insisted with her to have the liberty of washing at the river; and, as people pass, by, they divert themselves by talking very freely to them, like our codders, and other women, employed in the fields and gardens about London.

What I have said above, relating to their washing at the river in a hard frost may require an explanation, viz. the River Ness, like the lake from whence it comes, never freezes, from the great quantity of sulphur with which it is impregnated; but, on the contrary, will dissolve the icicles, contracted from other waters, at the horses' heels, in a very short space of time.

From the tolbooth, or county jail, the greatest part of the murderers and other notorious villains, that have been committed since I have been here, have made their escape; and I think this has manifestly proceeded from the furtherance or connivance of the keepers, or rather their keepers.

When this evil has been complained of, the excuse was, the prison is a weak old building, and the town is not in condition to keep it in repair: but, for my own part, I cannot help concluding, from many circumstances, that the greatest part of these escapes have been the consequence, either of clan interest or clannish terror. As for example, if one of the magistrates were a Cameron (for the purpose), the criminal (Cameron) must not suffer, if the clan be desirous he should be saved. In short, they have several other ties or attachments one to another, which occasion (like money in the south) this partiality.

When any ship in these parts is bound for the West Indies, to be sure a neighbouring chief, of whom none dares openly to complain, has several thieves to send prisoners to town.

It has been whispered, their crimes were only asking their dues, and suchlike offences; and I have been well assured, they have been threatened with hanging, or at least perpetual imprisonment, to intimidate and force them to sign a contract for their banishment, which they seldom refused to do, as knowing there would be no want of witnesses against them, however innocent they were; and then they were put on board the ship, the master paying so much a head for them.

Thus two purposes were served at once, viz. the getting rid of troublesome fellows, and making money of them at the same time: but these poor wretches never escaped out of prison.

All this I am apt to believe, because I met with an example, at his own house, which leaves me no room to doubt it.

As this chief was walking alone, in his garden, with his dirk and pistol by his side, and a gun in his hand (as if he feared to be assassinated), and, as I was reading in his parlour, there came to me by stealth (as I soon perceived), a young fellow, who accosted me with such an accent as made me conclude he was a native of Middlesex; and every now and then he turned about, as if he feared to be observed by any of the family.

He told me, that when his master was in London, he had made him promises of great advantage, if he would serve him as his gentleman; but, though he had been there two years, he could not obtain either his wages or discharge.

And, says he, when I ask for either of them, he tells me I know I have robbed him, and nothing is more easy for him than to find, among these Highlanders, abundant evidence against me (innocent as I am); and then my fate must be a perpetual jail or transportation: and there is no means for me to make my escape, being here in the midst of his clan, and never suffered to go far from home.

You will believe I was much affected with the melancholy circumstance of the poor young man; but told him, that my speaking for him would discover his complaint to me, which might enrage his master; and, in that case, I did not know what might be the consequence to him.

Then, with a sorrowful look, he left me, and (as it happened) in very good time.

This chief does not think the present abject disposition of his clan towards him to be sufficient, but entertains that tyrannical and detestable maxim – that to render them poor, will double the tie of their obedience; and accordingly he makes use of all oppressive means to that end.

To prevent any diminution of the number of those who do not offend him, he dissuades from their purpose all such as show an inclination to traffic, or to put their children out to trades, as knowing they would, by such an alienation, shake off at least good part of their slavish attachment to him and his family. This he does, when downright authority fails, by telling them how their ancestors chose to live sparingly, and be accounted a martial people, rather than submit themselves to low and mercenary employments like the Lowlanders, whom their forefathers always despised for the want of that warlike temper which they (his vassals) still retained, etc.

I shall say no more of this chief at present, because I may have occasion to speak of him again when I come to that part which is properly called Highlands; but I cannot so easily dismiss his maxim, without some little animadversion upon it.

It may, for aught I know, be suitable to clannish power, but, in general, it seems quite contrary to reason, justice, and nature, that any one person, from the mere accident of his birth, should have the prerogative to oppress a whole community, for the gratification of his own selfish views and inclinations: and I cannot but think, the concerted poverty of a people is, of all oppressions the strongest instigation to sedition, rebellion, and plunder.

The town hall is a plain building of rubble; and there is one room in it, where the magistrates meet upon the town business, which would be tolerably handsome, but the walls are rough, not white-washed, or so much as plastered; and no furniture in it but a table, some bad chairs, and altogether immoderately dirty.

The market cross is the exchange of the merchants, and other men of business.

There they stand in the middle of the dirty street, and are frequently interrupted in their negotiations by horses and carts, which often separate them one from another in the midst of their bargains or other affairs. But this is nothing extraordinary in Scotland; for it is the same in other towns, and even at the cross of Edinburgh.

Over-against the cross is the coffee-house. A gentleman, who loves company and play, keeps it for his diversion; for so I am told by the people of the town; but he has condescended to complain to me of the little he gets by his countrymen.

As to a description of the coffee room, the furniture, and utensils, I must be excused in that particular, for it would not be a very decent one; but I shall venture to tell you in general that the room appears

T. Jefferys sculp.

as it had never been cleaned since the building of the house; and, in frost and snow, you might cover the peat fire with your hands.

Near the extreme part of the town, toward the north, there are two churches, one for the English and the other for the Irish tongue, both out of repair, and much as clean as the other churches I have seen.

This puts me in mind of a story I was told by an English lady, wife of a certain lieutenant-colonel, who dwelt near a church in the low country on your side Edinburgh. At first coming to the place, she received a visit from the minister's wife, who, after some time spent in ordinary discourse, invited her to come to kirk the Sunday following. To this the lady agreed, and kept her word, which produced a second visit; and the minister's wife then asking her how she liked their way of worship, she answered, 'Very well'; but she had found two great inconveniences there, viz. that she had dirtied her clothes, and had been pestered with a great number of fleas. 'Now,' says the lady, 'if your husband will give me leave to line the pew, and will let my servant clean it against every Sunday, I shall go constantly to church.'

'Line the pew!' says the minister's wife: 'Troth, Madam, I cannot promise for that, for my husband will think it *rank Papery*.'

A little beyond the churches is the churchyard; where, as is usual in Scotland, the monuments are placed against the wall that encloses it, because, to admit them into the church, would be an intolerable ornament. The inscriptions, I think, are much upon a par with those of our country churchyards, but the monuments are some of them very handsome and costly. I cannot say much as to the taste, but they have a good deal of ornament about them.

Even the best sort of street houses, in all the great towns of the low country, are, for the most part contrived after one manner, with a staircase withoutside, either round or square, which leads to each floor, as I mentioned in my last letter.

By the way, they call a floor a 'house'; the whole building is called a 'land'; an alley, as I said before, is a wynde; a little court, or a turn-again alley, is a 'close'; round staircase, a 'turnpike'; and a square one goes by the name of a 'skale stair'. In this town the houses are so differently modelled, they cannot be brought under any general description; but commonly the back part, or one end, is turned toward the street, and you pass by it through a short alley into a little courtyard, to ascend by stairs above the first storey. This lowest stage of the building has a door toward the street, and serves for a shop or a warehouse, but has no communication with the rest.

The houses are for the most part low, because of the violent flurries of wind which often pour upon the town from the openings of the adjacent mountains, and are built with rubble-stone, as are all the houses in every other town of Scotland that I have seen, except Edinburgh, Glasgow, Perth, Stirling, and Aberdeen; where some of them are faced with ashler stone; but the four streets of Glasgow, as I have said before, are so from one end to the other.

The rubble walls of these houses are composed of stones of different shapes and sizes; and many of them, being pebbles, are almost round, which, in laying them, leave large gaps, and on the outside they fill up those interstices by driving in flat stones of a small size; and, in the end, face the work all over with mortar thrown against it with a trowel, which they call 'harling'.

This rough casting is apt to be damaged by the weather, and must be sometimes renewed, otherwise some of the stones will drop out.

It is true, this is not much unlike the way of building in some remote parts of England; only there, the stones are squarer, and more nearly proportioned one to another: but I have been thus particular, because I have often heard it said by some of the Scots in London, before I knew anything of Scotland, that the houses were all built with stone, as despising our bricks, and concealing the manner and appearance of their buildings.

This gave me a false idea of magnificence, both as to beauty and expense, by comparing them in my thoughts with our stone buildings in the south, which are costly, scarce, and agreeable to the eye

The chasms in the inside and middle of these walls, and the disproportionate quantity of mortar, by comparison, with the stone, render them receptacles for prodigious numbers of rats, which scratch their way from the inside of the house half through the wall, where they burrow and breed securely, and by that means abound every where in the small Scots towns, especially near the sea. But among the inner parts of the mountains I never saw or heard of any such thing, except, upon recollection, in a part called Coulnakyle, in Strathspey, to which place I have been told they were brought, in the year 1723, from a ship, among some London goods.

They were then thought by the inhabitants to be a sure presage of good luck; and so indeed they were, for much money followed: but when those works are at an end, I believe famine, or another transportation, must be the fate of the vermin.

I have been credibly informed, that when the rats have been increased to a great degree in some small villages, and could hardly subsist, they have crept into the little horses' manes and tails (which are always tangled and matted, being never combed), in order to be transported to other places, as it were, to plant new colonies, or to find fresh quarters, less burdened with numbers. And I was lately told by a countryman that lives about two miles off, who brought me a bundle of straw, that having slept in a stable here, he carried home one of them in his plaid. But such numbers of them are seen by the morning twilight in the streets, for water, after dry weather succeeded by a shower of rain, as is incredible: and (what at first seemed strange to me) among them several weasels. You will certainly say I was distressed for want of matter, when I dwelt so long upon rats; but they are an intolerable nuisance.

The houses of this town were neither sashed nor slated before the Union, as I have been informed by several old people: and to this day the ceilings are rarely plastered: nothing but the single boards serve for floor and ceiling, and the partitions being often composed of upright boards only, they are sometimes shrunk, and any body may not only hear, but see, what passes in the room adjoining.

When first I came to this country, I observed in the floor of several houses a good number of circles of about an inch diameter, and likewise some round holes of the same size, the meaning of which I did not then understand; but, not long after, I discovered the cause of those inconvenient apertures.

These, in great measure, lay the family below open to those that are above, who, on their part, are incommoded with the voices of the others.

The boards, when taken from the sawmill, are bored at a good distance from one end of them, for the conveniency of their way of carriage.

They put a cord (or a 'woodie' as they call it) through the holes of several of them, to keep them flat to the horses side, and the corners of the other end drag upon the ground; but before these boards are laid in the floor the holes are filled up with plugs, which they cut away, even with the surface on each side; and when these stopgaps shrink, they drop out, and are seldom supplied.

Those houses that are not sashed, have two shutters that turn upon hinges for the low half of the window, and only the upper part is glazed; so that there is no seeing anything in the street, in bad weather, without great inconvenience.

Asking the reason of this, I was told that these people still continue those shutters as an old custom which was at first occasioned by danger; for that formerly, in their clan quarrels, several had been shot from the opposite side of the way, when they were in their chamber, and by these shutters they were concealed and in safety; but I believe the true reason is, the saving the expense of glass, for it is the same in the outparts of all the towns and cities in the low country.

LETTER IV

———◆———

Inferior houses—Pavement—Want of cleanliness—A singular practice—
Remarkable inscriptions—Shops—Ridiculous affectation—Merchants—
Their vanity—Pride of birth in the lower class—Singular condescension—
Pride of birth exemplified in a piper—Ridiculous effect of this vanity on
strangers—Evil of such conceits—Lower class—Their wretched poverty—
Laborious occupation of women—Brogues—Carts—Drivers—Harness—
Horses unshod—Ill-contrived wheels—Public curiosity at a chariot—Scarcity
of pasture—Wretched state of horses in winter—Grass—Great scarcity of
hay—Fairs at Inverness—Poverty

WITHOUT any long preface, I shall make this letter a
continuation of the descriptions I have entered into; but,
at the same time, am not without fear that my former was rather
dry and tedious to you, than informing and diverting; and this I
apprehend the more, because good part of it was not agreeable to
myself.

What I have hitherto said, with respect to the buildings of this
town, relates only to the principal part of the streets; the middling
sort of houses, as in other towns, are very low, and have generally
a close wooden staircase before the front. By one end of this you
ascend, and in it above are small round or oval holes, just big
enough for the head to go through; and in summer, or when anything
extraordinary happens in the street to excite the curiosity of the
inhabitants, they look like so many people with their heads in the
pillory.

But the extreme parts of the town are made up of most miserably low, dirty hovels, faced and covered with turf, with a bottomless tub, or basket, in the roof for a chimney.

The pavement here is very good; but, as in other small towns where the streets are narrow, it is so much rounded, that when it is dry, it is dangerous to ride, insomuch that horses which are shod are often falling; and when it is dirty, and beginning to dry, it is slippery to the feet, for in Scotland you walk generally in the middle of the streets.

I asked the magistrates one day, when the dirt was almost above one's shoes, why they suffered the town to be so excessively dirty, and did not employ people to cleanse the street? The answer was, 'It will not be long before we have a shower'.

But as to the slipperiness, we have many principal towns in England paved with small pebbles, that, going down hill, or along a slope, are not less dangerous to ride over, especially in dry weather.

Some of the houses are marked on the outside with the first letters of the owner's name, and that of his wife if he be a married man. This is, for the most part, over the uppermost window; as for example, CM MM Charles Maclean, Margaret Mackenzie; for the woman writes her maiden name after marriage; and supposing her to be a widow that has had several husbands, if she does not choose to continue the use of her maiden name, she may take the name of either of her deceased husbands, as she thinks fit. This you may be sure has been the cause of many a joke among our countrymen, in supposing something extraordinary in that man above the rest, whose name, after all, she chose to bear.

Within doors, upon the chimney-piece of one of the rooms, in some houses, there are likewise initial letters of the proprietor's name, with a scrap of their poetry, of which I shall give you only two instances. One of them is as follows:

16 WMB   As with the Fire,   EMP 94
          So with thy God do stand;
             Keep not far off,
          Nor come thou too near Hand.

The other is:

16	Christ is my Life and Rent,	78
	His Promise is my Evident.	
LS		HF

The word 'evident' alludes to the owner's title to the house, the same signifying, in Scotland, a title-deed.

I had forgot to mention an inscription upon the outside of one of those houses, viz.

> Our Building is not here, but we
> Hope for ane better in Christ.

I was saying in my last letter, that here the ground floors are called warehouses; they are so, but they would seem very odd to you under that denomination.

There is, indeed, a shop up a pair of stairs, which is kept by three or four merchants in partnership, and that is pretty well stored with various sorts of small goods and wares, mostly from London. This shop is called, by way of eminence, 'the warehouse'; here (for the purpose) a hat, which with you would cost thirteen or fourteen shillings, goes by the established name of a 'guinea hat', and other things are much in the same proportion.

I remember to have read, in one of the *Tatlers* or *Spectators*, a piece of ridicule upon the French vanity, where it is said, that a barber writes upon his sign, *Magazin de Peruques*; and a cobbler upon an old boot, *La Botte Royale*, etc., but I am sorry to say, that, of late, something of this kind has crept into our proud metropolis; for here and there you may now see an ordinary shop dubbed with the important title of a 'warehouse': this I think is no good presage.

But to return to the general run of warehouses in this town. It is true some of them contain hogsheads of French wines, pieces of brandy, and other goods that will not be spoiled by dampness; but the cargo of others, that I have happened to see open, have consisted chiefly of empty casks and bottles, hoops, chalk (which last is not to be found in this country), and other merchandise of like value. On this side the Tweed many things are aggrandized, in imitation of their ancient allies (as they call them), the French.

A pedling shopkeeper, that sells a pennyworth of thread, is a 'merchant'; the person who is sent for that thread has received a 'commission'; and, bringing it to the sender, is making 'report'. A bill to let you know there, is a single room to be let, is called a 'placard'; the doors are 'ports'; an enclosed field of two acres is a 'park'; and the wife of a laird of fifteen pounds a year is a 'lady'; and treated with – 'your Ladyship'.

I am not unaware it may be objected, with respect to the word 'merchant', that in France it signifies no more than a shopkeeper, or other small dealer, and that the exporter and importer are called *un negociant*; and it may be said by these people, they use the word in the same sense; but, if that were granted, would it not be more proper, in correspondence, to make use of words suited to the acceptation of the country corresponded to?

A friend of mine told me, when I was last in London, that he had received, some time before, a bill of exchange from this country, directed to — , merchant, in London. You know it is deemed a kind of affront among real merchants, to be too particularly pointed out in a direction, as supposing them not well known, no not even at the Royal Exchange and post office. But, as I was saying, this Scots merchant was sought after for several days upon change, and the Scots walk in particular, but nobody knew anything of him; till at length, by mere accident, he was found to lodge up two pair of stairs, at a little house over against London Wall.

Would it not have been more reasonable to have given upon the bill a full direction to his place of abode (and called him 'Esquire', if his correspondent pleased), than to send people in this manner upon a wild-goose chase?

I will not suppose one part of the design in it to be the gaining time before the merchant could be found out; but there are evidently two other reasons for such blind directions, viz. they serve to give weight to their bills at home, and as they think, an air of importance to their correspondence and countrymen in London; but, in reality, all this serves but to render the drawer and accepter ridiculous in the end.

I am told once a week that the 'gentlewoman' that washes my linen is below, and frequently hear something or other of a 'gentleman' that keeps a 'change' not far from hence. They call an alehouse a change, and think a man of a good family suffers no diminution of his gentility to keep it, though his house and sale are too inconsiderable to be mentioned without the appearance of burlesque.

I was once surprised to see a neighbouring lord dismount from his horse, take an alehouse-keeper in his arms, kiss him, and make him as many compliments as if he had been a brother peer. I could not help asking his lordship the meaning of that great familiarity; and he told me that my landlord was of as good a family as any in Scotland, but that the *Laird* his father had a great many children, and but little to give them. By the way, in the Lowlands, where there are some few signs at public houses, I have seen written upon several – *Mr* Alexander, or *Mr* James Such a one: this is a token that the man of the house is a gentleman either by birth, or that he has taken his Master of Arts degree at the university.

I shall give you but one more instance of this kind of gentility.

At a town called Nairn, not far from hence, an officer who hoped to get a recruit or two (though contrary to an order to enlist no Scotsman while the regiment was in Scotland, because otherwise, in the course of several years, it might, by mortality, become almost a Scots regiment instead of English) – I say, this officer sent for a piper to play about the town before the sergeant, as more agreeable to the people than a drum.

After some time, our landlord came to us, and, for an introduction, told us the piper was a very good 'gentleman', thinking I suppose, that otherwise we should not show him due respect according to his rank. He then went out, and, returning with him, he introduced our musician to us, who entered the room, like a Spaniard, with a grave air and stately step: at first he seemed to expect we should treat him according to the custom of the country, by asking him to sit and take a glass with us; but we were not well enough bred for that, and let him stand, with a disappointed countenance, to hear what was to be his employment. This we partly did, as knowing we had in reserve a better way of making our court.

In the evening, when he returned with the sergeant, our landlord made him a kind of speech before us, telling him (for he came two miles) that we had sent to him rather than any other, having heard how excellent he was in his way, and at the same time stole into his hand the two shillings that were ordered him with as much caution as if he had been bribing at an election, or feeing an attorney-general before company.

'Twas now quite another countenance; and, being pleased with his reward (which was great in this country, being no less than one pound four shillings), he expressed his gratitude by playing a voluntary on his pipe for more than half an hour, as he strided backward and forward, outside the house, under our window.

Here is gentility in disguise; and I am sorry to say that this kind of vanity in people of no fortune makes them ridiculous to strangers, and I wish they could divest themselves of it, and apply to something more substantial than the airy notion of 'ancient family', which, by extending our thoughts, we shall find may be claimed by all mankind.

But it may be said that this pretention procures them some respect from those who are every way their equals, if not superior to them, except in this particular. This I grant, and there lies the mischief; for by that flattering conceit, and the respect shown them, they are brought to be ashamed of honest employments, which perhaps they want as much or more than the others, and which might be advantageous to them, their families, and country.

Thus you see a gentleman may be a mercenary piper, or keep a little alehouse where he brews his drink in a kettle; but to be of any working trade, however profitable, would be a disgrace to him, his present relations, and all his ancestry. If this be not a proper subject of ridicule, I think there never was any such thing.

But to return to town after my ramble: here is a melancholy appearance of objects in the streets – in one part the poor women, maid-servants, and children, in the coldest weather, in the dirt or in snow, either walking or standing to talk with one another, without stockings or shoes. In another place, you see a man dragging along a half-starved horse little bigger than an ass, in a cart, about the size of a wheelbarrow. One part of his plaid is wrapped round his body, and the rest is thrown over his left shoulder; and every now and then he turns himself about, either to adjust his mantle, when blown off by the wind or fallen by his stooping, or to thump the poor little horse with a great stick. The load in this cart, if compact, might be carried under his arm; but he must not bear any burden himself, though his wife has, perhaps, at the same time, a greater load on her loins than he has in his cart – I say on her loins, for the women carry fish, and other heavy burdens, in the same manner as the Scots pedlars carry their packs in England.

The poor men are seldom barefoot in the town, but wear 'brogues', a sort of pumps without heels, which keep them little more from the wet and dirt than if they had none, but they serve to defend their feet from the gravel and stones.

They have three several sorts of carts, according to the enclosed sketches, of which that species wherein they carry their peats (being a light kind of loading) is the largest; but as they too are very small, their numbers are sometimes so great, that they fill up one of the streets (which is the market for that fuel) in such manner, it is impossible to pass by them on horseback, and difficult on foot.

It is really provoking to see the idleness and inhumanity of some of the leaders of this sort of carts; for, as they are something higher than the horse's tail, in the motion they keep rubbing against it till the hair is worn off, and the dock quite raw, without any care being taken to prevent it, or to ease the hurt when discovered.

Some of these carts are led by women, who are generally barefoot, with a blanket for the covering of their bodies, and in cold or wet weather they bring it quite over them. At other times they wear a piece of linen upon their heads, made up like a napkin cap in an inn, only not tied at top, but hanging down behind.

Instead of ropes for halters and harness, they generally make use of sticks of birch twisted and knotted together; these are called 'woodies'; but some few have ropes made of the manes and tails of their horses, which are shorn in the spring for that purpose.

The horse-collar and crupper are made of straw-bands; and, to save the horse's back, they put under the cart-saddle a parcel of old rags.

Their horses are never dressed or shod, and appear, as we say, as ragged as colts. In short, if you were to see the whole equipage, you would not think it possible for any droll-painter to invent so perfect a picture of misery.

F. Garden Sculp.

If the horse carries any burden upon his back, a stick of a yard long goes across, under his tail, for a crupper; but this I have seen in prints of the loaded mules in Italy.

When the carter has had occasion to turn about one sort of these carts in a narrow place, I have seen him take up the cart, wheels and all, and walk round with it, while the poor little horse has been struggling to keep himself from being thrown.

The wheels, when new, are about about a foot and half high, but are soon worn very small: they are made of three pieces of plank, pinned together at the edges like the head of a butter-firkin, and the axletree goes round with the wheel; which having some part of the circumference with the grain and other parts not, it wears unequally, and in a little time is rather angular than round, which causes a disagreeable noise as it moves upon the stones.

I have mentioned these carts, horses, and drivers, or rather draggers of them, not as immediately relating to the town, but as they increase, in great measure, the wretched appearance in the streets; for these carters, for the most part, live in huts dispersed in the adjacent country. There is little need of carts for the business of the town; and when a hogshead of wine has been to be carried to any part not very far distant, it has been placed upon a kind of frame among four horses, two on a side, following each other; for not far off, except along the sea coast and some new road, the ways are so rough and rocky that no wheel ever turned upon them since the formation of this globe; and, therefore, if the townsmen were furnished with sufficient wheel-carriages for goods of great weight, they would be seldom useful.

The description of these puny vehicles brings to my memory how I was entertained with the surprise and amusement of the common people in this town, when, in the year 1725, a chariot with six monstrous great horses arrived here, by way of the sea coast. An elephant, publicly exposed in one of the streets of London, could not have excited greater admiration. One asked what the chariot was: another, who had seen the gentleman alight, told the first, with a sneer at his ignorance, it was a great cart to carry people in, and such like. But since the making of some of the roads, I have passed through them with a friend, and was greatly delighted to see the

Highlanders run from their huts close to the chariot, and, looking up, bow with their bonnets to the coachman, little regarding us that were within.

It is not unlikely they looked upon him as a kind of prime minister, that guided so important a machine; and perhaps they might think that we were his masters, but had delivered the reins into his hands, and, at that time, had little or no will of our own, but suffered ourselves to be conducted by him as he thought fit; and therefore their addresses were directed to the minister, at least in the first place; for motion would not allow us to see a second bow, if they were inclined to make it.

It is a common thing for the poorest sort hereabouts to lead their horses out in summer, when they have done their work, and attend them while they graze by the sides of the roads and edges of the cornfields, where there is any little grass to be had without a trespass; and generally they hold them all the while by the halter, for they are certainly punished if it be known they encroached ever so little upon a field, of which none are enclosed. In like manner, you may see a man tending a single cow for the greatest part of the day. In winter the horse is allowed no more provender than will barely keep him alive, and sometimes not even that; for I have known almost two hundred of them, near the town, to die of mere want, within a small compass of time. You will find in another letter how I came to know their numbers.

Certainly nothing can be more disagreeable than to see them pass the streets before this mortality, hanging down their heads, reeling with weakness; and having spots of their skins, of a foot diameter, appearing without hair, the effect of their exceeding poverty: but the mares, in particular, are yet a more unseemly sight.

When the grass in the season is pretty well grown, the country people cut it, and bring it green to the town for sale, to feed the horses that are kept in it; as others likewise do to Edinburgh, where there is a spacious street known by the name of the Grassmarket; and this is customary in all the parts of the low country where I have been, at the time of the year for that kind of marketing.

Hay is here a rare commodity indeed; sometimes there is none at all; and I have had it brought me forty miles by sea, at the rate of half a crown or three shillings a truss. I have given twenty pence for a bundle of straw, not more than one of our trusses, and oats have cost me at the rate of four shillings a bushel, otherwise I must have seen, as we say, my horses' skins stripped over their ears. But this is not always the case; for sometimes, after the harvest, oats and straw have been pretty reasonable.

A certain officer, soon after his arrival at this town, observing in what a miserable state the horses were, and finding his own would cost him more in keeping than was well consistent with his pay, shot them. And being asked why he did not rather choose to sell them, though but for a small matter, his answer was, they were old servants and his compassion for them would not suffer him to let them fall into the hands of such keepers. And indeed the town horses are but sparingly fed, as you may believe, especially when their provender is at such an extravagant price.

Here are four or five fairs in the year, when the Highlanders bring their commodities to market: but, good God! You could not conceive there was such misery in this island.

One has under his arm a small roll of linen, another a piece of coarse plaiding: these are considerable dealers. But the merchandise of the greatest part of them is of a most contemptible value, such are these, viz. two or three cheeses, of about three or four pounds weight apiece; a kid sold for six pence or eight pence at the most; a small quantity of butter, in something that looks like a bladder, and is sometimes set down upon the dirt in the street; three for four goatskins; a piece of wood for an axletree to one of the little carts, etc. With the produce of what each of them sells, they generally buy something, viz. a horn, or wooden spoon or two, a knife, a wooden platter, and suchlike necessaries for their huts, and carry home with them little or no money.

I am just now told the mail is about to be sealed, and therefore must refer you to my next, for the conclusion of this melancholy description.

P.S. You may see one eating a large onion without salt or bread; another gnawing a carrot, etc. These are rarities not to be had in their own parts of the country.

LETTER V

———◆———

Fairs continued—Dress—A curious precaution—Plaid the undress of ladies—Mode of wearing distinguish Whig and Tory—Handsome women —Maidservants—Their poverty—Their labour and small wages— Strange habits—Seldom wear shoes—Reflection on their condition— Children of the poor—Their wretched appearance—Their dress—Frequency of a loathsome distemper—Merchants and magistrates—Their narrow-mindedness—Suspicion—Mean artifices of shopkeepers—A candid proposal, and its effects—Will not lend without a pledge—Distinction between a measure for buying and selling—Jealousy—Soldiers the best tradesmen— Education

I ALMOST long for the time when I may expect your thoughts of my letters relating to this country, and should not at all be surprised to find you say, as they do after ten o'clock at night in the wynds and closes of Edinburgh, '—, haud your haunde'.

But if that should be the case, I can plead your injunction and the nature of the subject.

Upon second thoughts, I take it, we are just even with one another; for you cannot complain that these letters are not satisfactory, because I have been only doing the duty of a friend, by endeavouring to gratify your curiosity; nor can I find any cause of blame in you, since you could not possibly conceive the consequence of the task you enjoined on me. But, according to my promise, to continue my account of our Highland fair.

If you would conceive rightly of it, you must imagine you see two or three hundred half-naked, half-starved creatures of both sexes, without so much as a smile or any cheerfulness among them, stalking about with goods, such as I have described, up to their ankles in dirt; and at night numbers of them lying together in stables, or other outhouse hovels that are hardly any defence against the weather. I am speaking of a winter fair, for in summer the greatest part of them lie about in the open country.

The gentlemen, magistrates, merchants, and shopkeepers, are dressed after the English manner, and make a good appearance enough, according to their several ranks, and the working tradesmen are not very ill clothed; and now and then, to relieve your eyes yet more from these frequent scenes of misery, you see some of their women of fashion: I say sometimes, for they go seldom abroad; but, when they appear, they are generally well dressed in the English mode.

As I have touched upon the dress of the men, I shall give you a notable instance of precaution used by some of them against the tailor's purloining.

This is to buy everything that goes to the making of a suit of clothes, even to the staytape and thread; and when they are to be delivered out, they are, all together, weighed before the tailor's face.

And when he brings home the suit, it is again put into the scale with the shreds of every sort, and it is expected the whole shall answer the original weight. But I was told in Edinburgh of the same kind of circumspection, but not as a common practice.

The plaid is the undress of the ladies; and to a genteel woman, who adjusts it with a good air, is a becoming veil. But as I am pretty sure you never saw one of them in England, I shall employ a few words to describe it to you. It is made of silk or fine worsted, chequered with various lively colours, two breadths wide, and three yards in length; it is brought over the head, and may hide or discover the face according to the wearer's fancy or occasion: it reaches to the waist behind; one corner falls as low as the ankle on one side; and the other part, in folds, hangs down from the opposite arm.

I have been told, in Edinburgh, that the ladies distinguish their political principles, whether Whig or Tory, by the manner of wearing their plaids; that is, one of the parties reverses the old fashion, but which of them it is, I do not remember, nor is it material.

I do assure you we have here, among the better sort, a full proportion of pretty women, as indeed there is all over Scotland. But,
pray remember, I now anticipate the jest, that 'women grow handsomer and handsomer the longer one continues from home'.

The men have more regard to the comeliness of their posterity,
than in those countries where a large fortune serves to soften the
hardest features, and even to make the crooked straight; and, indeed,
their definition of a fine woman seems chiefly to be directed to that
purpose; for, after speaking of her face, they say, 'She's a fine, healthy,
straight, strong, strapping lassie'.

I fancy now I hear one of our delicate ladies say, ''Tis just so they
would describe a Flander's mare'. I am not for confounding the
characters of the two sexes one with another; but I should not care
to have my son a valetudinary being, partaking of his mother's nice
constitution.

I was once commending to a lady of fortune in London, the
upright, firm, yet easy manner of the ladies walking in Edinburgh.
And when I had done, she fluttered her fan, and with a kind of
disdain, mixed with jealousy to hear them commended, she said,
'Mr —, I do not at all wonder at that, they are used to walk.'

My next subject is to be the servants. I know little remarkable of
the men, only that they are generally great lovers of ale; but my
poor maids, if I may judge of others by what passes in my own
quarters, have not had the best of chances, when their lots fell to be
born in this country. It is true they have not a great deal of household
work to do; but when that little is done, they are kept to spinning,
by which some of there mistresses are chiefly maintained. Sometimes
there are two or three of them in a house of no greater number of
rooms, at the wages of three half crowns a year each, a peck of
oatmeal for a week's diet; and happy she that can get the skimming
of a pot to mix with her oatmeal for better commons. To this
allowance is added a pair of shoes or two, for Sundays when they
go to kirk.

These are such as are kept at board-wages. In larger families, I
suppose, their standing wages is not much more, because they
make no better appearance than the others. But if any one of them
happens, by the encouragement of some English family, or one more

reasonable than ordinary among the natives, to get clothes something better than the rest, it is ten to one that envy excites them to tell her to her face, 'She must have been a heure, or she cou'd n'ere ha getten sic bonny geer'.

All these generally lie in the kitchen, a very improper place, one would think, for a lodging, especially of such who have not wherewithal to keep themselves clean.

They do several sorts of work with their feet. I have already mentioned their washing at the river. When they wash a room, which the English lodgers require to be sometimes done, they likewise do it with their feet.

First, they spread a wet cloth upon part of the floor; then, with their coats tucked up, they stand upon the cloth and shuffle it backward and forward with their feet; then they go to another part and do the same, till they have gone all over the room. After this, they wash the cloth, spread it again, and draw it along in all places, by turns, till the whole work is finished. This last operation draws away all the remaining water. I have seen this likewise done at my lodgings within a quarter of a mile of Edinburgh.

When I first saw it, I ordered a mop to be made, and the girls to be shown the use of it; but, as it is said of the Spaniards, there was no persuading them to change their old method.

I have seen women by the riverside washing parsnips, turnips, and herbs, in tubs, with their feet. An English lieutenant-colonel told me, that about a mile from the town he saw, at some little distance, a wench turning and twisting herself about as she stood in a little tub; and as he could perceive, being on horseback, that there was no water in it, he rode up close to her, and found she was grinding off the beards and hulls of barley with her naked feet, which barley, she said, was to make broth withal: and, since that, upon inquiry, I have been told it is a common thing.

They hardly ever wear shoes, as I said before, but on a Sunday; and then, being unused to them, when they go to church they walk very awkwardly: or, as we say, 'like a cat shod with walnut shells'.

I have seen some of them come out of doors, early in a morning, with their legs covered up to the calf with dried dirt, the remains of what they contracted in the streets the day before: in short, a stranger might think there was but little occasion for strict laws against low fornication.

When they go abroad, they wear a blanket over their heads, as the poor women do, something like the pictures you may have seen of some barefooted order among the Romish priests.

And the same blanket that serves them for a mantle by day, is made a part of their bedding at night, which is generally spread upon the floor: this, I think, they call a 'shakedown'.

I make no doubt you are, long before this, fully satisfied of the truth of my prediction in the first letter; for to make you thoroughly acquainted with these remote parts, you see I have been reduced to tittle-tattle as low as that of a gossiping woman: however as I am 'in for 't', I must now proceed.

Let those who deride the dirtiness and idleness of these poor creatures, which my countrymen are too apt to do, as I observed before; let them, I say, consider what inclination they can have to recommend themselves? What emulation can there proceed from mere despair? Cleanliness is too expensive for their small wages; and what inducement can they have, in such a station, to be diligent and obliging to those who use them more like Negroes than natives of Britain? Besides, it is not anything in nature that renders them more idle and uncleanly than others, as some would inconsiderately suggest; because many of them, when they happened to be transplanted into a richer soil, grow as good servants as any whatever; and this I have known by experience.

It is a happiness to infancy, especially here, that it cannot reflect and make comparisons of its condition; otherwise how miserable would be the children of the poor that one sees continually in the streets! Their wretched food makes them look pot-bellied; they are seldom washed; and many of them have their hair clipped, all but a lock that hangs down over the forehead, like the representation of old Time in a picture: the boys have nothing but a coarse kind of vest, buttoned down the back, as if they were idiots, and that their coats were so made, to prevent their often stripping themselves quite naked.

The girls have a piece of blanket wrapped about their shoulders, and are bareheaded like the boys; and both without stockings and shoes in the hardest of the seasons. But what seems to me the worst of all is, they are overrun with the itch, which continues upon them from year to year, without any care taken to free them from that loathsome distemper. Nor indeed is it possible to keep them long from it, except all could agree, it is so universal among them; and as the children of people in better circumstances are not nice in the choice of their companions and playfellows, they are most of them likewise infected with this disease; insomuch that, upon entering a room where there was a pretty boy or girl that I should have been pleased to have caressed and played with (besides the compliment of it to the father and mother), it has been a great disappointment to me to discover it could not be done with safety to myself: and though the children of the upper classes wear shoes and stockings in winter-time, yet nothing is more common than to see them barefoot in the summer.

I have often been a witness, that when the father or mother of the lesser children has ordered their shoes and stockings to be put on, as soon as ever they had an opportunity they have pulled them off, which, I suppose, was done to set their feet at liberty.

From the sight of these children in the streets, I have heard some reflect, that many a gay equipage, in other countries, has sprung from a bonnet and barefeet; but for my own part, I think a fortune obtained by worthy actions or honest industry does real honour to the possessor; yet the generality are so far misled by customary notions, as to call the founder of an honourable family an upstart; and a very unworthy descendant is honoured with that esteem which was withheld from his ancestor. But what is yet more extraordinary is, that every successor grows more honourable with time, though it be but barely on that account; as if it were an accepted principle, that a stream must needs run the clearer the further it is removed from the fountain-head. But antiquity gives a sanction to anything.

I have little conversation with the inhabitants of this town, except some few, who are not comprehended in anything I have said, or will be in anything I am about to say of the generality. The coldness between the magistrates and merchants and myself has arisen from a shyness in them towards me, and my disinclination to any kind of intimacy with them; and therefore, I think, I may freely mention the narrow way they are in, without the imputation of a spy, as some of them foolishly gave out I was in my absence when last in London.

If I had had any inclination to expose their proceedings in another place, for they were public enough here, I might have done it long ago, perhaps to my advantage; but those deceitful, boggy ways lie quite out of my road to profit or preferment.

Upon my return, I asked some of them how such a scandalous thought could ever enter into their heads, since they knew I had little conversation with them; and that on the contrary, if I resided here in that infamous capacity, I should have endeavoured to insinuate myself into their confidence, and put them upon such subjects as would enable me to perform my treacherous office; but that I never so much as heard there was any concern about them; for they were so obscure, I did not remember ever to have heard of Inverness till it was my lot to know it so well as I did; and, besides, that nothing could be more public than the reason of my continuance among them. This produced a denial of the fact from some, and in others a mortification, whether real or feigned is not much my concern.

I shall here take notice, that there is hardly any circumstance or description I have given you, but what is known to some one officer or more of every regiment in Britain, as they have been quartered here by rotation. And, if there were occasion, I might appeal to them for a justification (the interested excepted) that I have exaggerated nothing; and I promise you I shall pursue the same route throughout all my progress.

I wish I could say more to the integrity of our own lower order of shopkeepers, than truth and justice will allow me to do; but these, I think are 'sharper' (to use no worse an expression) in proportion as their temptations are stronger.

Having occasion for some Holland cloth, I sent to one of these merchants, who brought me two or three pieces, which I just looked upon, and told him that as I neither understood the quality, nor knew the price of that sort of goods, I would make him, as we say, both seller and buyer, reserving to himself the same profit as he would take from others. At first he started at the proposal; and having recollected himself, he said, 'I cannot deal in that manner'; I asked him why, but I could get nothing more from him, but that it was not their way of dealing.

Upon this, I told him it was apparently his design to have over-reached me, but that he had some probity left, which he did not seem to know of, by refusing my offer; because it carried with it a trust and confidence in his honesty: and thereupon we parted.

Since that, I made the same proposal to a mercer in Edinburgh, and was fairly and honestly dealt with.

But the instances some of these people give of their distrust one of another, in matters of a most trifling value, would fill any stranger with notions very disadvantageous to the credit of the generality.

I sent one day to a merchant's hard by for some little thing I wanted; which being brought me by my servant, he laughed and told me, that while he was in the shop, there came in the maidservant of another merchant with a message from her master, which was to borrow an ell to measure a piece of cloth, and to signify that he had sent a napkin, that is, a handkerchief, as a pledge for its being returned; that the maid took the ell, and was going away with it, without leaving the security; upon which the merchant's wife called out hastily and earnestly to her for the pawn, and then the wench pulled it out of her bosom and gave it to her, not without some seeming shame for her attempt to go away with it.

Speaking of an ell measure, brings to my mind a thing that passed a few weeks ago when I was present.

An English gentleman sent for a wright, or carpenter, to make him an ell; but before the workman came, he had borrowed one, and offered it as a pattern. 'No, Sir,' says the man, 'it must not be made by this; for yours, I suppose, is to be for buying, and this is to sell by.'

I have not myself entirely escaped suspicions of my honesty; for sending one day to a shop for some twopenny business, a groat was demanded for it; the two pence was taken, the thing was sent, but my boy's cap was detained for the remaining half of that considerable sum.

It is a common observation with the English, that when several of these people are in competition for some profitable business or bargain, each of them speaks to the disadvantage of his competitors.

Some time ago, there was occasion to hire ovens wherewith to bake bread for the soldiery then encamped near the town. The officer who had the care of providing those ovens, thought fit, as the first step towards his agreements, to talk with several of the candidates separately, at their own houses, and to see what conveniency they had wherewith to perform a contract of that nature. In the course of this inquiry, he found that every one of them was speaking not much to the advantage of the rest, and, in the conclusion, he cried out, 'Every one of these men tells me the others are rogues': and added with an oath, 'I believe them all.'

But, on the other hand, if we ask of almost any one of them, who is quite disinterested, the character of some working tradesmen, though the latter be not at all beholden to fame, the answer to our inquiry will be, 'There is not an honester lad in all Britain'. This is done in order to secure the profit to their own countrymen; for the soldiers rival them in many things, especially in handicraft trades. I take this last to be upon the principle (for certainly it is one with them) that every gain they make off the English is an acquisition to their country.

But I desire I may not be understood to speak of all in general, for there are several among them, whom I believe, in spite of education, to be very worthy, honest men – I say against education, because I have often observed, by children of seven or eight years old, that when they have been asked a question, they have either given an indirect answer at first, or considered for a time what answer was fittest for them to make. And this was not my observation alone, but that of several others, upon trial, which made us conclude that such precaution, at such an age, could not be other than the effect of precept.

P.S. I have several times been told, by gentlemen of this country with whom I have contracted acquaintance and friendship, that others have said it would have been but just that some native had had my appointment; and once it was hinted to me directly. This induced me to say (for I could not help it), I should readily agree to it, and cheerfully resign; and would further take upon me to answer for all my countrymen that they should do the same, provided no Scotsmen had any government employment be-south the Tweed; and then I doubted not that there would be ample room at home for us all. This I should not have chosen to say, but it was begged and I gave it.

LETTER VI

AS I am inclined to give you a taste of everything this country affords, I shall now step out of my way for a little while, to acquaint you, that the other day, in the evening, I made a visit to a laird's lady, who is much esteemed for her wit, and really not without some reason.

After a good deal of tea-table chat, she brought upon the carpet the subject of her own sex; and thence her ladyship proceeded to some comparisons between the conduct of the English and Scots women.

She began, in a sort of jeering manner, to tell me our females are great enemies to dust; which led me to answer – it was no wonder, for it spoiled their furniture, and dirtied their clothes.

In the next place she entertained me with a parallel between the amours of the English and the Scots women. The English, she said, often take liberties after they are married, and seldom before; whereas the Scots women, when they make a trip, it is while they are single, and very rarely afterwards: and, indeed, this last is not often known, except among those who think themselves above reputation and scandal.

Now as she had condescended to own that the Scottish females are frail as well as ours, though in different circumstances of life, which was, indeed, an acknowledgment beyond what I expected, I could not, for that reason, persuade myself to mention another difference, which is, that the English women are not so well watched.

There were many other things said upon this subject which I shall not trouble you with; but I must tell you, that this conversation reminds me of a passage which, perhaps, might otherwise never have recurred to my memory, or, at most, would have been little regarded.

One day, when I was in Edinburgh, I walked out with three married women, whose husbands, some time after dinner, retired to their respective avocations or diversions, and left them to my conduct. As we approached the fields, we happened to meet a woman with cherries: this gave me an opportunity to treat the ladies with some of that fruit; and as we were walking along, says one of them to me, 'Mr —, there is a good deal of difference between a married woman in Scotland and one in England. Here are now three of us, and I believe I may venture to say, we could not, all of us together, purchase one single pound of cherries.' You may be sure I thought their credit very low at that time, and I endeavoured to turn it off as an accident; but she told me that such kind of vacuities were pretty general among the married woman in Scotland; and, upon her appeal to the other two, it was confirmed.

I have often heard it said by the English, that the men are not our friends, but I think the females have no aversion to us; not that I fancy our persons are better made, or that we are more engaging in any respect than their own countrymen, but from the notion that prevails among them (at least such as I have been acquainted), viz. that the English are the kindest husbands in the world. Perhaps it may be said, I was their dupe, and did not discover the sneer at what they may think a too precarious confidence, of which their sex is, without doubt, the most competent judge.

But I have heard some of these ladies first accuse the English women, and then treat the chimera with such excessive virulence, that I have been tempted to suspect it proceeded from jealousy, not unattended by envy, at that liberty which may give opportunities for such unfaithfulness; for otherwise I think it might have been sufficient, even if the fact were true, barely to show their dislike of such a perfidious conduct. And, besides, I cannot say it has not happened in the world, that the most severe censure has been changed to a more charitable opinion from experience of human weakness, or that such virulence was never used as a means to excite a conquest. To conclude these remarks: I think it was not over complaisant in a stranger, to bring such a general accusation against his country-women; and if I had done as much by them it might have been deemed a national reflection. But to me it would be a new kind of knight-errantry, to fight with the gentlewomen in defence of the ladies, and therefore I contented myself with turning (in as genteel a manner as I could) their accusation and parade of virtue into ridicule.

But to return to my general purpose.

The working tradesmen, for the most part, are indolent, and no wonder, since they have so little incitement to industry, or profitable employment to encourage them to it.

If a bolt for a door be wanted, the dweller often supplies it with one of wood; and so of many other things, insomuch that the poor smith is sometimes hardly enabled to maintain himself in oatmeal.

The neatness of a carpenter's work is little regarded. If it will just answer the occasion, and come very cheap, it is enough. I shall not trouble you with further instances. But to show you what they might be, if they had encouragement, I shall mention a passage that related to myself. I sent one day for a wright (they have no such distinction as joiner) to make me an engine to chop straw withal for my horses; and told him it must be neatly made, and I would pay him accord-ingly; otherwise when it was done it would be his own. The young man, instead of being discouraged by the danger of losing his time and materials, was overjoyed at the conditions, and told me, at the same time, that he should be quite undone if he was long about work which he did for his countrymen, for in that case they would not pay him for his time. In fine, he made me the machine, which was more like the work of one of your cabinet-makers in London than that of an Inverness carpenter; and he brought it home in as little time as I could reasonably expect.

Here I may observe, that when a young fellow finds he has a genius for his trade or business, and has anything of spirit, he generally lays hold of the first occasion to remove to England, or some other country, where he hopes for better encouragement. Hence, I take it, arose a kind of proverb, that there never came a fool out of Scotland. Some, perhaps, would be giving this a different interpretation; but what I mean is, that the cleverest and most sprightly among them leave the narrow way of their own country; and from this may come, for aught I know, another saying, that they seldom desire to return home

This very man of whom I have been speaking took occasion to tell me, that in two or three months he should go to seek employment in London.

The fishermen would not be mentioned, but for their remarkable laziness; for they might find a sale for much more sea fish than they do, but so long as any money remains of the last marketing, and until they are driven out by the last necessity, they will not meddle with salt water.

At low ebb, when their boats lie off at a considerable distance from the shore, for want of depth of water, the women tuck up their garments to an indecent height, and wade to the vessels, where they receive their loads of fish for the market; and when the whole cargo is brought to land they take the fishermen upon their backs, and bring them on shore in the same manner.

There is here none of that emulation among the ordinary people, nor any of that pride which the meanest cottagers in England generally take in the cleanliness and little ornaments of their hovels; yet, at the same time, these poor wretches entertain a kind of pride which is, I think, peculiar to themselves.

The officers of a certain regiment kept here a pack of beagles; and suspecting some of them to be in danger of the mange, they sent to the boatmen to take them out a little way to sea, and throw them

T. Jefferys sculp.

overboard, imagining their swimming in salt water would cure them of the distemper, if they were infected. The servant offered them good hire for their trouble; but they gave him bad language, and told him they would not do it. Upon this, some of the officers went themselves, and, in hopes to prevail, offered them a double reward; but they said they would not, for any money do a thing so scandalous as to freight their boats with dogs; and absolutely refused it.

The poorest creature that loses a horse by death, would sell him for three pence to a soldier, who made it a part of his business to buy them; and he made not only six pence of the carcase to feed the hounds, but got two shillings or half a crown for the hide. But the owner would not flay the horse, though he knew very well how to do it, as almost every one here, and in the Highlands, is something of a tanner; and their reason is, that it is an employment only 'fit for the hangman'. Upon this principle, the soldier was frequently pursued in the streets by the children, and called by that opprobrious name.

Very often, if you ask questions of the ordinary people here and hereabouts, they will answer you by '*Haniel Sasson uggit*', i.e. they have, or speak, no Saxon (or English). This they do to save the trouble of giving other answers: but they have been frequently brought, by the officers, to speak that language by the same method that Moliere's faggot-binder was forced to confess himself a doctor of physic.

The lodgings of the ordinary people are indeed most miserable ones; and even those of some who make a tolerable appearance in the streets are not much better.

Going along with some company toward one of the outparts of the town, I was shown the apartment of a young woman, who looks pretty smart when abroad, and affects to adorn her face with a good many patches, but is of no ill fame.

The door of the house, or rather hut, being open, and nobody within, I was prevailed with to enter and observe so great a curiosity. Her bed was in one corner of the room upon the ground, made up with straw, and even that in small quantity, and upon it lay a couple of blankets, which were her covering and that of two children that lay with her. In the opposite corner was just such another bed for two young fellows, who lay in the same room.

At another time I happened to be of a party who had agreed to go five or six and twenty miles into the Highlands, a small part by land and the rest by water; but a person who was not agreeable to any of us, having, as we say, pinned himself upon us, and being gone home, it was resolved that, to avoid him, we should set out at ten o'clock the same night, instead of the next morning, as was at first intended. About twelve we arrived at the end of Loch Ness, where we were to wait for news from the vessel. We were soon conducted to a house where lives a brother to the pretender's famous brigadier; and upon entering a large room, by the candle, we discovered, on different parts of the floor, nine persons, including children, all laid in the manner above described; and among the rest, a young woman, as near as I could guess about seventeen or eighteen, who, being surprised at the light and the bustle we made, between sleeping and waking, threw off part of the blankets, and started up, stared at us earnestly, and, being stark naked, scratched herself in several parts till thoroughly wakened.

After all this, I think I need not say anything about the lodgings of the meanest sort of people.

I shall not go about to deny, because I would not willingly be laughed at, that the English luxury is in everything carried to an exorbitant height; but if there were here a little of that vice, it would be well for the lower order of people, who, by that means, would likewise mend their commons in proportion to it.

By accounts of the plenty and variety of food at the tables of the luxurious in England, the people, who have not eaten with the English, conclude they are likewise devourers of great quantities of victuals at a meal, and at other times talk of little else besides eating. This is their notion of us, but particularly of our gormandizing. I shall give you one instance:

Some years ago I obtained the favour and great conveniency to board, for a time, with an English gentleman in a house near Edinburgh, of which the proprietor retained the uppermost floor to himself and family.

It seems, by what follows, that this gentleman had amused himself sometimes by observing what passed among us; and being one day invited to our table, after dinner he told us very frankly, that he had been watching us all the time we were eating, because he had thought we must necessarily have large stomachs to consume the quantity of victuals brought so often from the market; but that now he concluded we were as moderate as any.

Thus the wonder had been reciprocal; for while he was surprised at our plenty (not knowing how much was given away), we were at a loss to think how he and his family could subsist upon their slender provision.

For my own part, I never dined in a mixed company of Scots and English, but I found the former not only eat as much as the others, but seemed as well pleased with the delicacy and diversity of the dishes; but I shall make no inference from thence.

It is from this notion of the people that my countrymen, not only here, but all over Scotland, are dignified with the title of 'Poke Pudding', which, according to the sense of the word among the natives, signifies a glutton.

Yet this reproach should not deter me from giving you an account of our way of living in this country, that is of our eating, supposing every one that charges us with that swinish vice were to read this letter.

Our principal diet, then, consists of such things as you in London esteem to be the greatest rarities, viz. salmon and trout just taken out of the river, and both very good in their kind: partridge, grouse, hare, duck, and mallard, woodcocks, snipes, etc., each in its proper season. And yet for the greatest part of the year, like the Israelites who longed for the garlic and onions of Egypt, we are hankering after beef, mutton, veal, lamb, etc.

It is not only me, but every one that comes hither, is soon disgusted with these kinds of food, when obliged to eat them often for want of other fare, which is not seldom our case.

There is hardly any such thing as mutton to be had till August, or beef till September – that is to say, in quality fit to be eaten; and both go out about Christmas. And, therefore, at or about Martinmas (the 11th of November), such of the inhabitants, who are anything beforehand with the world, salt up a quantity of beef, as if they were going a voyage. And this is common in all parts of Scotland where I have been.

It would be tedious to set down the price of every species of provision. I shall only say, that mutton and beef are about a penny a pound; salmon, which was at the same price, is, by a late regulation of the magistrates, raised to two pence a pound, which is thought by many to be an exorbitant price. A fowl, which they, in general, call a hen, may be had at market for two pence or two pence halfpenny, but so lean they are good for little. It would be too ludicrous to say that one of them might almost be cut up with the breast of another, but they are so poor, that some used to say they believed the oats were given them out by tale.

This brings to my remembrance a story I have heard of a foreigner, who being newly arrived in this country, at a public house desired something to eat. A fowl was proposed, and accepted; but when it was dressed and brought to table, the stranger showed a great dislike to it, which the landlord perceiving, brought him a piece of fresh salmon, and said, 'Sir, I observe you do not like the fowl; pray what do you think of this?' 'Think', says the guest, 'why I think it is very fine salmon, and no wonder, for that is of God Almighty's feeding; if it had been fed by you, I suppose it would have been as lean as this poor fowl, which I desire you will take away.'

We have, in plenty, variety, and good perfection, roots and greens, which you know have always made a principal part of my luxury.

This, I think, has been chiefly owing to a communication with the English: and I have been told by old people in Edinburgh, that no longer ago than forty years, there was little else but kale in their greenmarket, which is now plentifully furnished with that sort of provision, and I think altogether as good as in London.

Pork is not very common with us, but what we have is good.

I have often heard it said that the Scots will not eat it. This may be ranked among the rest of the prejudices; for this kind of food is common in the Lowlands, and Aberdeen, in particular, is famous for furnishing families with pickled pork for winter provision, as well as their shipping.

I own I never saw any swine among the mountains, and there is good reason for it: those people have no offal wherewith to feed them; and were they to give them other food, one single sow would devour all the provisions of a family.

It is here a general notion, that where the chief declares against pork, his followers affect to show the same dislike; but of this affectation I happened once to see an example.

One of the chiefs, who brought hither with him a gentleman of his own clan, dined with several of us at a public house, where the chief refused the pork, and the laird did the same; but some days afterward, the latter being invited to our mess, and under no restraint, he ate it with as good an appetite as any of us all.

The little Highland mutton, when fat, is delicious, and certainly the greatest of luxuries. And the small beef, when fresh, is very sweet and succulent, but it wants that substance which should preserve it long when salted. I am speaking of these two sorts of provision when they are well fed; but the general run of the market here, and in other places too, is such as would not be suffered in any part of England that I know of.

We (the English) have the conveniency of a public house (or tavern, if you please), kept by a countrywoman of ours, where everything is dressed our own way, but sometimes it has been difficult for our landlady to get anything for us to eat except some sort of food so often reiterated as almost to create a loathing. And one day I remember she told us there was nothing at all to be had in the town. This you may believe was a melancholy declaration to a parcel of 'Poke Puddings'; but for some relief, a Highlander soon after happened to bring to town some of the moor-game to sell, which (in looking out sharp) she secured for our dinner.

Hares and the several kinds of birds above-mentioned, abound in the neighbouring country near the town, even to exuberance; rather too much, I think, for the sportsman's diversion, who generally likes a little more expectation; so that we never need to want that sort of provision of what we may kill ourselves; and, besides, we often make presents of them to such of the inhabitants who are in our esteem; for none of them, that I know of, will bestow powder and shot upon any of the game.

It is true, they may sometimes buy a partridge for a penny, or less, and the others in proportion – I say sometimes, for there are not very many brought to market, except in time of snow, and then indeed I have seen sacks full of them.

I remember that the first hard weather after I came, I asked the magistrates why such poaching was suffered within their district; and their answer was, that there was enough of them, and if they were not brought to market they should get none themselves.

The river is not less plentiful in fish. I have often seen above a hundred large salmon brought to shore at one haul. Trout is as plenty, and a small fish the people call a little trout, but of another species, which is exceedingly good, called in the north of England a 'branlin'. These are so like the salmon fry, that they are hardly to be distinguished; only the scales come off the fry in handling, the others have none.

It is, by law, no less than transportation to take the salmon fry; but, in the season, the river is so full of them that nobody minds it, and those young fish are so simple the children catch them with a crooked pin. Yet the townsmen are of opinion that all such of them as are bred in the river, and are not devoured at sea by larger fish, return thither at the proper season; and as a proof, they affirm they have taken many of them, and, by way of experiment, clipped their tails into a forked figure, like that of a swallow, and found them with that mark when full grown and taken out of the cruives.

Eels there are, and very good, but the inhabitants will not eat of them any more than they will of a pike, for which reason some of these last, in the standing lakes, are grown to a monstrous size; and I do assure you, I have eaten of trouts taken in those waters each of fifteen or sixteen pounds weight.

I am surprised the townsmen take no delight in field-exercises or fishing, in both of which there is health and diversion, but will rather choose to spend great part of their time in the wretched coffee-room, playing at backgammon, or hazard, mostly for half-pence.

But I must ingenuously confess to you that they might retaliate this accusation, so far as it relates to mis-spending of time, if they had but the opportunity to let you know they have seen me throwing haddocks' and whitings' heads into the river from the parapet of the bridge, only to see the eels turn up their silver bellies in striving one with another for the prey. At other times they might tell you they saw me letting feathers fly in the wind, for the swallows that build under the arches (which are ribbed withinside), to make their circuits in the air, and contend for them to carry them to their nests. I have been jestingly reproached by them, *en passant*, for both these amusements, as being too juvenile for me. This I have returned in their own way, by telling them I thought myself at least as well employed as they, when tumbling over and over a little cube made out of a bone, and making every black spot on the faces of it a subject of their fear and hope. Nor did I think the Emperor Domitian's ordinary diversion was anything more manly than mine; but I think myself, this instant, much better employed by endeavouring to contribute to your amusement.

The meanest servants, who are not at board-wages, will not make a meal upon salmon if they can get anything else to eat. I have been told it here, as a very good jest, that a Highland gentleman, who went to London by sea, soon after his landing passed by a tavern where the larder appeared to the street, and operated so strongly upon his appetite that he went in – that there were among other things a rump of beef and some salmon: of the beef he ordered a steak for himself, 'But,' says he, 'let Duncan have some salmon.' To be short, the cook who attended him humoured the jest, and the master's eating was eight pence, and Duncan's came to almost as many shillings.

I was speaking of provisions in this town according to the ordinary markets, but their prices are not always such to us. There are two or three people, not far from the town, who, having an eye to our mess, employ themselves now and then in fattening fowls, and sometimes a turkey, a lamb, etc. These come very near, if not quite, as dear as they are in London.

I shall conclude this letter with an incident which I confess is quite foreign to my present purpose, but may contribute to my main design.

Since my last, as I was passing along the street, I saw a woman sitting with a young child lying upon her lap, over which she was crying and lamenting, as in the utmost despair concerning it. At first I thought it was want, but found she was come from Fort William, and that the ministers here had refused to christen her child, because she did not know who was the father of it; then she renewed her grief, and, hanging down her head over the infant, she talked to it, as if it must certainly be damned if it should die without baptism. To be short, several of us together prevailed to have the child christened, not that we thought the infant in danger, but to relieve the mother from her dreadful apprehensions.

I take this refusal to be partly political, and used as a means whereby to find out the male transgressor; but that knowledge would have been to little purpose in this case, it being a regimental child: and, indeed, this was our principal argument, for any dispute against the established rules of the Kirk would be deemed impertinence if not profaneness.

LETTER VII

———✦———

Complaint against the English—Cheapness of provisions—Curious law respecting the green plover—Highland baronet—Hospitality—Meanness—Highland cookery—Anecdote—Comparison with the English—French claret—Brandy—The laird of Culloden—His hospitality—Humorous contrivance—Hounds, and harehunting—Foxes—Beggars, numerous and importunate—Police—A Frenchman's comment—Highland thriftiness—A diverting instance of—Common sayings—Kitchens filthy—An instance of, and remarks on—Butter—Filthy state of public inns—Landlords—Their want of ceremony—Pride of family—A ridiculous instance of

THE inhabitants complain loudly that the English, since the Union, have enchanced the rates of everything by giving extravagant prices; and I must own, in particular, there has been seven pence or eight pence a pound given by some of them for beef or mutton that has been well-fed and brought to them early in the season. But the townspeople are not so nice in the quality of these things; and to some the meat is good enough if it will but serve for soup.

As to their complaint, I would know what injury it is to the country in general, that strangers especially are lavish in their expenses; does it not cause a greater circulation of money among them, and that too brought from distant places, to which but a very small part of it ever returns?

But it is in vain to tell these people that the extraordinary cheapness of provisions is a certain token of the poverty of a country; for that would insinuate they are gainers by the Union, which they cannot bear to hear of.

As an instance of the low price of provisions formerly, I have been told by some old people that, at the time of the revolution, General Mackay was accustomed to dine at one of these public houses, where he was served with great variety, and paid only two shillings and six pence Scots – that is, two pence halfpenny for his ordinary.

When I was speaking of game and wildfowl in my last letter, it did not occur to me to have often heard in this country of an old Scottish Act of Parliament for encouragement to destroy the green plover, or pewit, which, as said, is therein called the 'ungrateful' bird; for that it came to Scotland to breed, and then returned to England with its young to feed the enemy, but I never could obtain any satisfaction in this point, although a certain baronet, in the shire of Ross, who is an advocate, or counsellor-at-law, mentioned it to me at his own house in that county as a thing certain; and he seemed then to think he could produce the Act of Parliament, or at least the title of it in one of his catalogues; but he sought a long while to no purpose, which, as well as my own reason, made me conclude there was nothing in it; though, at the same time, it was matter of wonder to me that the knight should seem so positive he could produce evidence of a fact, and earnestly seek it, which, if found, would have been an undeniable ridicule upon the legislature of his own country.

What kind of food this bird is I do not know, for, although I have shot many of them here, I never made any other use of them than to pluck off the crown or crest to busk my flies for fishing, and gave the bird to the next poor Highlander I met withal; but perhaps you may have partaken of this advantage, which was so much envied by the Scots according to the tradition.

I would, but cannot, forbear to give you, *en passant*, a specimen of this Highland baronet's hospitality at the time above-mentioned.

He had known me both at Inverness and Edinburgh, and I, being out with an English officer sporting near his house, proposed to make him a visit.

After the meeting-compliments were over, he called for a bottle of wine; and, when the glass had once gone about, 'Gentlemen,' says he, pretty abruptly, 'this wine is not so good as you drink at Inverness.' We assured him it was, and repeated it several times; but he still insisted it was not, took it away himself, and set a bottle of ale before us in its stead, which we just tasted out of pure civility: but we were no losers by this, for the benefit of refreshment by his wine after fatigue would have been the least of trifles, compared with the diversion we had in going home, at this – what shall I call it? This barefaced – I don't know what!

From the provisions of this country it would be an easy natural transition to the cookery, but it might be disagreeable; and it would be almost endless to tell you what I know and have heard upon that subject. I do not mean as to the composition of the dishes, but the uncleanliness by which they are prepared. But how should you think it otherwise, when you recollect what has been said of the poor condition of the female servants, and what would you think to have your dinner dressed by one of them? I do assure you that, being upon a journey in these parts, hard eggs have been my only food for several days successively.

Shall I venture at one only instance of cookery? I will, and that a recent one, and therefore comes first to hand; but it does not come up to many others that I know, and are not fit to be told to any one that has not an immoveable stomach.

An officer, who arrived here a few days ago with his wife and son, a boy of about five or six years old, told me, that, at a house not far distant from this place, as they were waiting for dinner, the child, who had been gaping about the kitchen, came running into the room and fell a-crying, of which the mother asking the reason, he sobbed, and said, 'Mamma, don't eat any of the greens!' This occasioned a further inquiry; by which it appeared, the maid had been wringing the kale with her hands, as if she was wringing a dish-clout, and was setting it up in pyramids round the dish by way of ornament, and that her hands were very dirty, and her fingers in a lamentable condition with the itch.

Soon after the coleworts were brought to table just as the child had described their figure and situation, and the wench's hands convinced them that his whole complaint was just and reasonable.

But I would not be thought by this to insinuate that there is nothing but cleanliness in England; for I have heard of foul practices there, especially by the men cooks in the kitchens of persons of distinction; among whom I was told by one, that, happening to go into his kitchen, where he had hardly ever been before, probably by some information, he observed his cook had stuck upon the smoky chimneypiece a large lump of butter, and (like the pot of pigeons at Kelso) had raked part of it off with his fingers by handfuls as he had occasion to throw them into the saucepan.

We have one great advantage, that makes amends for many inconveniences, that is, wholesome and agreeable drink – I mean French claret, which is to be met with almost every where in public houses of any note, except in the heart of the Highlands, and sometimes even there; but the concourse of my countrymen has raised the price of it considerably. At my first coming it was but sixteen pence a bottle, and now it is raised to two shillings, although there be no more duty paid upon it now than there was before, which, indeed, was often none at all.

French brandy, very good, is about three shillings and six pence or four shillings a gallon, but in quantities, from hovering ships on the coast, it has been bought for twenty pence.

Lemons are seldom wanting here; so that punch, for those that like it, is very reasonable; but few care to drink it, as thinking the claret a much better liquor – in which I agree with them.

There lives in our neighbourhood, at a house (or castle) called Culloden, a gentleman whose hospitality is almost without bounds. It is the custom of that house, at the first visit or introduction, to take up your freedom by cracking his nut (as he terms it), that is, a cocoa-shell, which holds a pint filled with champagne, or such other sort of wine as you shall choose. You may guess by the introduction, at the contents of the volume. Few go away sober at any time; and for the greatest part of his guests, in the conclusion, they cannot go at all.

This he partly brings about by artfully proposing, after the public healths (which always imply bumpers) such private ones as he knows will pique the interest or inclinations of each particular person of the company, whose turn it is to take the lead to begin it in a brimmer;

and he himself being always cheerful, and sometimes saying good things, his guests soon lose their guard, and then – I need say no more.

For my own part, I stipulated with him, upon the first acquaintance, for the liberty of retiring when I thought convenient; and, as perseverance was made a point of honour, that I might do it without reproach.

As the company are disabled one after another, two servants who are all the while in waiting, take up the invalids with short poles in their chairs, as they sit (if not fallen down), and carry them to their beds; and still the hero holds out.

I remember one evening an English officer, who has a good deal of humour, feigned himself drunk, and acted his part so naturally, that it was difficult to distinguish it from reality; upon which the servants were preparing to take him up and carry him off. He let them alone till they had fixed the machine, and then raising himself upon his feet, made them a sneering bow, and told them he believed there was no occasion for their assistance; whereupon one of them, with sang-froid and a serious air, said, 'No matter, sir, we shall have you by and by.' This laird keeps a plentiful table, and excellent wines of various sorts and in great quantities; as, indeed, he ought, for I have often said I thought there was as much wine spilt in his hall, as would content a moderate family. We gave to a hound puppy that is now pretty well grown, in honour of him, the name of 'Bumper': another we called 'Nancy', after our most celebrated toast; so that, shortly, in our eagerest chase we shall remember love and the bottle – you know to what this alludes.

I think a pack of hounds were never kept cheaper than here (as you may believe from the mortality of horses I have already mentioned), or that there is better hare hunting in any part of Britain than hereabouts; though it be pretty rough riding in some places, and the ground mostly hilly. We never go far from the town, or beat long for the game, or indeed have much regard to seasons, for none here trouble themselves about it; insomuch that we might hunt at any time of the year without censure. Yet I have heard of a gentleman of this country, who was so scrupulous a sportsman, that when word was brought him that his servant was drowned in passing a Highland ford, he cried out, 'I thought the fellow would come to an untimely end – for he shot a hare in her form!'

In some parts, within less than ten miles of us, near the coast, the hares are in such numbers there is but little diversion in hunting, for one being started soon turns out a fresh one; then the pack is divided, and must be called off, etc., insomuch that a whole day's hunting has been entirely fruitless. The country people are very forward to tell us where the 'maukin' is, as they call a hare, and are pleased to see them destroyed, because they do hurt to their kaleyards.

Besides the hares, there are numbers of foxes; but they take to the mountains, which are rocky, and sometimes inaccessible to the dogs, of which several have been lost by falling from precipices in the pursuit; for the fox in his flight takes the most dangerous way. But when we happen to kill one of them, it is carried home, through the blessings of the people, like a dangerous captive in a Roman triumph.

In this little town there are no less than four natural fools. There are hardly any crooked people (except by accidents), because there has been no care taken to mend their shapes when they were young.

The beggars are numerous, and exceedingly importunate, for there is no parish allowance to any.

I have been told that, before the Union, they never presumed to ask for more than a bodle (or the sixth part of a penny), but now they beg for a 'baubee' (or halfpenny). And some of them, that they may not appear to be ordinary beggars, tell you it is to buy snuff. Yet still it is common for the inhabitants (as I have seen in Edinburgh), when they have none of the smallest money, to stop in the street, and giving a halfpenny, take from the beggar a 'plack', i.e. two bodles (or the third part of a penny) in change. Yet, although the beggars frequently receive so small an alms from their benefactors, I don't know how it is, but they are generally shod, when the poor working women go barefoot. But here are no idle young fellows and wenches begging about the streets, as with you in London, to the disgrace of all order, and, as the French call it, 'police'. By the way, this police is still a great office in Scotland; but, as they phrase it, is grown into disuetude, though the salaries remain.

Having mentioned this French word more by accident than choice, I am tempted (by way of chat) to make mention likewise of a Frenchman who understood a little English.

Soon after his arrival in London, he had observed a good deal of dirt and disorder in the streets; and asking about the police, but finding none that understood the term, he cried out, 'Good Lord! How can one expect order among these people, who have not such a word as "police" in their language!'

By what I have seen, the people here are something cleaner in their houses than in other parts of this country where I have been; yet I cannot set them up as patterns of cleanliness.

But in mere justice to a laird's lady, my next-door neighbour, I must tell you that in her person, and every article of her family, there is not, I believe, a cleaner woman in all Britain; and there may be others the same, for aught I know, but I never had the satisfaction to be acquainted with them.

I shall not enter into particulars; only they are, for the most part, very cautious of wearing out their household utensils of metal; insomuch that I have sometimes seen a pewter vessel to drink out of not much unlike in colour to a leaden pot to preserve tobacco or snuff.

I was one day greatly diverted with the grievous complaint of a neighbouring woman, of whom our cook had borrowed a pewter pudding pan (for we had then formed a mess in a private lodging), and when we had done with it, and she came for her dish, she was told, by the servants below stairs, that it should be cleaned, and then sent home.

This the woman took to be such an intended injury to her pan, that she cried out, 'Lord! You'll wear it out!' and then came upstairs to make her complaint to us, which she did very earnestly.

We perceived the jest, and gravely told her it was but reasonable and civil, since it was borrowed, to send it home clean. This did not at all content her, and she left us; but at the foot of the stairs, she peremptorily demanded her moveable; and when she found it had been scoured before it was used, she lost all patience, saying she had had it fifteen years, and it had never been scoured before; and she swore she would never lend it again to any of our country. But why not to any? Sure the woman in her rage intended that same *any* as a national reflection. And, without a jest, I verily think it was as much so as some words I have heard over a bottle, from which some wrong-headed, or rather rancorous, coxcombs have wrested that malicious inference; though, at the same time, the affront was not discovered by any other of the company. But this does not happen so often with them on this side the Tweed as in London, where I have known it to have been done several times apparently to raise a *querelle d'Allemand*.

Not only here, but in other parts of Scotland, I have heard several common sayings very well adapted to the inclination of the people to save themselves pains and trouble; as, for one instance, 'A clean kitchen is a token of poor housekeeping'. Another is, 'If a family remove from a house, and leave it in a clean condition, the succeeding tenant will not be fortunate in it'. Now I think it is intended the reverse of both these proverbs should be understood, viz. that 'a foul kitchen is a sign of a plentiful table' (by which one might conclude that some live like princes); and that a dirty house will be an advantage to him that takes it. But I shall give you an example of the fallacy of both these maxims, i.e. from a filthy kitchen without much cookery, and the new tenant's ill fortune to be at the expense of making a dirty house clean (I cannot say sweet), and paying half a years rent without having any benefit from it. This happened to a friend of mine.

Some few years ago he thought it would be his lot to continue long in the Lowlands; and accordingly he took a house, or floor, within half a quarter of a mile of Edinburgh, which was then about to be left by a woman of distinction; and it not being thought proper he should see the several apartments while the lady was in the house, for he might judge of them by those beneath, he, immediately after her removal, went to view his bargain. The floor of the room where she saw company was clean, being rubbed every morning according to custom; but the insides of the corner cupboards, and every other part out of sight, were in a dirty condition; but, when he came to the kitchen, he was not only disgusted at the sight of it, but sick with the smell, which was intolerable; he could not so much as guess whether the floor was wood or stone, it was covered over so deep with accumulated grease and dirt, mingled together. The drawers under the table looked as if they were almost transparent with grease; the walls near the servants' table, which had been white, were almost covered with snuff spit against it; and bones of sheeps' heads lay scattered under the dresser.

His new landlord was, or affected to be, as much moved with the stench as he himself; yet the lodging apartment of the two young ladies adjoined to this odoriferous kitchen.

Well, he hired two women to cleanse this Augean part, and bought a vast quantity of sweet herbs wherewith to rub it every where; and yet he could not bear the smell of it a month afterwards. Of all this I was myself a witness.

You know very well that a thorough neatness, both in house and person, requires expense; and therefore such as are in narrow circumstances may reasonably plead an excuse for the want of it; but when persons of fortune will suffer their houses to be worse than hogsties, I do not see how they differ in that particular from Hottentots, and they certainly deserve a verbal punishment, though I could very willingly have been excused from being the executioner; but this is only to you; yet, if it were made public (reserving names), I think it might be serviceable to some in whatever part of this island they may be.

As to myself, I profess I should esteem it as a favour rather than an offence, that any one would take the trouble to hold up a mirror to me, in which I could see where to wipe off those spots that would otherwise render me ridiculous.

I shall only trouble you with one more of these saving sayings, which is, that 'if the butter has no hairs in it the cow that gave the milk will not thrive'. But on this occasion I cannot forbear to tell you it falls out so *à propos*, that an English gentleman, in his way hither, had some butter set before him in which were a great number of hairs; whereupon he called to the landlady, desiring she would bring him some butter upon one plate and the hairs upon another, and he would mix them himself, for he thought they were too many in proportion for the quantity of butter that was before him.

Some of the inns in these remote parts, and even far south of us, are not very inviting: your chamber, to which you sometimes enter from without doors, by stairs as dirty as the streets, is so far from having been washed, it has hardly ever been scraped, and it would be no wonder if you stumbled over clods of dried dirt in going from the fireside to the bed, under which there often is lumber and dust that almost fill up the space between the floor and the bedstead. But it is nauseous to see the walls and inside of the curtains spotted, as if every one that had lain there had spit straight forward in whatever position they lay.

Leonardo da Vinci, a celebrated painter, and famous for his skill in other arts and sciences, in a treatise written by himself on the art of painting, advises those of his profession to contemplate the spots on an old wall, as a means to revive their latent ideas; and he tells them they may thereby create new thoughts, which might produce something purely original. I doubt not he meant in the same manner as people fancy they see heads and other images in a decaying fire. This precept of his has sometimes come in my mind when I cast my eye on the various forms and colours of the spots I have been speaking of; and a very little attention has produced the effect proposed by the painter.

My landlord comes into the room uninvited, and though he never saw you before, sits himself down and enters into conversation with you, and is so sociable as to drink with you; and many of them will call, when the bottle is out, for another; but, like mine host at Kelso, few will stir to fetch anything that is wanting.

This behaviour may have been made, by custom, familiar to their own countrymen; but I wonder they do not consider that it may be disagreeable to strangers of any appearance, who have been used to treat their landlords in quite another manner, even permitting an innkeeper, worth thousands, to wait at table and never show the least uneasiness at his humility; but it may be said he was no gentleman.

Pride of family, in mean people, is not peculiar to this country, but is to be met with in others; and indeed it seems natural to mankind, when they are not possessed of the goods of fortune, to pique themselves upon some imaginary advantage. Upon this remark I shall so far anticipate (by way of postscript) my Highland account as to give you a low occurrence that happened when I was last among the hills.

A young Highland girl in rags, and only the bastard daughter of a man very poor and employed as a labourer, but of a family so old that, with respect to him and many others, it was quite worn out. This girl was taken in by a corporal's wife, to do any dirty work in an officer's kitchen, and, having been guilty of some fault or neglect, was treated a little roughly; whereupon the neighbouring Highland women loudly clamoured against the cook, saying, 'What a monster is that to maltreat a *gentleman's* bairn!' and the poor wretch's resentment was beyond expression upon that very account.

LETTER VIII

———◆———

Correspondence interrupted—Reason of—Visit to a Highland chief—
Account of the excursion—Occurrences on the way—Arrival at the castle
—Reception—Entertainment—Musicians—Style of dinner—Ostentation—
Number of Highlanders in attendance—Chief engrosses the conversation
—Departure—Return—Remarks—Wretched stables—Trial of patience
—Highland ale—The pint stoop—A dialogue—English spoken at
Inverness—Irish in the Lowlands—Herring fishery—Instance of a plentiful
season—Fraud on salt duty—Appointment of a new officer—Is bribed—
Intimidated by a smuggler—Curious consequences—Importations—Attempt
to prohibit brandy—Scarcity of port—Soldiers—Wretched quarters—A
complaint—Honour among merchants—Ministers and their stipends—Style
of discourses—Strongly object to personal decoration—Force of flattery

AS I have, in point of time, till the last post, been perfectly punctual
in this my tattling correspondence, though not so exact in
my letters upon other subjects, you may possibly expect I should
give you a reason for this failure, at least I am myself inclined to do
so.

Several of us (the English) have been, by invitation, to dine with
an eminent chief, not many miles from hence, in the Highlands; but
I do assure you it was his importunity (the effect of his interest) and
our own curiosity, more than any particular inclination, that induced
us to a compliance.

We set out early in the morning without guide or interpreter, and
passed a pretty wide river, into the county of Ross, by a boat that

we feared would fall to pieces in the passage. This excursion was made in order to a short visit on that side the Moray Firth, and to lengthen out the way, that we might not be too early with our noble host.

Our first visit being dispatched, we changed our course, and as the sailor says, 'stood' directly, as we thought, for the castle of our inviter; but we soon strayed out of our way among the hills, where there was nothing but heath, bogs, and stones, and no visible track to direct us, it being across the country.

In our way we inquired of three several Highlanders, but could get nothing from them but '*Haniel Sasson uggit*'. We named the title of our chief, and pointed with the finger; but he was known to none of them, otherwise than by his patronymic, which none of us knew at that time. (I shall have something to say of this word, when I come to speak of the Highlands in general.) But if we had been never so well acquainted with his ancestry name, it would have stood us in little stead, unless we had known likewise how to persuade some one of those men to show us the way. At length we happened to meet with a gentleman, as I supposed, because he spoke English, and he told us we must go west apiece (though there was no appearance of the sun), and then incline to the north; that then we were to go along the side of a hill, and ascend another (which to us was then unseen), and from the top of it we should see the castle.

I should have told you, that in this part of our peregrination we were upon the borders of the mountains only; and the hills, for the most part, not much higher than Hampstead or Highgate.

No sooner had he given us this confused direction, but he skipped over a little bog, that was very near us, and left us to our perplexed consultations. However, at last we gained the height; but when we were there, one of our company began to curse the Highlander for deceiving us, being prepossessed with the notion of a castle, and seeing only a house hardly fit for one of our farmers of fifty pounds a year; and in the courtyard a parcel of low outhouses, all built with turf, like other Highland huts.

When we approached this castle, our chief with several attendants (for he had seen us on the hill), came a little way to meet us; gave us a welcome, and conducted us into a parlour pretty well furnished.

After some time, we had notice given us that dinner was ready in another room; where we were no sooner sat down to table, but a band of music struck up in a little place out of sight, and continued playing all the time of dinner.

These concealed musicians he would have had us think were his constant domestics; but I saw one of them, some time after dinner, by mere chance, whereby I knew they were brought from this town to regale us with more magnificence.

Our entertainment consisted of a great number of dishes, at a long table, all brought in under covers, but almost cold. What the greatest part of them were I could not tell, nor did I inquire, for they were disguised after the French manner; but there was placed next to me a dish, which I guessed to be boiled beef – I say that was my conjecture, for it was covered all over with stewed cabbage, like a smothered rabbit, and over all a deluge of bad butter.

When I had removed some of the encumbrance, helped myself, and tasted, I found the pot it was boiled in had given it too high a *goût* for my palate, which is always inclined to plain eating.

I then desired one of the company to help me to some roasted mutton, which was indeed delicious, and therefore served very well for my share of all this inelegant and ostentatious plenty.

We had very good wine, but did not drink much of it; but one thing I should have told you was intolerable, viz. the number of Highlanders that attended at table, whose feet and foul linen, or woollen, I don't know which, were more than a match for the odour of the dishes.

The conversation was greatly engrossed by the chief, before, at, and after dinner; but I do not recollect anything was said that is worth repeating.

There were, as we went home, several descants upon our feast; but I remember one of our company said he had tasted a pie, and that many a peruke had been baked in a better crust.

When we were returned hither in the evening we supped upon beefsteaks, which some, who complained they had not made a dinner, rejoiced over, and called them a luxury.

I make little doubt but, after our noble host had gratified his ostentation and vanity, he cursed us in his heart for the expense, and that his family must starve for a month to retrieve the profusion; for this is according to his known character.

Toward the conclusion of my last letter I gave you some account of the lodging rooms of many of the inns in this country, not forgetting my landlord; and now I shall descend to the stables, which are often wretched hovels, and, instead of straw for litter, are clogged with such an accumulated quantity of dung, one might almost think they required another Hercules to cleanse them.

There is another thing very inconvenient to the traveller, which I had omitted. He is made to wait a most unreasonable while for everything for which he has occasion. I shall give you only one instance among a hundred.

At the Blairatholl, benighted, tired, and hungry, I came to the inn, and was put into a room without any light; where, knowing the dilatory way of those people, I sat patiently waiting for a candle near half an hour; at last, quite tired with expectation, I called pretty hastily, and, I must confess, not without anger, for a light and some wine; this brought in a servant maid, who, as usual, cried out, 'What's your will?' I then again told her my wants; but had no other answer than that her mistress had the keys, and was at supper, and she could not be disturbed. Her mistress, it is true, is a gentlewoman, but before she was married to the stately beggar who keeps that house she lived in this town, and was humble enough to draw twopenny.

The 'twopenny', as they call it, is their common ale; the price of it is two pence for a Scots pint, which is two quarts.

In sliding thus from the word twopenny to a description of that liquor, there came to my memory a ridiculing dissertation upon such kind of transitions in one of the *Tatlers*, for those books I have with me, which, indeed, are here a good part of my library.

This liquor is disagreeable to those who are not used to it; but time and custom will make almost anything familiar. The malt, which is dried with peat, turf, or furzes, gives to the drink a taste of that kind of fuel: it is often drank before it is cold out of a cap, or 'coif', as they call it: this is a wooden dish, with two ears or handles, about the size of a tea-saucer, and as shallow, so that a steady hand is necessary to carry it to the mouth, and, in windy weather, at the door of a change, I have seen the liquor blown into the drinker's face. This drink is of itself apt to give a diarrhoea; and therefore, when the natives drink plentifully of it, they interlace it with brandy or whisky.

I have been speaking only of the common ale; for in some few gentlemen's houses I have drank as good as I think I ever met with in any part of England, but not brewed with the malt of this country.

The mention of their capacious pint pot, which they call a 'stoup', puts me in mind of part of a dialogue between two footmen, one English the other Scots.

Says the English fellow, 'Ye sorry dog, your shilling is but a penny.' 'Aye,' says Sawny, who, it seems, was a lover of ale, ''tis true; but the De'el tak him that has the least pint stoup.'

They tell me, that in Edinburgh and other great towns, where there are considerable brewings, they put salt into the drink, which makes it brackish and intoxicating.

The natives of this town speak better English than those of any other part of Scotland, having learned it originally from the troops in the time of Oliver Cromwell; but the Irish accent that sometimes attends it is not very agreeable.

The Irish tongue was, I may say lately, universal even in many parts of the Lowlands; and I have heard it from several in Edinburgh, that, before the Union, it was the language of the shire of Fife, although that county be separated from the capital only by the Firth of Forth, an arm of the sea, which from thence is but seven miles over; and, as a proof, they told me, after that event (the Union) it became one condition of an indenture, when a youth of either sex was to be bound on the Edinburgh side of the water, that the apprentice should be taught the English tongue.

This town is not ill situated for trade, and very well for a herring fishery in particular; but except the shoals would be so complaisant as to steer into some part of the Moray Firth near them, they may remain in safety from any attempts of our adventurers: yet, notwithstanding they do not go out to sea themselves, they are continually complaining of the Dutch, who, they say, with their vast number of busses, break and drive the shoals from coming nearer to them.

There was lately a year in which they made a considerable advantage (I think they say five or six thousand pounds) from the quantity of fish, which, as I may say, fell into their mouths; but this happens very rarely, and then their nets and vessels are in a bad condition. Their excuse is, that they are poor; and when they have been asked, why then does not a greater number contribute to a stock sufficient to carry on a fishery effectually to this they have answered frankly, that they could not trust one another.

Some of the honester sort have complained, that when they had a good quantity of fish to send abroad (for the sake of the bounty on salt exported), the herrings have not swam much thicker in the barrel than they did before in the sea, and this brought their ships into disrepute at foreign markets.

I have heard, from good authority, of a piece of finesse that was practised here, which must have been the product of some very fertile brain, viz. the screwing of wool into a cask, and laying over it some pieces of pickled salmon, separated by a false head, and by that means, and an oath, obtaining the bounty upon salt exported, as if the whole was salmon, and at the same time running the wool; but to this, the connivance of the collector of the customs was necessary.

This fraud (among others) was made a handle to procure the appointment of an inspector-general at the salary of £200 per annum, which was done at the representation and request of a certain M— of D—, who had been, as the cant is, a good boy for many years, and never asked for anything; but at first the M—r made strong objections to it, as it was to be a new-created place, which was generally the cause of clamour, and particularly with respect to the person proposed, who had formerly been condemned to be hanged for perjury relating to the customs, and was a Jacobite. But, in order to remove all these scruples, the gentleman who solicited the affair first acknowledged all that to be true. 'But, sir,' said he, 'the Laird is familiar with the man's wife.' 'Nay then,' says the M—r, 'he must have it.'

Not long afterwards, there was information given that a considerable quantity of wine and brandy was run, and lodged in a house on the north side of the Moray Firth, and the new-made officer applied accordingly for a sergeant and twelve men to support him in making the seizure. When he arrived at the place, and had posted his guard at some small distance from the house, he went in and declared his business: whereupon the owner told him, that if he proceeded further he would ruin him; for that he knew of a sum of money he had taken, on the other side of the water, for his connivance at a much greater cargo.

Upon this, with guilt and surprise, the custom-house officer said, 'But what must I do with the soldiers?' 'Nay,' says the other, 'do you look to that.'

Then he went out, and having mused awhile, he returned in better spirits, and said, 'Now I have got it! You have firearms, I suppose?' 'Yes,' says the other. 'Then do you arm yourself and your servants, and come resolutely to the door, and swear to me that you will all die upon the spot rather than your house should be ransacked, unless an authentic warrant be produced for that purpose.'

This was done; and the officer immediately fell to fumbling in his pockets, till he had gone through the whole order of them; and then, turning to the sergeant, he cried out, 'What an unfortunate dog am I! What shall I do? I have left my warrant at home!' To conclude: after all this farce had been well acted, he told the sergeant there could nothing be done, by reason of this unlucky accident, but to return to Inverness, giving him half a crown, and to each of the soldiers one shilling.

Some time ago insurance was the practice, which the Royal Exchange soon discovered; but this imputation was brought upon the town, as I have been assured, by one single person.

But what am I talking of? I am mentioning to you four or five illicit dealers, when you can tell me of great part of our own coast, where almost all degrees of men are either practising, encouraging, or conniving at the same iniquity.

The principal importation of these parts consists in wines, brandy, tea, silks, etc., which is no great advantage to those who deal that way, when their losses by bad debts, seizures, and other casualties, are taken into the account: and it is injurious to the community, by exchanging their money for those commodities which are consumed among themselves, excepting the soldiery and a few strangers, who bring their money with them.

Every now and then, by starts, there have been agreements made among the landed men, to banish, as much as in them lay, the use of brandy in particular. By those contracts they have promised to confine themselves to their own growth, and to enjoin the same to their families, tenants and other dependants; but, like some salutary laws made for the public, these resolutions have not been regarded long.

I wish the reformation could be made for the good of the country (for the evil is universal); but I cannot say I should even be contented it should extend to the claret, till my time comes to return to England and humble port, of which, if I were but only inclined to taste, there is not one glass to be obtained for love or money, either here or in any other part of Scotland that has fallen within my knowledge: but this does not at all excite my regret. You will say I have been giving you a pretty picture of patriotism in miniature, or as it relates to myself.

Sometimes they export pretty handsome quantities of pickled salmon, and the money expended by the troops is a good advantage to the town and the country hereabouts; of which they are so sensible, that, unlike our own countrymen who think the soldiery a burden, they have several times solicited for more companies to be quartered in the town; though, God knows, most of the quarters are such as, with you, would hardly be thought good enough for a favourite dog.

It was but the other day that a grenadier came to the commanding officer, and begged of him to take a view of his bed; and, with tears in his eyes told him he had always been a clean fellow (for those were his words), but here he could not keep himself free from vermin.

As I happened to be present, the officer desired me to go along with him. I did so; and what the man called a bed proved to be a little quantity of straw, not enough to keep his sides from the hardness of the ground, and that too laid under the stairs very near the door of a miserable hovel. And though the magistrates have often been applied to, and told that the very meanest among the soldiers have never been used to such lodging, yet their favourite townspeople have always been excused, and these most wretched quarters continued to them. And I cannot doubt but this has contributed greatly to the bloody flux, which sweeps away so many of them, that, at some seasons, for a good while together, there has hardly a day passed but a soldier has been buried. Thus are they desirous to make their gains of the poor men without any regard to their ease or their health, which I think is something to the purpose of a profligate saying I have heard, 'Give me the fortune, and let the devil take the woman!' But when the new barracks are completed, the soldiers will have warm quarters, and the town lose great part of their profit by provision made for them from more distant parts.

There is one practice among these merchants which is not only politic but commendable, and not to be met with every where, which is, that if a bill of exchange be drawn upon any one of them, and he fails in cash to make payment in due time, in that case the rest of them will contribute to it rather than the town should receive any discredit.

In a former letter I took notice that there are two churches in this town, one for the English, the other for the Irish tongue. To these there are three ministers, each of them, as I am told, at one hundred pounds a year.

It is a rule in Scotland, or at least is generally understood to be so, that none shall have more than that stipend, or any less than fifty; yet I have been likewise informed, that some of the ministers in Edinburgh and other cities make of it near two hundred, but how the addition arises has not come to my knowledge. What I shall say of the ministers of this town is, that they are men of good lives and sober conversation, and less stiff in many indifferent matters than most of their brethren in other parts of Scotland; and, to say the truth, the Scottish clergy (except some rare examples to the contrary) lead regular and unblamable lives.

What I have further to say on this head shall be more general, but nothing of this kind can be applied to all.

The subjects of their sermons are, for the most part, grace, freewill, predestination, and other topics hardly ever to be determined; they might as well talk Hebrew to the common people, and I think to anybody else. But 'Thou shalt do no manner of work', they urge with very great success. The text relating to Caesar's tribute is seldom explained, even in places where great part of the inhabitants live by the contrary of that example. In England, you know, the minister, if the people were found to be negligent of their clothes when they came to church, would recommend decency and cleanliness, as a mark of respect due to the place of worship; and indeed, humanly speaking, it is so to one another. But, on the contrary, if a woman, in some parts of Scotland, should appear at kirk dressed, though not better than at an ordinary visit, she would be in danger of a rebuke from the pulpit, and of being told she ought to purify her soul, and not employ part of the Sabbath in decking out her body; and I must needs say, that most of the females in both parts of the kingdom follow, in that particular, the instructions of their spiritual guides religiously.

The minister here in Scotland would have the ladies come to kirk in their plaids, which hide any loose dress, and their faces, too, if they would be persuaded, in order to prevent the wandering thoughts of young fellows, and perhaps some young old ones too; for the minister looks upon a well-dressed woman to be an object unfit to be seen in the time of divine service, especially if she be handsome.

The before-mentioned writer of *A Journey through Scotland*, has borrowed a thought from the *Tatler* or *Spectator*, I do not remember which of them.

Speaking of the ladies' plaids, he says, 'They are striped with green, scarlet, and other colours, which, in the middle of a church on a Sunday, look like a *parterre de fleurs*.' Instead of striped he should have said chequered, but that would not so well agree with his flowers; and I must ask leave to differ from him in the simile, for at first I thought it a very odd sight; and as to outward appearance, more fit to be compared with an assembly of harlequins than a bed of tulips.

But I am told this traveller through Scotland was not ill paid for his adulation by the extraordinary call there has been for his last volume. The other two, which I am told relate to England, I have not seen, nor did I ever hear their character.

They tell me this book is more common in this country than I shall say; and this, in particular, that I have seen was thumbed in the opening where the 'pretty town of Inverness' is mentioned, much more than the book we saw at a painter's house in Westminster some years ago; which you will remember (to our diversion) was immoderately soiled in that important part where mention was made of himself.

O, Flattery! Never did any altar smoke with so much incense as thine! Thy female votaries fall down reversed before thee; the wise, the great – whole towns, cities, provinces, and kingdoms – receive thy oracles with joy, and even adore the very priests that serve in thy temples!

LETTER IX

———❦———

Ministers appear to disregard morality in their sermons—Their prayers—Extempore preaching—Danger of—Mistakes in—An instance of—Approval of a Minister at Edinburgh—Extracts from a sermon—Lilly the astrologer —Improvement of young ministers—Ministers circumscribed in their intercourse—Their strict observance of the Sabbath—Are much revered by the people—Their strictness—Instance of—In synod assume great authority—Neglect of the Kirk—Its consequences—Meeting of synod—Whimsical saying—Watchful of the female character—Singular marriage by declara-tion—Power of the Kirk to compel—Routine for enforcing—Penance—Injudicious application of—Fatal occurrence—Power of the presbytery—Instance of—Doing penance—Style of ministerial rebuke—Power of ministers with the bulk of the people—Instance of—Kirk treasurer—His spies—Frequent service on Sunday—Kirk bell—Music bells

I WISH these ministers would speak oftener, and sometimes more civilly than they do of morality.

To tell the people they may go to Hell with all their morality at their back – this surely may insinuate to weak minds, that it is to be avoided as a kind of sin – at best that it will be of no use to them: and then no wonder they neglect it, and set their enthusiastic notions of grace in the place of righteousness. This is in general; but I must own, in particular, that one of the ministers of this town has been so careful of the morals of his congregation that he earnestly exhorted them, from the pulpit, to fly from the example of a wicked neighbouring nation.

Their prayers are often more like narrations to the Almighty than petitions for what they want; and the 'sough', as it is called (the whine), is unmanly, and much beneath the dignity of their subject.

I have heard of one minister so great a proficient in this sough, and his notes so remarkably flat and productive of horror, that a master of music set them to his fiddle, and the wag used to say, that in the most jovial company, after he had played his tune but once over, there was no more mirth among them all the rest of that evening than if they were just come out of the cave of Trophonius.

Their preaching extempore exposes them to the danger of exhibiting undigested thoughts and mistakes; as, indeed, it might do to any others who make long harangues without some previous study and reflection; but that some of them make little preparation, I am apt to conclude from their immethodical ramblings.

I shall mention one mistake – I may call it an absurdity:

The minister was explaining to his congregation the great benefits arising from the Sabbath. He told them it was a means of frequently renewing their covenant, etc.; and, likewise, it was a worldly good, as a day of rest for themselves, their servants, and cattle. Then he recounted to them the different days observed in other religions, as the seventh day by the Jews, etc. 'But,' says he, 'behold the particular wisdom of our institution, in ordaining it to be kept on the first for if it were any other day, it would make a broken week!'

The cant is only approved of by the ignorant (poor or rich), into whom it instils a kind of enthusiasm, in moving their passions by sudden starts of various sounds. They have made of it a kind of art not easy to attain; but people of better understanding make a jest of this drollery, and seem to be highly pleased when they meet with its contrary. The latter is manifest to me by their judgment of a sermon preached at Edinburgh by a Scots minister, one Mr Wishart.

Several of us went to hear him, and you would not have been better pleased in any church in England.

There was a great number of considerable people, and never was there a more general approbation than there was among them at going from the kirk.

This gentleman, as I was afterwards informed, has set before him Archbishop Tillotson for his model; and, indeed, I could discover several of that prelate's thoughts in the sermon.

How different was that of another Edinburgh minister, who, in one of his sermons, made use of an extraordinary comparison, surely not fit for a congregation to hear, viz. Christians, with respect to grace, are like a maid; it's hard to get it into them, difficult to make them keep it, and painful for them to part with it. But it may be supposed, that when Mess John had stumbled upon the simile, he thought it too *à propos* to be concealed.

And I have been told, that in explaining to a poor sinner upon the stool of repentance, the heinousness of the sin of fornication, some of them, in their extemporary admonitions, have stumbled upon descriptions not much tending to promote chastity in the congregation.

One of the ministers of this town (an old man, who died some time ago) undertook one day to entertain us with a dialogue from the pulpit relating to the fall of man, in the following manner, which cannot so well be conveyed in writing as by word of mouth:

First he spoke in a low voice – 'And the L. G. came into the garden, and said — '

Then loud and angrily – 'Adam, where art?'

Low and humbly – 'Lo, here am I, Lord!'

Violently – 'And what are ye deeing there?'

With a fearful trembling accent – 'Lord, I was nacked, and I hid mysel.'

Outrageously – 'Nacked! And what then? Hast thou eaten', etc.

Thus he profanely (without thinking so) described the omniscient and merciful God in the character of an angry master, who had not patience to hear what his poor offending servant had to say in excuse of his fault. And this they call speaking in a familiar way to the understandings of the ordinary people.

But perhaps they think what the famous astrologer, Lilly, declared to a gentleman, who asked him how he thought any man of good sense would buy his predictions. This question started another, which was – what proportion the men of sense bore to those who could not be called so, and at last they were reduced to one in twenty.

'Now,' says the conjuror, 'let the nineteen buy my prophecies, and then', snapping his fingers, 'That! For your one man of good sense.'

Not to trouble you with any more particulars of their oddities from the pulpit, I shall only say, that, since I have been in this country, I have heard so many, and of so many, that I really think there is nothing set down in the book, called *Scots Presbyterian Eloquence*, but what, at least, is probable. But the young ministers are introducing a manner more decent and reasonable, which irritates the old stagers against them; and therefore they begin to preach at one another.

If you happen to be in company with one or more of them, and wine, ale, or even a dram is called for, you must not drink till a long grace be said over it, unless you could be contented to be thought irreligious and unmannerly.

Some time after my coming to this country I had occasion to ride a little way with two ministers of the Kirk; and, as we were passing by the door of a change, one of them, the weather being cold, proposed a dram.

As the alehouse-keeper held it in his hands, I could not conceive the reason of their bowing to each other, as pleading by signs to be excused, without speaking one word.

I could not but think they were contending who should drink last, and myself, a stranger, out of the question; but, in the end, the glass was forced upon me, and I found the compliment was which of them should give the preference to the other saying grace over the brandy. For my part, I thought they did not well consider to whom they were about to make their address, when they were using all this ceremony one to another in his presence; and, to use their own way of argument, concluded they would not have done it in the presence at St James's.

They seem to me to have but little knowledge of men, being restrained from all free conversation, even in coffee-houses, by the fear of scandal, which may be attended with the loss of their livelihood; and they are exceedingly strict and severe upon one another in everything which, according to their way of judging, might give offence.

Not long ago, one of them, as I am told, was suspended for having a shoulder of mutton roasted on a Sunday morning; another for powdering his peruke on that day. Six or seven years ago, a minister (if my information be right) was suspended by one of the presbyteries – the occasion this:

He was to preach at a kirk some little way within the Highlands, and set out on the Saturday; but, in his journey, the rains had swelled the rivers to such a degree, that a ford which lay in his way was become impassable.

This obliged him to take up his lodging for that night at a little hut near the river; and getting up early the next morning, he found the waters just enough abated for him to venture a passage, which he did with a good deal of hazard, and came to the kirk in good time, where he found the people assembled and waiting his arrival.

This riding on horseback of a Sunday was deemed a great scandal. It is true, that when this affair was brought, by appeal, before the General Assembly in Edinburgh, his suspension was removed, but not without a good many debates on the subject.

Though some things of this kind are carried too far, yet I cannot but be of opinion, that these restraints on the conduct of the ministers, which produce so great regularity among them, contribute much to the respect they meet with from the people; for although they have not the advantage of any outward appearance, by dress, to strike the imagination, or to distinguish them from other men who happen to wear black or dark gray, yet they are, I think I may say, ten times more reverenced than our ministers in England.

Their severity likewise to the people, for matters of little consequence, or even for works of necessity, is sometimes extraordinary.

A poor man who lodged in a little house where (as I have said) one family may often hear what is said in another; this man was complained of to the minister of the parish by his next neighbour, that he had talked too freely to his *own wife*, and threatened her with such usage as we may reasonably suppose she would easily forgive.

In conclusion, the man was sentenced to do penance for giving scandal to his neighbours: a pretty subject for a congregation to ruminate upon!

The informer's wife, it seems, was utterly against her husband's making the complaint; but it was thought she might have been the innocent occasion of it, by some provoking words or signs that bore relation to the criminal's offence. This was done not far from Edinburgh.

One of our more northern ministers, whose parish lies along the coast between Spey and Findhorn, made some fishermen do penance for Sabbath-breaking, in going out to sea, though purely with endeavour to save a vessel in distress by a storm. But behold how inconsistent with this pious zeal was his practice in case relating to his own profit.

Whenever the director of a certain English undertaking in this country fell short of silver wherewith to pay a great number of workmen, and he was therefore obliged on pay-day to give gold to be divided among several of them, then this careful guardian of the Sabbath exacted of the poor men a shilling for the change of every guinea, taking that exorbitant advantage of their necessity.

In business, or ordinary conversation, they are, for the most part, complaisant; and I may say, supple, when you talk with them singly – at least I have found them so; but when collected in a body at a presbytery, or synod, they assume a vast authority, and make the poor sinner tremble.

Constantly attending ordinances, as they phrase it, is a means with them of softening vices into mere frailties; but a person who neglects the Kirk, will find but little quarter.

Some time ago two officers of the army had transgressed with two sisters at Stirling: one of these gentlemen seldom failed of going to kirk, the other never was there. The affair came to a hearing before a presbytery, and the result was, that the girl who had the child by the kirk-goer was an impudent baggage, and deserved to be whipped out of town for seducing an honest man; and that he who never went to kirk, was an abandoned wretch for debauching her sister.

Whether the ordinary people have a notion that when so many holy men meet together upon any occasion, the evil spirits are thereby provoked to be mischievous, or what their whimsical fancy is I cannot tell, but it is with them a common saying, that when the clergy assemble the day is certainly tempestuous.

If my countrymen's division of the year were just, there would always be a great chance for it without any supernatural cause; for they say, in these northern parts, the year is composed of nine months winter and three months bad weather; but I cannot fully agree with them in their observation, though, as I have said before, the neighbouring mountains frequently convey to us such winds as may not improperly be called tempests.

In one of my journeys hither, I observed, at the first stage on this side Berwick, a good deal of scribbling upon a window; and among the rest, the following lines, viz.

> Scotland! Thy weather's like a modish wife,
> Thy winds and rains for ever are at strife;
> So termagant, awhile her bluster tries,
> And when she can no longer scold – she cries!
>
> A. H.

By the two initial letters of a name, I soon concluded it was your neighbour, Mr Aaron Hill, but wondered at his manner of taking leave of this country, after he had been so exceedingly complaisant to it, when here, as to compare its subterraneous riches with those of Mexico and Peru.

There is one thing I always greatly disapproved, which is, that when anything is whispered, though by few, to the disadvantage of a woman's reputation, and the matter be never so doubtful, the ministers are officiously busy to find out the truth, and by that means make a kind of publication of what, perhaps, was only a malicious surmise – or if true, might have been hushed up; but their stirring in it possesses the kind of every one, who has any knowledge of the party accused, to her disadvantage: and this is done to prevent scandal! I will not say what I have heard others allege, that those who are so needlessly inquisitive in matters of this nature must certainly feel a secret pleasure in suchlike examinations; and the joke among the English is, that they highly approve of this proceeding, as it serves for a direction where to find a loving girl upon occasion.

I have been told, that if two or more of these ministers admonish, or accuse a man, concerning the scandal of suspected visits to some woman, and that he, through anger, peevishness, contempt, or desire to screen the woman's reputation, should say, 'She is my wife', then the ministers will make a declaration upon the spot to this purpose, viz.

'In the Name of the Father, Son, and Holy Ghost, we pronounce you, A. B. and C. D., to be man and wife'; and the marriage is valid, at least so far as it relates to Scotland; but whether this kind of coupling would be binding when the parties are in any other country has not come to my knowledge.

If a woman of any consideration has made a slip which becomes visible, and her lover be a man of some fortune, and an inhabitant, the Kirk will support her, and oblige him either to marry her, to undergo the penance, or leave the country; for the woman in that circumstance always declares she was deceived under promise of marriage: and some of them have spread their snares with design by that means to catch a husband. Nay, I have known English gentlemen, who have been in government employments, that, after such an affair, have been hunted from place to place, almost from one end of Scotland to the other, by the women, who, wherever they came, have been favoured by the clergy; and, at best, the man has got rid of his embarrassment, by a composition: and, indeed, it is no jesting matter; for although his stay in this country might not be long enough to see the end of the prosecution, or, by leave of absence, he might get away to England, yet the process being carried on from a kirk session to a presbytery, and thence to a synod, and from them to the General Assembly, which is the *dernier ressort* in these cases; yet from thence the crime and contempt may be represented above; end how could any particular person expect to be upheld in the continuance of his employment, against so considerable a body as a national clergy, in transgression against the laws of the country, with a contempt of that authority by which those laws are supported? I mention this, because I have heard several make a jest of the Kirk's authority.

When a woman has undergone the penance, with an appearance of repentance, she has wiped off the scandal among all the godly; and a female servant, in that regenerated state, is as well received into one of those families as if she had never given a proof of her frailty.

There is one kind of severity of the Kirk which I cannot but think very extraordinary; and that is, the shameful punishment by penance for ante-nuptial fornication, as they call it; for the greatest part of male transgressors that way, when they have gratified their curiosity, entertain a quite different opinion of the former object of their desire from what they had while she retained her innocence, and regard her with contempt if not with hatred. And therefore one might think it a kind of virtue, at least honesty, in the man who afterwards makes the only reparation he can for the injury done, by marrying the woman he has otherwise brought to infamy. Now may not this public shame deter many from making that honest satisfaction? But the great offence is against the office, which formerly here was the prerogative of the civil magistrate as well as the minister, till the former was jostled out of it by clamour.

There happened, a very few years ago, a fatal instance of the change of opinion above-mentioned:

A young gentleman (if he may deserve the title) made his addresses to the only daughter of a considerable merchant in a city of the Lowlands; and one evening as the young people were alone together, being supposed to be just upon the eve of marriage, and the young woman's father and mother in the next room, which was separated only by a slight partition, the eager spark made his villainous attempt with oaths and imprecations, and using common plea, that they were already man and wife before God, and promising the ceremony should be performed the next day, and perhaps he meant it at that instant. By these means he put the poor girl under a dilemma, either to give herself up, or, by resisting the violence, to expose her lover to the fury of her parents. Thus she was – what shall I say? – one must not say undone, for fear of a joke, though not from you. And as that kind of conquest, once obtained renders the vanquished a slave to her conqueror, the wedding was delayed, and she soon found herself with child. At length the time came when she was delivered, and in that feeble state she begged she might only speak to her deceiver; who, with great difficulty, was prevailed with to see her. But when she put him in mind of the circumstances she was in when he brought her to ruin, he, in a careless, indolent manner, told her she was as willing as himself; upon which she cried out, 'Villain, you know yourself to be a liar!' and immediately jumped out of bed, and dropped down dead upon the floor.

But I must go a little further, to do justice to the young gentlemen of that town and the neighbourhood of it; for as soon as the melancholy catastrophe was known, they declared to all keepers of taverns and coffee-houses where they came, that if ever they entertained that fellow they would never after enter their doors.

Thus, in a very little time, he was deprived of all society, and obliged to quit the country.

I am afraid your smart ones in London would have called this act of barbarity only a piece of gallantry, and the betrayer would have been as well received among them as ever before.

I know I should be laughed at by the libertines, for talking thus gravely upon this subject, if my letter were to fall into their hands. But it is not in their power, by a sneer, to alter the nature of justice, honour, or honesty, for they will always be the same.

What I have said is only for repairing the effect of violence, deceit, and perjury; and of this, every one is a conscious judge of himself.

If any one be brought before a presbytery, etc., to be questioned for 'sculduddery', i.e. fornication or adultery, and shows a neglect of their authority, the offender is not only brought to punishment by their means, but will be avoided by his friends, acquaintance, and all that know him and his circumstance in that respect.

I remember a particular instance in Edinburgh, where the thing was carried to an extraordinary height.

A married footman was accused of adultery with one of the wenches in the same family where he served; and, before a kirk session, was required to confess, for nothing less will satisfy; but he persisted in denial of the fact.

This contempt of the clergy and lay elders, or, as they say, of the Kirk, excited against him so much the resentment and horror of the ordinary people (who looked upon him as in a state of damnation while the anathema hung over his head), that none of them would drink at the house where his wife kept a change.

Thus the poor woman was punished for the obstinacy of her husband, notwithstanding she was innocent, and had been wronged the other way.

I was told in Edinburgh that a certain Scots colonel, being convicted of adultery (as being a married man), and refusing to compound, he was sentenced to stand in a hair cloth at the kirk door every Sunday morning for a whole year, and to this he submitted.

At the beginning of his penance he concealed his face as much as he could, but three or four young lasses passing by him, one of them stooped down, and cried out to her companions, 'Lord! It's Colonel —.' Upon which he suddenly threw aside his disguise, and said, 'Miss, you are right; and if you will be the subject of it, I will wear this coat another twelvemonth.'

Some young fellows of fortune have made slight of the stool of repentance, being attended by others of their age and circumstances of life, who to keep them in countenance, stand with them in the same gallery or pew fronting the pulpit; so that many of the spectators, strangers especially, cannot distinguish the culprit from the rest. Here is a long extemporary reproof and admonition, as I said before, which often creates mirth among some of the congregation.

This contempt of the punishment has occasioned, and more especially of late years, a composition in money with these young rakes, and the kirk treasurer gives regular receipts and discharges for such and such fornications.

As I have already told you how much the ministers are revered, especially by the commonalty, you will readily conclude the mob are at their devotion upon the least hint given for that purpose; of which there are many riotous instances, particularly at the opening of the Playhouse in Edinburgh, to which the clergy were very averse, and left no stone unturned to prevent it.

I do not, indeed, remember there was much disturbance at the institution of the ball or assembly, because that meeting is chiefly composed of people of distinction; and none are admitted but such as have at least a just title to gentility, except strangers of good appearance. And if by chance any others intrude they are expelled upon the spot, by order of the directrice, or governess, who is a woman of quality. I say, it is not in my memory there was any riot at the first of these meetings: but some of the ministers published their warnings and admonitions against promiscuous dancing; and in one of their printed papers, which was cried about the streets, it was said that the devils are particularly busy upon such occasions. And Asmodeus was pitched upon as the most dangerous of all in exciting to carnality. In both these cases, viz. the Playhouse and the assembly, the ministers lost ground to their great mortification; for the most part of the ladies turned rebels to their remonstrances, notwithstanding their frightful danger.

I think I never saw so many pretty women of distinction together as at that assembly, and therefore it is no wonder that those who know the artful insinuations of that fleshly spirit should be jealous of so much beauty.

But I have not done with my kirk treasurer – this in Edinburgh is thought a profitable employment.

I have heard of one of them (severe enough upon others) who, having a round sum of money in his keeping, the property of the Kirk, marched off with the cash, and took his neighbour's wife along with him to bear him company and partake of the spoil.

There are some rugged hills about the skirts of that city, which, by their hollows and windings, may serve as screens from incurious eyes; but there are sets of fellows, enemies to love and lovers of profit, who make it a part of their business, when they see two persons of different sexes walk out to take the air, to dog them about from place to place, and observe their motions, while they themselves are concealed. And if they happen to see any kind of freedom between them, or perhaps none at all, they march up to them and demand the 'bulling siller' (alluding to the money usually given for the use of a bull); and if they have not something given them (which to do would be a tacit confession), they, very likely, go and inform the kirk treasurer of what perhaps they never saw, who certainly makes the man a visit the next morning. And as he (the treasurer), like our informing justices formerly, encourages these wretches, people lie at the mercy of villains who would perhaps forswear themselves for six pence apiece.

The same fellows, or such like, are peeping about the streets of Edinburgh in the night-time, to see who and who are together;

and sometimes affront a brother and sister, or a man and his wife.

I have known the town guard, a band of men armed and clothed in uniforms like soldiers, to beset a house for a whole night, upon an information that a man and a woman went in there, though in the daytime. In short, one would think there was no sin, according to them, but fornication; or other virtue besides keeping the Sabbath.

People would startle more at the humming or whistling part of a tune on a Sunday, than if anybody should tell them you had ruined a family.

I thought I had finished my letter; but stepping to the window, I saw the people crowding out of the kirk from morning service; and the bell begins to ring, as if they were to face about and return. And now I am sitting down again to add a few words on that subject – but you have perceived that such occasional additions have been pretty common in the course of this prattle.

This bell is a warning to those who are going out, that they must soon return; and a notice to such as are at home, that the afternoon service is speedily to begin. They have a bell in most of the Lowland kirks; and as the Presbyterians and other sectaries in England are not allowed to be convened by that sound (of their own), so neither are those of the Episcopal Church in Scotland. But I need not tell you, that every where the reigning church will be paramount, and keep all other communities under. The people, in the short interval between the times of service, walk about in the churchyard, the neighbouring fields, or step home and eat an egg or some little ready-dressed morsel, and then go back to their devotions. But they fare better in the evening; which has given rise to a common saying in Scotland, viz. 'If you would live well on the Sabbath, you must eat an Episcopal dinner and a Presbyterian supper'. By this it should seem, that the Episcopalians here provide a dinner, as in England – I say it seems so, for I never was at one of their meetings, or dined with any of them at their houses on a Sunday.

I have just now taken notice that each church has but one bell; which leads me to acquaint you, that on a joy-day, as the King's birthday, etc. (we will suppose in Edinburgh, where there are nine churches), the bells are all rung at a time, and almost all of them within hearing. This causes a most disagreeable jangling, by their often clashing one with another. And thus their joy is expressed by the same means as our sorrow would be for the death of a good king.

But their music bells (as they call them) are very entertaining, and a disgrace to our clockwork chimes.

They are played at the hours of exchange, that is, from eleven to twelve, upon keys like an organ or harpsichord; only as the force in this case must be greater than upon those instruments, the musician has a small cushion to each hand, to save them from bruising.

He plays Scots, English, Irish, and Italian tunes to great perfection, and is heard all over the city. This he performs every weekday, and, I am told, receives from the town, for this service, a salary of fifty pounds a year.

LETTER X

———❖———

A progress among the mountains—Guide and his discourse—Mountain scenery—Extravagant gratitude of a Highlander—Reflection on the condition of Highlanders—Curious letter from a young Highlander in America—Remarks on

I AM now to acquaint you that I have not at this time sufficient provision for your usual repast. But, by the way, I cannot help accusing myself of some arrogance, in using such a metaphor; because your ordinary fare has been little else beside 'brochan', 'cale', 'stirabout', 'sowings', etc. (oatmeal varied in several shapes): but, that you may be provided with something, I am now about to give you a 'haggass', which would be yet less agreeable, were it not to be a little seasoned with variety.

The day before yesterday, an occasion called me to make a progress of about six or seven miles among the mountains; but before I set out, I was told the way was dangerous to strangers, who might lose themselves in the hills if they had not a conductor. For this reason, about two miles from hence, I hired a guide, and agreed with him for six pence to attend me the whole day. This poor man went barefoot, sometimes by my horse's side, and in dangerous places leading him by the bridle, winding about from side to side among the rocks, to such gaps where the horses could raise their feet high enough to mount the stones, or stride over them.

In this tedious passage, in order to divert myself (having an interpreter with me), I asked my guide a great many questions relating to the Highlands, all which he answered very properly.

In his turn, he told me, by way of question, to hear what I would say, that he believed there would be no war; but I did not understand, his meaning till I was told. By 'war' he meant rebellion; and then, with a dismal countenance, he said he was by trade a weaver, and that in the year 1715, the 'seidir roy', or red soldiers, as they call them (to distinguish them from the Highland companies, whom they call 'seider dou', or the black soldiers) – I say he told me, that they burnt his house and his loom, and he had never been in a condition since that time to purchase materials for his work, otherwise he had not needed to be a guide; and he thought his case very hard, because he had not been in the affair, or the 'scrape', as they call it all over Scotland, being cautious of using the word rebellion. But this last declaration of his, I did not so much depend on.

When he had finished his story, which, by interpreting, took up a good deal of time, I recounted to him the fable of the pigeon's fate that happened to be among the jackdaws, at which he laughed heartily, notwithstanding his late grief for his loss; and doubtless the fable was to him entirely new.

I then asked his reason why he thought there would not be another war (as he called it); and his answer was, he believed the English did not expect one, because they were fooling away their money, in removing great stones and blowing up of rocks.

Here he spoke his grievance as a guide; and indeed, when the roads are finished according to the plan proposed, there will be but little occasion for those people, except such as can speak English, and may by some be thought necessary for interpreters in their journeys: I say they will be useless as guides alone, reckoning from the south of Scotland to this town the mountain way (for along the coast hither, the road can hardly be mistaken), and counting again from the Lowlands to the west end of the opening among the mountains that run from hence quite across the island.

But all the Highlands north of this town and the said opening will remain as rugged and dangerous as ever.

At length I arrived at the spot, of which I was to take a view, and found it most horrible; but in the way, that I went, being the shortest cut going southward, it is not to be avoided.

This is a deep, narrow hollow, between very steep mountains, into which huge parts of rocks have fallen. It is a terrifying sight to those who are not accustomed to such views; and at bottom is a small but dangerous burn, running wildly among the rocks, especially in times of rain. You descend by a declivity in the face of the mountain, from whence the rocks have parted (for they have visibly their decay), and the rivulet is particularly dangerous, when the passenger is going along with the stream, and pursued by the torrent. But you have not far to go in this bottom before you leave the current, which pursues its way, in continued windings, among the feet of the mountains; and soon after you ascend by a steep and rocky hill, and when the height is attained, you would think the most rugged ways you could possibly conceive to be a happy variety.

When I had returned to the hut where I took my guide, being pleased with the fellow's good humour, and frankness in answering my questions, instead of six pence I gave him a shilling. At first he could not trust his own eyes, or thought I was mistaken; but being told what it was, and that it was all his own, he fell on his knees and cried out, he never, in all his life before, knew anybody give more than they bargained for. This done, he ran into his hut, and brought out four children almost naked, to show them to me, with a prayer for the English. Thus I had, for so small a price as one six pence, the exquisite pleasure of making a poor creature happy for a time.

Upon my Highlander's lamentation of his loss and present bad circumstances, I could not forbear to reflect and moralize a little, concluding, that ruin is ruin, as much to the poor as to those that had been rich.

Here's a poor Highlandman (whose house, loom, and all his other effects were, it is likely, not worth thirty shillings) as effectually undone, by the loss he sustained, as one that had been in the possession of thousands; and the burning of one of their huts, which does not cost fifteen shillings in building, is much worse to them than the loss of a palace by fire is to the owner. And were it not for their fond attachment to their chiefs, and the advantage those gentlemen take of their slave-like notions of patriarchal power, I verily believe there are but few among them that would engage in an enterprise so dangerous to them as rebellion; and as some proof of this, I have been told by several people of this town, that in the year 1715, the then Earl of Mar continued here for near two months together before he could muster two hundred Highlanders, so unwilling were these poor people to leave their little houses and their families to go a king-making.

But when a number sufficient for his present purpose had been corrupted by rewards and promises, he sent them out in parties from hut to hut, threatening destruction to such as refused to join with them.

But it may be necessary to let you know that these men of whom I have been speaking, were not such as were immediately under the eye of their respective chiefs, but scattered in little dwellings about the skirts of the mountains.

Here follows the copy of a Highlander's letter, which has been lately handed about this town, as a kind of curiosity.

When I first saw it, I suspected it to be supposititious, and calculated as a lure, whereby to entice some Highlanders to the colony from whence it was supposed to be written; but I was afterwards assured, by a very credible person, that he knew it to be genuine.

Endorsed – letter from Donald McPherson a young Highland lad, who was sent to Virginia with Captain Toline, and was born near the house of Culloden where his father lives.

Portobago in Marilante, 2 June 17—

Teer lofen kynt Fater,

Dis is te let ye ken, dat I am in quid Healt, plessed be Got for dat, houpin te here de lyk frae yu, as I am yer nane Sin, I wad a bine ill leart gin I had na latten yu ken tis, be Kaptin Rogirs Skep dat geangs to Innerness, per cunnan I dinna ket sika anither apertunti dis Towmen agen. De Skep dat I kam in was a lang tym o de See cumin oure heir, but plissit pi Got for à ting wi à kepit our Heels unco weel, pat Shonie Magwillivray dat hat ay a Sair Heet. Dere was saxty o's à kame inte te Quintry hel a lit an lim an nane o's à dyit pat

Shonie Magwillivray an an otter Ross lad dat kam oure wi's an mai
pi dem twa wad a dyit gin tey hed bitten at hame.

Pi mi fait I kanna komplin for kumin te dis Quintry, for mestir
Nicols, Lort pliss hem, pat mi till a pra Mestir, dey ca him Shon
Bayne, an hi lifes in Marylant in te rifer Potomak, he nifer gart mi
wark ony ting pat fat I lykit mi sel: de meast o à mi Wark is waterin
a pra stennt Hors, an pringin Wyn an Pread ut o de seller te mi
Mestir's Tebil.

Sin efer I kam til him I nefer wantit a Pottle o petter ele nor is in à
shon glass hous, for I ay set toun wi de Pairns te Dennir.

Mi Mestir seys till mi, fan I can speck lyk de fouk hier dat I sanna
pe pidden di nating pat gar his Plackimors wurk, for de fyt fouk
dinna ise te wurk pat te first yeer aftir dey kum in te de Quintry. Tey
speck à lyk de Sogers in Innerness.

Lofen Fater, fan de Sarvants trier he deen wi der mestirs, dey
grou unco rich, an its ne wonter for day mak a hantil tombako; an
des Sivites an Apels an de Sheries an de Pires grou in de wuds wantin
Tyks apout dem. De Swynes te Ducks an Durkies geangs en de Wuds
wantin Mestirs.

De Tombako grous shust lyk de Dockins en de bak o de lairts
yart an de Skeps dey cum fra ilka Place an bys dem an gies a hantel
o Silder and Gier for dem.

Mi nane Mestir kam til de Quintry a Sarfant an weil I wot hi's
nou wort mony a susan punt. Fait ye mey pelive mi de pirest Plantir
hire lifes amost as weil as de Lairt o Collottin. Mai pi fan mi Tim is
ut I wel kom hem an sie yu pat not for de furst nor de neest Yeir till
I gater somting o mi nane, for fan I ha dun wi mi Mestir, hi maun gi
mi a Plantashon to set mi up, its de Quistium hier in dis Quintry; an
syn I houp to gar yu trink wyn insteat o Tippeni in Innerness.

I wis I hat kum our hier twa or tri Yiers seener nor I dit, syn I
wad ha kum de seener hame, pat Got bi tanket dat I kam sa seen as
I dit.

Gin yu koud sen mi owr be ony o yur Innerness skeps, ony tiny te
mi, an it war as muckle Clays as mak a Quelt it wad, mey pi, gar my
Meister tink te mere o mi. It's trw I ket clays eneu fe him bat oni
ting fe yu wad luck weel an Pony, an ant plese Got gin I life, I sal
pey yu pack agen.

Lofen fater, de Man dat vryts dis Letir for mi is van Shams
Macheyne, hi lifes shust a Myl fe mi, hi hes pin unko kyn te mi sin
efer I kam te de Quintrie. Hi wes Porn en Petic an kam our a sarfant
fe Klesgou an hes peen hes nane Man twa yeirs, an has Sax Plackimors
wurkin til hem alrety makin Tombako ilka Tay. Heil win hem, shortly
an à te Geir dat he hes wun hier an py a LERTS KIP at hem. Luck
dat yu duina forket te vryt til mi ay, fan yu ket ony ocashion.

Got Almichte pliss you Fater an a de leve o de hous, for I hana
forkoten nane o yu, nor dinna yu forket mi, for plise Got I sal kum
hem wi Gier eneuch te di yu à an mi nane sel guid.

I weit you will be very vokie, fan yu sii yur nane Sins Fesh agen,
for I heive leirt a hantle hevens sin I sau yu an I am unco buick leirt.

A tis is fe yur lofen an Opetient Sin,

TONAL MACKAFERSON

For Shames Mackaferson neir te Lairt o Collottin's hous, neir
Innerness en de Nort o Skotlan.

This letter is a notable instance of those extravagant hopes that
often attend a new condition. Yet Donald, notwithstanding all his
happiness, desires his father to send him some clothes; not that he
wants, or shall want them, but that they would look 'bonny' and
recommend him to his master. But I shall not further anticipate that
difficulty, which I know will not be unpleasing to you.

If you should think poor Donald's sentiments of his change to be
worth your notice, and at the same time find yourself at a loss to
make out any part of his letter, your friend Sir Alexander, who is
very communicative, will be pleased with the office of your interpreter.

There is one thing I should have told you at first, which is, that
where I have marked the single (a) thus (à), it must be pronounced
(au), which signifies (all).

LETTER XI

Episcopalians—Remarkable instance of disloyalty—Nonjuring ministers
—Political cast of their instructions—Weddings—Penny, or servant's
weddings—Do not use the ring—Custom of plunging infants into water—
Christening—Admonition to parents—Funerals—Mode of invitation to—
Of procession—Bagpipe—Funerals among the higher class—Entertainment
at—Excessive drinking—Minister has no demand for christening, marrying, or burial—Inconvenience of burial fees in England—Oliver Cromwell's
fort—His army—His colours

NEAR the conclusion of my last letter but one, I happened to
say a word or two concerning the Episcopalians of this
country, of whom I do not remember to have known one that is not
a professed Jacobite, except such as are in the army, or otherwise
employed under the Government, and therefore I must suppose all
those who have accepted of commissions or places were in their hearts
of revolutional principles before they entered into office, or that they
changed for them on that occasion.

You know my true meaning; but many people in this country
render the word 'revolution' a very equivocal expression – nor,
among many, is it free from ambiguity in the south.

Their ministers here are all nonjurors, that I know, except those
of the chief baron's chapel in Edinburgh, and the Episcopal church
at Aberdeen; but whether there is any qualified Episcopal minister
at Glasgow, St Andrews, etc., I do not know.

The nonjuring ministers generally lead regular lives; and it behoves them so to do, for otherwise they would be distanced by their rivals.

I saw a flagrant example of the people's disaffection to the present government in the above mentioned church of Aberdeen, where there is an organ, the only one I know of, and the service is chanted as in our cathedrals.

Being there, one Sunday morning, with another English gentleman, when the minister came to that part of the litany where the king is prayed for by name, the people all rose up as one, in contempt of it, and men and women set themselves about some trivial action, as taking snuff, etc., to show their dislike, and signify to each other they were all of one mind; and when the responsal should have been pronounced, though they had been loud in all that preceded, to our amazement there was not one single voice to be heard but our own, so suddenly and entirely were we dropped.

At coming out of the church we complained to the minister (who, as I said before, was qualified) of this rude behaviour of his congregation, who told us he was greatly ashamed of it, and had often admonished them, at least, with more decency.

The nonjuring ministers have made a kind of linsey-woolsey piece of stuff of their doctrine, by interweaving the people's civil rights with religion, and teaching them, that it is as unChristian not to believe their notions of government as to disbelieve the gospel. But I believe the business, in a great measure is to procure and preserve separate congregations to themselves, in which they find their account by inciting State enthusiasm, as others do Church fanaticism, and, in return, their hearers have the secret pleasure of transgressing under the umbrage of duty.

I have often admired the zeal of a pretty well-dressed Jacobite, when I have seen her go down one of the narrow, steep wyndes in Edinburgh, through an accumulation of the worst kind of filth, and whip up a blind staircase almost as foul, yet with an air as *degagé* as if she were going to meet a favourite lover in some poetic bower: and, indeed, the difference between the generality of those people and the Presbyterians, particularly the women, is visible when they come from their respective instructors, for the former appear with cheerful countenances, and the others look as if they had been just before convicted and sentenced by their gloomy teachers.

I shall now, for a while, confine myself to some customs in this town; and shall not wander, except something material starts in my way.

The evening before a wedding there is a ceremony called the 'feet-washing', when the bridesmaids attend the future bride, and wash her feet.

They have a penny-wedding – that is, when a servant maid has served faithfully, and gained the goodwill of her master and mistress, they invite their relations and friends, and there is a dinner or supper on the day the servant is married, and music and dancing follow to complete the evening.

The bride must go about the room and kiss every man in the company, and in the end everybody puts money into a dish, according to their inclination and ability. By this means a family in good circumstances, and respected by those they invite, have procured for the new couple wherewithal to begin the world pretty comfortably for people of their low condition. But I should have told you, that the whole expense of the feast and fiddlers is paid out of the contributions. This and the former are likewise customs all over the Lowlands of Scotland.

I never was present at one of their weddings, nor have I heard of anything extraordinary in that ceremony, only they do not use the ring in marriage, as in England. But it is a most comical farce to see an ordinary bride conducted to church by two men, who take her under the arms, and hurry the poor unwilling creature along the streets, as you may have seen a pickpocket dragged to a horse-pond in London. I have somewhere read of a kind of force, of old, put upon virgins in the article of marriage, in some eastern country, where the practice was introduced to conquer their modesty; but I think, in this age and nation, there is little occasion for any such violence; and, perhaps, with reverence to antiquity, though it often reproaches our times, it was then only used to save appearances.

The moment a child is born, in these northern parts, it is immerged in cold water, be the season of the year never so rigorous. When I seemed at first a little shocked at the mention of this strange extreme, the good women told me the midwives would not forego that practice if my wife, though a stranger, had a child born in this country.

At the christening, the husband holds up the child before the pulpit, from whence the minister gives him a long extemporary admonition concerning its education. In most places the infant's being brought to the church is not to be dispensed with, though it be in never so weak a condition; but here, as I said before, they are not so scrupulous in that and some other particulars.

For inviting people to ordinary buryings, in all parts of the low country as well as here, a man goes about with a bell, and, when he comes to one of his stations (suppose the deceased was a man), he cries, 'All brethren and sisters, I let you to wot, that there is a brother departed this life, at the pleasure of Almighty God; they called him', etc. – He lived at', etc. And so for a woman, with the necessary alterations. The corpse is carried, not upon men's shoulders, as in England, but underhand upon a bier; and the nearest relation to the deceased carries the head, the next of kin on his right hand, etc., and, if the churchyard be anything distant, they are relieved by others as occasion may require. The men go two and two before the bier, and the women, in the same order, follow after it; and all the way the bellman goes tinkling before the procession, as is done before the host in popish countries.

Not long ago a Highlandman was buried here. There were few in the procession besides Highlanders in their usual garb; and all the way before them a piper played on his bagpipe, which was hung with narrow streamers of black crape.

When people of some circumstance are to be buried, the nearest relation sends printed letters signed by himself, and sometimes, but rarely, the invitation has been general, and made by beat of drum.

The friends of the deceased usually meet at the house of mourning the day before the funeral, where they sit a good while, like Quakers at a silent meeting, in dumb show of sorrow; but in time the bottle is introduced, and the ceremony quite reversed.

It is esteemed very slighting, and scarcely ever to be forgiven, not to attend after invitation, if you are in health; the only means to escape resentment is to send a letter, in answer, with some reasonable excuse.

The company, which is always numerous, meets in the street at the door of the deceased; and when a proper number of them are assembled, some of those among them, who are of highest rank or most esteemed, and strangers, are the first invited to walk into a room, where there usually are several pyramids of plum cake, sweetmeats, and several dishes, with pipes and tobacco; the last is according to an old custom, for it is very rare to see anybody smoke in Scotland.

The nearest relations and friends of the person to be interred attend, and, like waiters, serve you with wine for about a quarter of an hour; and no sooner have you accepted of one glass but another is at your elbow, and so a third, etc. There is no excuse to be made for not drinking, for then it will be said, 'You have obliged a brother, or my cousin Such a one; pray, sir, what have I done to be refused?' When the usual time is expired, this detachment goes out and another succeeds; and when all have had their tour, they accompany the corpse to the grave, which they generally do about noon.

The minister, who is always invited, performs no kind of funeral service for those of any rank whatever, but most commonly is one of the last that leaves the place of burial.

When the company are about to return, a part of them are selected to go back to the house, where all sorrow seems to be immediately banished, and the wine is filled about as fast as it can go round, till there is hardly a sober person among them. And, by the way, I have been often told, that some have kept their friends drinking upon this occasion for more days together than I can venture to mention.

In the conclusion, some of the sweetmeats are put into your hat, or thrust into your pocket, which enables you to make a great compliment to the women of your acquaintance.

This last homage they call the 'dredgy'; but I suppose they mean the dirge – that is, a service performed for a dead person some time after his death; or this may be instead of a lamentation sung at the funeral; but I am sure it has no sadness attending it, except it be for an aching head the next morning. The day following, every one that has black puts it on, and wears it for some time afterwards; and if the deceased was anything considerable, though the mourners' relation to him was never so remote, it serves to soothe the vanity of some, by inciting the question, 'For whom do you mourn?' 'My cousin, the Laird of Such a place,' or 'My Lord Such a one,' is the answer to the question begged by the sorrowful dress. I have seen the doors and gates blacked over in token of mourning.

I must confess I never was present at more than one of these funerals, though afterwards invited to several, and was pretty hard put to it to find out proper excuses; but I never failed to enquire what had passed at those assemblies, and found but little difference among them.

You know I never cared to be singular when once engaged in company, and in this case I thought it best, being a stranger, to comply with their customs, though I could not but foresee the inconvenience that was to follow so great an intimacy with the bottle.

You will, perhaps, wonder why I have continued so long upon this subject, none of the most entertaining; but as the better sort here are almost all of them related to one another in some degree, either by consanguinity, marriage, or clanship, it is to them, as it were, a kind of business, and takes up good part of their time. In short, they take a great pride and pleasure in doing honours to their dead.

The minister or parish has no demand for christening, marrying, or burying. This last expense, particularly, I have ever thought unreasonable to be charged upon the poorer sort in England. A poor industrious man, for example, who has laboured hard for fifty years together, brought up a numerous family, and been at last reduced to necessity by his extraordinary charge, age, and long sickness, shall not be entitled to his length and breadth under the ground of that parish where he had lived, but his poor old widow must borrow or beg to pay the duties, or (which to her, perhaps, is yet worse) be forced to make her humble suit to an imperious parish officer, whose insolence to his inferiors (in fortune) was ever increasing with the success he met with in the world; besides the disgrace and contumely the poor wretch must suffer from her neighbours in the alley, for that remarkable state of poverty, viz. being reduced to beg the ground. And none more ready than the poor to reproach with their poverty any whom they have the pleasure to think yet poorer than themselves.

This to her may be as real distress as any dishonour that happens to people of better condition.

Before I proceed to the Highlands (i.e. the mountains), I shall conduct you round this town, to see if there be anything worth your notice in the adjacent country.

Toward the north-west, the Highlands begin to rise within a mile of the town. To some other points (I speak exclusive of the coast way) there are from three to five or six miles of what the natives call a flat country, by comparison with the surrounding hills; but to you, who have been always accustomed to the south of England, this plain (as they deem it) would appear very rough and uneven.

I shall begin with the ruins of a fort built by Oliver Cromwell in the year 1653 or 1654, which, in his time, commanded the town, the mouth of the river, and part of the country on the land sides of it where there are no hills. It lies something to the north-east of us, and is washed by a navigable part of the Ness, near its issue in to the Moray Firth.

The figure of the outwork is a pentagon of two hundred yards to a side, surrounded to landward with a fosse, now almost filled up with rubbish. The rampart is not unpleasant for a walk in a summer's evening, and among the grass grow carraways that have so often regaled my palate, and of which the seeds are supposed to have been scattered, by accident, from time out of mind.

Oliver had 1,200 men in and near this citadel, under the command of one Colonel Fitz, who had been a tailor, as I have been informed by a very ancient laird, who said he remembered every remarkable passage which happened at that time, and, most especially, Oliver's colours, which were so strongly impressed on his memory, that he thought he then saw them spread out by the wind, with the word Emmanuel (God with us) upon them, in very large golden characters.

LETTER XII

———✦———

The name of Cromwell disliked by the Highlanders—His success—Inverness quay—A remarkable hill, said to be inhabited by fairies and frequented by witches—Notion of judges respecting witches—Trial at Hertford—Trial of two Highland women, a mother and daughter, accused of witchcraft—Their condemnation and reputed confession—Gross absurdity of such imputations—Said to have been used as an engine of political power—Danger of exposing this notion—Island on the River Ness—Plantation—Moorstones—Soldiers raise immense blocks of stone—Anecdote—The Laird of Fairfield—Frequency of mortgage—Daughter's portion—Usury prohibited

THE name of Oliver, I am told, continues still to be used in some parts, as a terror to the children of the Highlanders; but, that is so common a saying of others who have rendered themselves formidable, that I shall lay no stress upon it. He invaded the borders of the Highlands, and shut the natives up within their mountains. In several parts he penetrated far within, and made fortresses and settlements among them; and obliged the proudest and most powerful of the chiefs of clans, even such as had formerly contended with their kings, to send their sons and nearest relations as hostages for their peaceable behaviour.

But, doubtless this success was owing, in great measure, to the good understanding there was at that time between England and France; otherwise it is to be supposed that the ancient ally of Scotland, as it is called here, would have endeavoured to break those measures, by hiring and assisting the Scots to invade our borders, in order to divert the English troops from making so great a progress in this part of the island.

Near the fort is the quay, where there are seldom more than two or three ships, and those of no great burden.

About a mile westward from the town, there rises, out of a perfect flat, a very regular hill; whether natural or artificial, I could never find by any tradition; the natives call it 'tomman-heurach'. It is almost in the shape of a Thames wherry, turned keel upwards, for which reason they sometimes call it Noah's Ark.

The length of it is about four hundred yards, and the breadth at bottom about one hundred and fifty. From below, at every point of view, it seems to end at top in a narrow ridge; but when you are there, you find a plain large enough to draw up two or three battalions of men.

Hither we sometimes retire in a summer's evening, and sitting down on the heath, we beat with our hands upon the ground, and raise a most fragrant smell of wild thyme, pennyroyal, and other aromatic herbs, that grow among the heath: and as there is likewise some grass among it, the sheep are fed the first; and when they have eaten it bare, they are succeeded by goats, which browse upon the sweet herbs that are left untouched by the sheep.

I mention this purely because I have often heard you commend the Windsor mutton, supposing its delicacy to proceed from those herbs; and, indeed, the notion is not uncommon.

But this is not the only reason why I speak of this hill; it is the weak credulity with which it is attended, that led me to this detail; for as anything, ever so little extraordinary, may serve as a foundation (to such as are ignorant, heedless, or interested) for ridiculous stories and imaginations, so the fairies within it are innumerable, and witches find it the most convenient place for their frolics and gambols in the night-time.

I am pleased when I reflect, that the notion of witches is pretty well worn out among people of any tolerable sense and education in England; but here it remains even among some that sit judicially; and witchcraft and 'charming' (as it is called) make up a considerable article in the recorded Acts of the General Assembly.

I am not unaware that here the famous trial at Hertford, for witchcraft, may be objected to me.

It is true the poor woman was brought in guilty by an ignorant, obstinate jury, but it was against the sentiments of the judge, who, when the minister of the parish declared, upon the faith of a clergyman, he believed the woman to be a witch, told him in open court, that therefore, upon the faith of a judge, he took him to be no conjuror.

Thus you see, by the example of this clergyman, that ignorance of the nature of things may be compatible with what is generally called learning; for I cannot suppose that, in a case of blood, there could be any regard had to the interest of a profession.

But perhaps the above assertion may be thought a little too dogmatical – I appeal to reason and experience.

After all, the woman was pardoned by the late queen (if any one may properly be said to be forgiven a crime they never committed), and a worthy gentleman in that county gave her an apartment over his stables, sent her victuals from his table, let her attend his children and she was looked upon, ever after, by the family as an honest good-natured old woman.

But I shall now give an instance (in this country) wherein the judge was not so clear-sighted.

In the beginning of the year 1727, two poor Highland women (mother and daughter), in the shire of Sutherland, were accused of witchcraft, tried, and condemned to be burnt. This proceeding was in a court held by the deputy-sheriff. The young one made her escape out of prison, but the old woman suffered that cruel death in a pitch barrel, in June following, at Dornoch, the head borough of that county.

In the introduction to the chapter under the title of witchcraft, in *Nelson's Justice*, which I have by me, there are these words: 'It seems plain that there are witches, because laws have been made to punish such offenders, though few have been convicted of witchcraft.' Then he quotes one single statute, viz. 1 Jac. c. 23.

May not any one say, with just as much reason, it seems plain there has been a phoenix, because poets have often made it serve for a simile in their writings, and painters have given us the representation of such a bird in their pictures?

It is said those Highland women confessed; but, as it is here a maxim that wizards and witches will never acknowledge their guilt so long as they can get anything to drink, I should not wonder if they owned themselves to be devils, for ease of so tormenting a necessity, when their vitals were ready to crack with thirst.

I am almost ashamed to ask seriously how it comes to pass that in populous cities, among the most wicked and abandoned wretches, this art should not be discovered; and yet that so many little villages and obscure places should be nurseries for witchcraft? But the thing is not worth speaking of, any further than that it is greatly to be wished that any such law should be annulled, which subjects the lives of human creatures to the weakness of an ignorant magistrate or jury, for a crime of which they never had the power to be guilty; and this might free them from the miseries and insults these poor wretches suffer when unhappily fallen under the imputation. In this county of Sutherland, as I have been assured, several others have undergone the same fate within the compass of no great number of years.

I must own it is possible there may be some, oppressed by poverty, and actuated by its concomitant envy, who may malign a thriving neighbour so far as to poison his cattle, or privately do him other hurt in his property, for which they may deserve the gallows as much as if they did the mischief by some supernatural means; but for such wicked practices, when discovered, the law is open, and they are liable to be punished according to the quality of the offence.

Witchcraft, if there were such a crime, I think would be of a nature never to be proved by honest witnesses: for who could testify they saw the identical person of such a one riding in the dark upon a broomstick through the air – a human body, composed of flesh and bones, crammed through a keyhole – or know an old woman through the disguise of a cat? These are some of the common topics of your wise witchmongers!

But to be more serious: we have reason to conclude, from several authentic relations of facts, that this supposed crime has sometimes been made a political engine of power, whereby to destroy such persons as were to be 'taken off', which could not otherwise be done with any seeming appearance of justice: and who should be fitter instruments to this purpose, than such, who would be so wicked as for hire, and assurance of indemnity, to own themselves accomplices with the party accused?

Notwithstanding this subject has led me further than I at first intended to go, I must add to it a complaint made to me about two months since, by an Englishman who is here in a government employment.

As he was observing the work of some carpenters, who were beginning the construction of a large boat, there came an old woman to get some chips, who, by his description of her, was indeed ugly enough. One of the workmen rated her, and bid her be gone, for he knew she was a witch. Upon that, this person took upon him to vindicate the old woman, and, unluckily, to drop some words as if there were none such. Immediately two of them came up to him, and held their axes near his head, with a motion as if they were about to cleave his skull, telling him he deserved death; for that he was himself a warlock or wizard, which they knew by his taking the witch's part. And he, observing their ignorance and rage, got away from them as fast as he could, in a terrible fright, and with a resolution to lay aside all curiosity relating to that boat, though the men were at work not far from his lodgings.

The greatest ornament we have in all the adjacent country, is about a quarter of a mile from the town, but not to be seen from it, by reason of the castle hill. It is an island about six hundred yards long, surrounded by two branches of the River Ness, well planted with trees of different kinds, and may not unaptly be compared with the island in St James's Park; all, except fruit trees, gravel-walks, and grass-plots; for I speak chiefly of its outward appearance, the beauty whereof is much increased by the nakedness of the surrounding country and the blackness of the bordering mountains. For in any view hereabouts there is hardly another tree to be seen, except about the houses of two or three lairds, and they are but few.

Hither the magistrates conduct the judges and their attendants, when they are upon their circuit in the beginning of May; and sometimes such other gentlemen, to whom they do the honours of the corporation by presenting them with their freedom, if it happens to be in the salmon season.

The entertainment is salmon, taken out of the cruives just by, and immediately boiled and set upon a bank of turf, the seats the same, not unlike one of our country cockpits; and during the time of eating, the heart of the fish lies upon a plate in view, and keeps in a panting motion all the while, which to strangers is a great rarity. The cruives above the salmon leap (which is a steep slope composed of large loose stones) are made into many divisions by loose walls, and have about three or four feet of water. These render such a number of fish as they contain an agreeable sight, being therein confined, to be ready at any time for the barrel or the table.

I am told there was formerly a fine planted avenue from the town to this island; but one of the magistrates, in his solitary walk, being shot by a Highlander from behind the trees, upon some clan quarrel, they were soon after cut down; and indeed I think such kind of walks, unless very near a house, are not the most suitable to this country: I do not mean on account of robberies, but revenge.

In several places upon the heaths, at no great distance from this town, and in other parts of the country, there are large moorstones, set up in regular circles one within another, with a good space between each round. In some of these groups there are only two such circles, in others three; and some of the stones on the outermost ring are nine or ten feet high above the surface of the ground, and in bulk proportionable.

How long time they have been in that situation nobody knows, or for what purpose they were disposed in that order; only some pretend, by tradition, they were used as temples for sacrifices in the time of the Romans; and others have been taught, by that variable instructor, that they were tribunals for the trials of supposed criminals in a Roman army.

What matter of wonder and curiosity their size might be upon Hounslow Heath I do not know; but here among these rocks, by comparison, they make no figure at all. Besides, the soldiers, by the force of engines and strength, have raised stones as large or larger, that lay more than half buried under ground, in the lines marked out for the new projected roads; and they have likewise set them upright along the sides of those ways.

Having chanced to mention the stones raised out of the ground by the troops, I cannot forbear a little tattle concerning two officers that are employed upon the new roads, as directors of the work in different parts of the Highlands; and, if you please, you may take it for a piece of Highland news, for I am sure your public papers often contain paragraphs altogether as trifling, and not so true.

Upon one of these stones (surprisingly large to be removed) one of those gentlemen employed a soldier, who is a mason by trade, to engrave an inscription of his making, in Latin, fearing, perhaps his own renown might wear out with our language. The substance of it is, the date of the year, time of the reign, director's name, etc.

Some little time after this was done, the other officers party of men having raised out of the ground a stone, as he thought, yet bigger than the former, he began to envy his competitor's foundation for fame, and applied himself to a third officer (who had done several little poetical pieces) to think of some words for his stone. But I should tell you, that before he did so, it had been remarked, he had too often boasted of the exploit in the first person, viz. 'I raised a larger stone than —', etc.

The poet officer told him he would satisfy him offhand, and it should be in English, which would be understood by more people than the other's Latin, and by that means he would have the advantage of his rival at least in that particular.

But instead of his real name, I shall insert a feigned one, and under that only disguise give you the proposed inscription as follows:

> Hibern alone
> Rais'd up this stone;
> Ah! Hone, Ah Hone.

Upon this, the hero turned ridiculously grave; and says he, 'The soldiers did the slavish part only with their hands, but, in effect, it was I that did it with my head: and therefore I do not like any burlesque upon my performance.'

One thing, which I take to be a curiosity in its kind, had like to have escaped me, viz. a single enclosed field, nearly adjoining to the suburbs of this town, containing, as near as I can guess, about five or six acres, called Fairfield. This to the owner gives the title of Laird of Fairfield, and it would be a neglect or kind of affront to call him by his proper name, but only Fairfield. For those they call lairds in Scotland do not go by their surname; but, as in France, by the name of their house, state, or part of it. But if the lairdship be sold, the title goes along with it to the purchaser, and nothing can continue the name of it to the first possessor but mere courtesy.

There are few estates in this country free from mortgages and encumbrances (I wish I could not say the same of England); but the reason given me for it, by some gentlemen of pretty good estates, seems to be something extraordinary.

They do not care to ascribe it to the poverty of their tenants, from the inconsiderable farms they occupy, or other disadvantages incident to these parts; but say it has proceeded from the fortunes given with their daughters. Now the portion or 'tocker', as they call it, of a laird's eldest daughter, is looked upon to be a handsome one if it amounts to one thousand merks, which is £55 11s 1⅓d sterling; and ten thousand merks, or £555 11s 1⅓d is generally esteemed no bad tocker for a daughter of the lower rank of quality.

The Scots merk is thirteen pence and one-third of a penny of our money.

Having touched upon mortgages, which in Scotland are called 'wadsetts', I shall say a few words on that article.

By the canon law of Scotland all kind of usury is prohibited; but as the forbidding it is very incommodious to a country, on account of trade and husbandry, as well as to particular persons, and besides, a law most easily evaded; there was a method contrived by the people, whereby to sell their estates, with a conditional right of redemption. This is called a 'proper wadsett', where the mortgagee takes into possession so much land as will secure the principal and interest of the money lent, and sometimes more; for which he is never to give account, though there should be a surplus, but only to return the lands to the former proprietor when the principal sum is paid off.

LETTER XIII

---◆◆◆---

Castle of Culloden—Female courage—Parks—Disappoint an English officer—Arable land—Plowing—Poverty of labourers—Corn cut while green—Wages of labourers—Kinds of grain—Scanty produce—Trades—Improved by communication with the soldiers—Partiality of the Scotch for their countrymen—Distress during scarcity—Anecdote—Description of Fort William and Maryburgh—Houses built of wood—These letters designed to contain nothing that may be found elsewhere—Answer to an inquiry—Account of Inverness and country around concluded—White hares and small birds on the snowy mountains

I SHALL now return to the neighbouring country. Here are but two houses of any note within many miles of us, on this side the Moray Firth; one is the house of Culloden, which I have mentioned in a former letter.

This is about two miles off, and is a pretty large fabric, built with stone, and divided into many rooms, among which the hall is very spacious.

There are good gardens belonging to it, and a noble planted avenue, of great length, that leads to the house, and a plantation of trees about it.

This house (or castle) was besieged, in the year 1715, by a body of the rebels; and the laird being absent in Parliament, his lady baffled all their attempts with extraordinary courage and presence of mind.

Nearly adjoining are the parks – that is, one large tract of ground, surrounded with a low wall of loose stones, and divided into several parts by partitions of the same. The surface of the ground is all over heath, or, as they call it, 'heather', without any trees; but some of it has been lately sown with the seed of firs, which are now grown about a foot and a half high, but are hardly to be seen for the heath.

An English captain, the afternoon of the day following his arrival here from London, desired me to ride out with him, and show him the parks of Culloden, without telling me the reason of his curiosity. Accordingly we set out, and when we were pretty near the place, he asked me, 'Where are these parks? For', says he, 'there is nothing near in view but heath, and, at a distance, rocks and mountains.' I pointed to the enclosure; and, being a little way before him, heard him cursing in soliloquy, which occasioned my making a halt, and asking if anything had displeased him. Then he told me, that, at a coffee-house in London, he was one day commending the park of Studley, in Yorkshire, and those of several other gentlemen in other parts of England, when a Scots captain, who was by, cried out, 'Ah, sir! But if you were to see the parks at Culloden, in Scotland!'

This my companion repeated several times with different modulations of voice; and then, in an angry manner, swore, if he had known how grossly he had been imposed on, he could not have put up with so great an affront. But I should have told you, that every one of the small divisions above-mentioned is called a separate park, and that the reason for making some of the inner walls has been to prevent the hares, with which, as I said before, the country abounds, from cropping the tender tops of these young firs, which, indeed, effectually spoils their regular growth.

The other house I spoke of is not much further distant from the contrary side of the town, and belongs to the younger brother of the gentleman above-mentioned; he is Lord-Advocate, or Attorney-General, for Scotland: it is a good old building, but not so large as the other; and near it there is a most romantic wood, whereof one part consists of great heights and hollows; and the brushwood at the foot of the trees, with the springs that issue out of the sides of the hills, invite the woodcocks, which, in the season, are generally there in great numbers, and render it the best spot for cock-shooting that ever I knew. Neither of these houses are to be seen from any part near the town.

The gentleman, of whose house I have last been speaking, were it not for a valetudinary state of health, and the avocations of his office, would be as highly pleased to see his friends about him at table and over a bottle as his hospitable brother.

In the spots of arable land near the town the people sometimes plough with eight small beasts, part oxen and part cows. They do not drive them with a goad, as in England, but beat them with a long stick, making a hideous Irish noise in calling to them as they move along.

The poverty of the field labourers hereabouts is deplorable. I was one day riding out for air and exercise, and in my way I saw a woman cutting green barley in a little plot before her hut: this induced me to turn aside and ask her what use she intended it for, and she told me it was to make bread for her family.

The grain was so green and soft that I easily pressed some of it between my fingers; so that when she had prepared it, certainly it must have been more like a poultice than what she called it, bread. There was a gentleman with me, who was my interpreter; and though he told me what the woman said, yet he did not seem greatly to approve of my curiosity.

Their harvest labourers are often paid in kind, viz. oats or barley; and the person thus paid goes afterwards about with the sheaves, to sell them to such as will purchase them. If they are paid in money, their wages is two pence halfpenny or three pence a day and their dinner, which I suppose is oatmeal.

There is no other sort of grain hereabouts, besides oats, barley, and beer, which last is an inferior species of barley, but of greater increase. A field of wheat would be as great a rarity as a nightingale in any part of Scotland, or a cat-o'-mountain in Middlesex. And yet I have seen good wheat in some of the Lowland part of the shire of Moray; which is, indeed, but a narrow space between the sea and the mountains not very far south of us. It is true, a certain gentleman, not far from the coast, in the county of Ross, which is further north than we are, by favour of an extraordinary year, and a piece of new ground, raised some wheat; but he made so much parade of it, that the stack stood in his courtyard till the rats had almost devoured it. This, and a good melon he treated me with, which was raised under a rock facing the south, and strongly reflecting the heat of the sun, so equally flattered him, that he afterwards made use of me as a witness of both upon several occasions. But melons may be produced in Lapland.

In the Lowlands of Scotland I have seen, in many places, very fertile land, good wheat, and oats in particular, much better than ever I saw in the growth of England. But, perhaps, you will imagine that, as oatmeal serves for bread, and, in other shapes, for most part of the rest of the ordinary people's diet, they are more careful in the choice of the seed than our farmers are, who know their oats are chiefly used as provender for cattle; but, I think, in some parts of the country, the soil is peculiarly adapted to that kind of grain.

In some remote parts of England I have seen bread for the field labourers, and other poor people, so black, so heavy, and so harsh, that the 'bonnack', as they call it (a thin oatmeal cake baked on a plate over the fire), may, by comparison, be called a piecrust.

By the small proportion the arable lands hereabouts bear to the rocky grounds and barren heaths, there is hardly a product of grain sufficient to supply the inhabitants, let the year be ever so favourable; and, therefore, any ill accident that happens to their growth, or harvest, produces a melancholy effect. I have known, in such a circumstance, the town in a consternation for want of oatmeal, when shipping has been retarded, and none to be procured in these parts (as we say) for love or money.

There are but few in this town that eat wheat-bread, besides the English and those that belong to them, and some of the principal inhabitants, but not their servants. Among the English, I think I may include good part of the private soldiers, that are working men.

All the handicraft tradesmen have improved their skill in their several occupations, by example of the workmen among the troops, who are often employed by the inhabitants as journeymen; and in particular the bakers, whose bread, I think, is not inferior to that of London, except when their flour is grown, or musty, when imported. This sometimes happens; but they are too national to hold any correspondence but with their countrymen, who, I think, have not the same regard for them, but study too carefully their own extraordinary profit – I am speaking of such as have their goods from England.

This brings to my remembrance an observation I met with in London a good many years ago, and that is, what an advantage the Scots, the Quakers, and the French refugees, have over the generality of trading people in England, since they all confine the profit of their dealings, so far as ever they can, within their respective circles; and moreover have an equal chance for trading profit with all others who make no such partial distinction; and therefore it was no wonder they throve accordingly.

I happened lately, upon a certain occasion, to mention this to an old officer in the army, who thereupon told me he had observed, through all the quarters in England, that if there were any Scots tradesmen or shopkeepers in a country town, the newcomers of that nation soon found them out, and would deal with no others, so far as they could be served or supplied by them.

This, I think, is carrying it too far, and teaching an ill lesson against themselves. And we, on the other hand, are accused of the contrary extreme, which is an unnational neglect (if I may use such an expression) of one another, when we happen to meet in foreign countries.

But to return. When the flour is musty, they mingle seeds with the dough, to overcome the disagreeable smell and taste. This I have likewise met with in Edinburgh and other great towns of the low country.

About the time of one great scarcity here, the garrison of Fort William, opposite to us on the west coast, was very low in oatmeal, and the little hovel town of Maryburgh, nearly adjoining to it, was almost destitute.

Some affairs at that time called me to the fort; and, being at the governor's house, one of the townswomen came to his lady, and besought her to use her interest that she might be spared out of the stores, for her money, or to repay it in kind, only one peck of oatmeal to keep her children from starving; for that there was none to be sold in the town, or other food to be had whatever. The lady, who is one of the best and most agreeable of women, told her she feared her husband could not be prevailed on to part with any at that time.

This she said, as knowing that kind of provision was almost exhausted, and a great number of mouths to be fed; that there was but a very precarious dependence upon the winds for a supply, and that other sea accidents might happen; but to show her goodwill, she gave her a shilling. The poor woman, holding up the money, first looked at that in a musing manner, then at the lady, and bursting out into tears, cried 'Madam, what must I do with this? My children cannot eat it!' And laid the shilling down upon the table in the greatest sorrow and despair. It would be too trite to remark upon the uselessness of money, when it cannot be bartered for something absolutely necessary to life. But I do assure you I was hardly ever more affected with distress than upon this occasion, for I never saw such an example of it before.

I must not leave you in suspense. The governor, commiserating the poor woman's circumstances, spared her that small quantity; and then the passion of joy seemed more unruly in the poor creature's breast than all her grief and fear had been before.

Some few days afterwards, a ship that had lain wind-bound in the Orkneys, arrived; and upon my return hither, I found there had been a supply likewise by sea from the low country.

I shall make no apology for going a little out of my way to give you a short account of the fortress of Fort William, and the town of Maryburgh that belongs to it; because, upon a like occasion, you give me a hint in one of your letters, that such sudden starts of a variety were agreeable to you.

The fort is situated in Lochaber, a country which, though bordering upon the western ocean, yet is within the shire of Inverness. Oliver Cromwell made there a settlement, as I have said before; but the present citadel was built in the reign of King William and Queen Mary, and called after the name of the king. It was in great measure originally designed as a check upon the chief of the Camerons, a clan which, in those days, was greatly addicted to plunder, and strongly inclined to rebellion.

It stands in a most barren rocky country, and is washed on one of the faces of the fortification by a navigable arm of the sea. It is almost surrounded, on the land sides, with rivers, not far distant from it, which though but small, are often impassible from their depth and

rapidity. And lastly, it is near the foot of an exceedingly high mountain, called Ben Nevis, of which I may have occasion to say something in some future letter, relating particularly to the high country. The town was erected into a barony in favour of the governor of the fort for the time being, and into a borough bearing the name of Queen Mary. It was originally designed as a sutlery to the garrison in so barren a country, where little can be had for the support of the troops.

The houses were neither to be built with stone nor brick, and are to this day composed of timber, boards, and turf. This was ordained, to the end they might the more suddenly be burnt, or otherwise destroyed, by order of the governor, to prevent any lodgment of an enemy that might annoy the fort; in case of rebellion or invasion.

In your last letter you desire to know of me what is the qualification of fortune required of the elector and elected to a seat in Parliament for a county or borough in Scotland.

This induces me to believe the baronet is either gone into Bedfordshire, or come to Edinburgh.

What you now require of me is one, among many, of those articles I have left out of my account, concluding you might have met with it in some treatise of the constitution of Scotland; for I intended, from the beginning, to give you nothing but what I suppose was no where else to be found. And now I shall endeavour to satisfy your curiosity in that point, according to the best information I have obtained.

One and the same qualification is required of a voter and a candidate for a county, which is £400 Scots, or £33 6s 8d sterling per annum, according to the old rent, or as they stand rated on the king's books. These are called barons, and none others vote for the shires, except some few in the county of Sutherland, where several of the old voters, refusing to pay their quota of £6 13s 4d Scots, or 11s 1⅓d sterling per diem, for the maintenance of their representative in time of the session, others were willing to be taxed in their stead, providing they might have the privilege of voting, which they obtained thereby, to the exclusion of the former.

The magistrates and town council elect members to represent the boroughs, or corporation towns; and there is neither land nor money qualification required either of the candidate or electors.

This letter brings you the conclusion of my chat, in relation to this town and the country near it, having at present exhausted my memory as well as my written remarks on that head. In my next I shall begin my account of the Highlands, which I hope will be something more grateful to your curiosity than I think the former could possibly be; but if, in my mountain progress, anything new and worth your notice relating to these parts should happen, either by occurrence or recollection, you may expect a separate letter by way of supplement. But what am I saying? This very moment a thought has obtruded, which tells me, that, when I was speaking of our hunting and fowling, I did not remember to acquaint you that it is no uncommon thing, when the mountains are deep in snow, for us to see hares almost as white, which descend into these plains for sustenance; but although we have hunted several of them for awhile, yet always without success, for they keep near the feet of the hills, and, immediately on being started, make to the heights, where the scent is lost, and they baffle all pursuit.

As white rabbits are common in England, and our ideas arise from what we know, you may think, perhaps, we have been deceived; but that cannot be, for there is not a rabbit in all the country; and besides, if there were any, we have been too near those hares at starting to be mistaken in that particular: but this is not the only thing of the kind; snow sends down from the mountains large flights of small birds, about the size of larks or something bigger, and very white, which they are not in summer, any more than the mountain hare. These have here no other name than 'snow birds'.

It should seem as if nature changed the coats of these creatures, that they might not be too easy a prey to the foxes, wild cats, eagles, and hawks, as they would be from distant views, in time of snow, if they retained in winter their natural colour: but in general nature has been provident in rendering difficult the finding of animals pleasing to mankind for food, diversion, and exercise, as you may have observed in England; the hare, the partridge, woodcock, fieldfare, etc., are all, by their clothing, in good measure suited to their respective haunts and places of concealment; and some of them, one might almost think, were sensible of the advantage, when we see them lie without motion till they are almost trod upon, as if knowing that action, would catch the eye, and being motionless, they should continue concealed by their resembling colour.

I shall never entertain the least doubt of your sincere intentions in everything; but, since I received your last letter, which relates to this prattle, I cannot but be apprehensive your favourable opinion of it proceeds less from your satisfaction than a friendly partiality to —, etc.

LETTERS

FROM

A Gentleman in the North of *Scotland*

TO

His FRIEND in *London*;

CONTAINING

The Defcription of a Capital Town in that
Northern Country;

WITH

An Account of fome uncommon Cuftoms
of the Inhabitants:

LIKEWISE

An Account of the HIGHLANDS, with the
Cuftoms and *Manners* of the HIGHLANDERS.

To which is added,

A LETTER relating to the MILITARY WAYS
among the Mountains, began in the Year 1726.

The Whole interfpers'd with *Facts* and *Circumftances*
intirely New to the Generality of People in *England*,
and little known in the Southern Parts of *Scotland*.

In TWO VOLUMES.

VOL. II.

LONDON:
Printed for S. BIRT, in *Ave-Maria-Lane.*

MDCCLIV.

LETTER XIV

Account of a Highlander executed for murder—Causes of its perpetration
—His desperate resistance and concealment—Is visited by ministers—
His singular conduct—His execution and desperate conduct—Incendiaries
in Glengarry—Origin of the occurrence—Failure of the attack—Visit to
a laird—The company—Witchcraft—Minister's opinion—A controversy—
Ludicrous story of a witch and a Highland laird—Certified by four
ministers—Author's incredulity—His remarks—Reply—Arguments—Witch
of Endor—Copernicus and Psalms of David—Egotism excused—Moliere's
physician—Bigotry of the clergy to received notions

IN my last letter relating to this northern part of the low country,
I promised (notwithstanding I should be engaged on the subject
of the Highlands) to give you an account of anything else that should
fall out by the way, or recur to my memory; but whether this letter
is to be placed to the high or low country I leave you to determine,
and I think it is not very material.

Some time ago a Highlander was executed here for murder, and I
am now about to give you some account of his education, character,
and behaviour; and I flatter myself I shall do it at least as much to
your satisfaction as the Reverend Historiographer of Newgate.

You know I have rallied you several times before now upon your
bestowing, as I thought too much attention upon that kind of
narrative, viz. the session papers and last dying speeches.

This man was by trade a smith, and dwelt near an English foundry
in Glengarry, which lies between this town and Fort William, of

which ironwork I shall have some occasion to speak more particularly before I conclude this letter.

The director of that work had hired a smith from England, and as it is said that kings and lovers can brook no partners, so neither could the Highlander suffer the rivalship of one of his own trade, and therefore his competitor was by him destined to die. One night he came armed to the door of the Englishman's hut with intent to kill him; but the man being for some reason or other, apprehensive of danger, had fastened the door of his hovel more firmly than usual, and, while the Highlander was employed to force it open, he broke away through the back wall of his house and made his escape, but, being pursued, he cried out for assistance; this brought a Lowland Scots workman to endeavour to save him, and his generous intention cost him his life. Upon this several others took the alarm and came up with the murderer, whom they tried to secure; but he wounded some of them, and received several wounds himself; however, he made his escape for that time. Three days afterwards he was hunted out, and found among the heath (which was then very high), where he had lain all that time with his wounds rankling, and without any sustenance, not being able to get away because a continual search was made all round about both night and day, and for the most part within his hearing; for it is more difficult to find a Highlander among the heather, except newly tracked, than a hare in her form.

He was brought to this town and committed to the tolbooth, where sentinels were posted to prevent his second escape, which otherwise, in all probability, would have been effected.

Sometime afterwards the judges, in their circuit, arrived here, and he was tried and condemned. Then the ministers of the town went to the jail to give him their ghostly advice, and endeavoured to bring him to a confession of his other sins, without which they told him he could not hope for redemption. For, besides this murder, he was strongly suspected to have made away with his former wife, with whose sister he was known to have had too great a familiarity. But when the ministers had said all that is customary concerning the merit of confession, he abruptly asked them, if either or all of them could pardon him, in case he made a confession; and when they had answered, 'No, not absolutely,' he said, 'You have told me, God can forgive me.' They said it was true. 'Then,' said he, 'as you cannot pardon me, I have nothing to do with you, but will confess to Him that can.'

A little while after, a smith of this town was sent to take measure of him, in order to make his irons (for he was to be hanged in chains), and, while the man was doing it, the Highlander, with a sneer, said, 'Friend, you are now about to do a job for a better workman than yourself; I am certain I could fit you better than you can me.'

When the day for his execution came (which by a late law, could not be under forty days after his condemnation), and I had resolved to stay at home, though perhaps I should have been the only one in the town that did so – I say having taken that resolution, a certain lieutenant-colonel, who is come into these parts to visit his friends, and is himself a Highlander, for whom I have the greatest esteem; he came to me, and would have me bear him company, declaring, at the same time, that although he had a great desire to see how the criminal would behave, yet he would wave all that, unless I would go with him; and, therefore, rather than disoblige my friend, I consented, but I assure you with reluctancy.

The criminal was a little fellow, but a fearless desperado; and having annexed himself to the clan of the Camerons, the magistrates were apprehensive that some of the tribe might attempt his rescue; and therefore they made application to the commanding officer for a whole company of men to guard him to the place of execution with greater security.

Accordingly they marched him in the centre, with two of the ministers, one on each side, talking to him by turns all the way for a mile together. But I, not being accustomed to this sort of sights, could not forbear to reflect a little upon the circumstance of a man walking so far on foot to his own execution.

The gibbet was not only erected upon the summit of a hill, but was itself so high that it put me in mind of Haman's gallows.

Being arrived at the place, and the ministers having done praying by him, the executioner, a poor helpless creature, of at least eighty years of age, ascended the ladder. Then one of the magistrates ordered the malefactor to go up after him; upon which the fellow turned himself hastily about; says he, 'I did not think the magistrates of Inverness had been such fools, as to bid a man go up a ladder with his hands tied behind him.' And, indeed, I thought the great burgher looked very silly, when he ordered the fellow's hands to be set at liberty.

When the knot was fixed, the old hangman (being above the criminal) began to feel about with his feet to find some footing whereby to come down beside the other, in order to turn him off, which I think could hardly have been done by a young fellow the most nimble and alert, without getting under the ladder, and coming down chiefly by his hands.

Thus the Highlander, feeling the executioner fumbling about him, in a little time seemed to lose all patience; and turning himself about, with his face from the ladder, and his cap over his eyes, he cried out upon the Trinity, which I daresay he had never heard of before he was committed prisoner for this fact, and then jumped off the ladder. And though his hands were free, there did not appear in them, or any other part of his body, the least motion or convulsion, any more than if he had been a statue.

It is true, I could not compare this with other things of the same kind, but I thought it a very bungling execution, yet liked the cause of their unskilfulness.

His mother, who, it seems, is a very vile woman, and had bred him up in encouragement to thieving and other crimes, was present, lying on the heath at some little distance, when he leaped from the ladder; and at that instant set up such a hideous shriek, followed by a screaming Irish howl, that everybody seemed greatly surprised at the uncommon noise; and those who knew the woman loaded her with curses for being the cause of this shameful end of her son, who, they said, was naturally a man of good sense.

To conclude this subject. The smith who had made the irons (I suppose frighted at the execution) had run away, leaving his tools behind him; and one of the magistrates was forced to rivet them, there being none other that would undertake so shameful a work for any reward whatever.

But I had forgot to acquaint you that my friend the colonel, as we stood together all the while, favoured me with the interpretation of that which passed, and most particularly what was said by the criminal, who could not speak one word of English.

You have now had a view of two tragic scenes, viz. one at Glengarry, and the other (being the catastrophe) near Inverness – at this time a new subject calls upon me to withdraw the latter scene, and restore the former which represents Glengarry.

Some few years ago, a company of Liverpool merchants contracted with the chieftain of this tribe, at a great advantage to him, for the use of his woods and other conveniences for the smelting of iron; and soon after, they put their project in execution, by building of furnaces, sending ore from Lancashire, etc.

By the way, I should tell you that those works were set up in this country merely for the sake of the woods, because iron cannot be made from the ore with sea or pit coal, to be malleable and fit for ordinary uses.

The dwelling-house of this chieftain had been burnt by the troops in the year 1715; but the walls, which were of stone, remained; and therefore the director of the above-mentioned works thought it convenient to fit it up with new timber, for the use of himself or his successors, during the term of the lease.

This being effectually done, a certain number of gentlemen of the tribe came to him one evening, on a seeming friendly visit, whom he treated in a generous manner, by giving them his best wines and provisions. Among other things (though a Quaker by his religious principles, yet is he a man of polite behaviour), he said to them something to this purpose (for he told me himself how he had been used): 'Gentleman, you have given me a great deal of pleasure in this visit; and when you all, or any of you, will take the trouble to repeat it, let it be when it will, you shall be welcome to anything that is in my house.'

Upon those two last words, one of them cried out, 'G—d d—n you, sir! *Your* house? I thought it had been Glengarry's house!' And upon those watchwords they knocked out the candles, fell upon him, wounded him, and got him down among them; but he being strong and active, and the darkness putting them in confusion lest they should wound one another, he made a shift to slip from them in the bustle, and to gain another room. This he immediately barricaded, and cried out at the window to his workmen, that were not far off, who running to arm themselves and hasten to his assistance, those 'gentlemen' made off.

It only now remains that I make some little animadversion upon this rancorous, treacherous, and inhospitable insult, which but for an accident, it is much more than probable, would have gone by another name.

Notwithstanding this house was repaired by consent of the chief, and, in course of time, he would have the benefit of so great an expense, yet an English trader dwelling in the 'castle', as they call it, when at the same time, the laird inhabited a miserable hut of turf, as he did, and does to this day – this, I say, was intolerable to their pride; and as it was apparently their design at first to raise a *quarrelle d'Allemand* (a wrong-headed quarrel), whatever other words he had used, they would have found some among them that they might wrest to their inhuman purpose. But those words, 'my house', unluckily served in an eminent degree to provoke their rage, as a lunatic, who is reasonable by intervals, returns to his ravings when any one touches upon the cause of his madness. However, some good arose from this evil; for, upon complaint made, the chieftain was threatened with a great number of troops to be quartered upon him, and by that means the Liverpool company obtained some new advantageous conditions to be added to their original contract, which have made some amends for the bad usage of their manager and partner: and since that time he has met with no ill treatment from any of the tribe, except some little pilferings, which might have happened any where else.

I am next to give you a conversation-piece, which, with its incidents, I foresee will be pretty spacious; but I shall make no apology for it, because I know your leisure hours to be as many as my own.

I have often heard it urged, as an undeniable argument for the truth of incredible stories, that the number and reputed probity of the witnesses to the truth of a fact is, or ought to be, sufficient to convince the most incredulous. And I have known the unbeliever to be treated by the greatest part of a company as an infidel, or, at best, as a conceited sceptic; and that only because he could not, without a hypocritical complaisance, own his assent to the truth of relations the most repugnant to reason and the well-known laws and operations of nature.

The being accused of unreasonable unbelief was, some time ago, my own circumstance; and perhaps I have suffered in my character, as a Christian (though Christianity has nothing to do with it), by disputing the truth of a tale, which I thought nobody above the ordinary run of unthinking people could have believed – if upon trust, without examination, may be called believing.

Upon making my first visit to a certain lord not many miles from this town, I found there one of our ministers of the Gospel; for so they called themselves, very probably for a distinction between them and ministers of state.

This gentleman being in a declining way in his constitution, had been invited by our Lord (who I make no doubt has some particular view in making his court to Presbyterian clergy) – I say this invitation to him was, to pass some time in the hills for the benefit of the mountain air. But this was not a compliment to him alone, but likewise to the whole town; for I do assure you none could be more esteemed than this minister, for his affable temper, exemplary life, and what they call sound doctrine. And for my own part, I verily think, from some of what I am about to recite, that he was a true believer; for I do not in the least suspect him of falsehood, it being so foreign to his known character.

In the evening, our noble host, with the minister and myself, sat down to a bottle of champagne. And after the conversation had turned upon several subjects (I do not remember how), but witchcraft was brought upon the carpet. By the way, I did intend, after what I have formerly said upon that frivolous subject, never to trouble you with it again. But to my present purpose.

After the minister had said a good deal concerning the wickedness of such a diabolical practice as sorcery; and that I, in my turn, had declared my opinion of it which you knew many years ago; he undertook to convince me of the reality of it by an example, which is as follows.

A certain Highland laird had found himself at several times deprived of some part of his wine, and having so often examined his servants about it, and none of them confessing, but all denying it with asseverations, he was induced to conclude they were innocent.

The next thing to consider was, how this could happen. 'Rats there were none to father the theft. Those, you know, according to your philosophical next-door neighbour, might have drawn out the corks with their teeth, and then put in their tails, which, being long and spongeous, would imbibe a good quantity of liquor. This they might suck out again, and so on, till they had emptied as many bottles as were sufficient for their numbers and the strength of their heads.' But to be more serious – I say, there was no suspicion of rats, and it was concluded it could be done by none but witches.

Here the new inquisition was set on foot, and who they were was the question; but how should that be discovered? To go the shortest way to work, the laird made choice of one night, and an hour when he thought it might be watering-time with the hags; and went to his cellar without a light, the better to surprise them. Then with his naked broadsword in his hand, he suddenly opened the door, and shut it after him, and fell to cutting and slashing all round about him, till, at last, by an opposition to the edge of his sword, he concluded he had at least wounded one of them. But I should have told you, that although the place was very dark, yet he made no doubt, by the glare and flashes of their eyes that they were cats; but, upon the appearance of a candle, they were all vanished, and only some blood left upon the floor. I cannot forbear to hint in this place at Don Quixotte's battle with the borachios of wine.

There was an old woman, that lived about two miles from the laird's habitation, reputed to be a witch: her he greatly suspected to be one of the confederacy, and immediately he hasted away to her hut; and, entering, he found her lying upon her bed, and bleeding excessively.

This alone was some confirmation of the justness of his suspicion; but casting his eye under the bed, there lay her leg in its natural form!

I must confess I was amazed at the conclusion of this narration: but ten times more when, with the most serious air, he assured me that he had seen a certificate of the truth of it, signed by four ministers of that part of the country, and could procure me a sight of it in a few days, if I had the curiosity to see it.

When he had finished his story, I used all the arguments I was master of, to show him the absurdity to suppose a woman could be transformed into the shape and diminutive substance of a cat; to vanish like a flash of fire; carry her leg home with her, etc.: and I told him, that if a certificate of the truth of it had been signed by every member of the General Assembly, it would be impossible for me (however strong my inclination were to believe) to bring my mind to assent to it. And at last I told him, that if it could be supposed to be true, it might be ranked in one's imagination among the most eminent miracles. Upon this last word (like 'my house' at Glengarry) my good lord, who had been silent all this while, said to the minister, 'Sir, you must not mind Mr —, for he is an atheist.'

I shall not remark upon the politeness, good sense, and hospitality of this reflection; but this imputation, although perhaps it might have passed with me for a jest, or unheeded, before another, induced me, by my present situation, to justify myself to the Kirk; and therefore it put me upon telling him, I was sorry his lordship knew me no better, for that I thought there was nothing in the world, that is speculative, would admit of the thousandth part of the reasons for its certainty, as would the being of a divine providence; and that the visible evidences were the stupendous contrivance and order of the universe, the fitness of all the parts of every individual creature for their respective occasions, uses, and necessities, etc.; and concluded, that none but an idiot could imagine that senseless atoms could jumble themselves into this wonderful order and economy. To this, and a good deal more to the same purpose, our host said nothing; perhaps he was conscious he had given his own character for mine.

Then I turned to the minister, and told him, that, for my own part, I could not think there was anything irreligious in denying the supernatural power of witchcraft, because I had, early in my youth, met with such arguments as then convinced me, that the Woman of Endor was only an impostor, like our astrologers and fortune-tellers, and not a witch, in the present acceptation of the word; and, if my memory did not deceive me, the principal reasons were, that to support herself in her dishonest profession, she must have been a woman of intelligence, and intrigue, and therefore knew what passed in the world, and could not be ignorant of Saul's unhappy and abandoned state at that time. Nor could she be unacquainted with the person and dress of the prophet in his lifetime, and therefore might easily describe him; and that Saul saw nothing, though he was in the same room, but took it all from the woman's declaration.

Besides, I told him I might quote the case of Copernicus, who was not far from suffering death for broaching his new system of the earth, because it seemed to contradict a text in the Psalms of David, although the same is now become unquestionable among the astronomers, and is not at all disproved by the divines. And to this I told him I might add an inference relating to the present belief of the plurality of habitable worlds. Thus tenderly did I deal with a man of his modesty and ill state of health.

I should have been ashamed to relate all this egotism to any other than a truly bosom-friend, to whom one may and ought to talk as to one's self; for otherwise it is, by distrust, to do him injustice.

Some of these ministers put me in mind of Moliere's physicians who were esteemed by the faculty according as they adhered to, or neglected the rules of Hippocrates and Galen; and these, like them, will not go a step out of the old road, and therefore have not been accustomed to hear anything out of the ordinary way, especially upon subjects which, in their notion, may have any relation even to their traditional tenets. And I think this close adherency to principles, in themselves indifferent, must be owing, in good measure, to their fear of the dreadful word heterodoxy. But this gentleman heard all that I had to say against his notion of witchcraft with great attention, either for the novelty of it, or by indulgence to a stranger, or both. And I am fully persuaded it was the newness of that opposition which tempted him to sit up later than was convenient for him – I say his sitting up only, because I think the very little he drank could make no alteration in his health; but not many days after, I heard of his death, which was much lamented by the people of this town and the surrounding country.

LETTER XV

———— ❦ ————

Retrospect—Difference between inhabitants of the Highlands and Lowlands—Extent of the Highlands—Natural Division—Language cannot describe scenery of—Appearance of the hills—Summits covered with snow—Proof of the deluge—Hills covered with heath—Trees, difficulty of removing—Bridge of Snow—Deep hollows—Grey Mare's Tail—Tremendous waterfall—Similarity of Highland scenery—Terrific view of hills from east to west—Ben Nevis—Travellers seldom reach the top—Difficulties of travelling—Contrast—Minerals—Use of mountains—The strath—The glen—Journal of two days' progress among the hills—Monts—Their immense number—Preparations for the journey—Servant and guide—Danger of being lost—The ferry—Ancient boat—Horses swim well

I HAVE hitherto been speaking only of the part of Scotland where I am, viz. the eastern side of this island, bordering upon the northern mountains, which part I take to be a kind of medium between the Lowlands and Highlands, both by its situation, and as it partakes of the language and customs of both those extremes.

In England the name of Scotsman is used indiscriminately to signify any one of the male part of the natives of North Britain; but the Highlanders differ from the people of the low country in almost every circumstance of life. Their language, customs, manners, dress, etc., are unlike, and neither of them would be contented to be taken for the other, insomuch that in speaking of an unknown person of this country (I mean Scotland) as a Scotsman only, it is as indefinite as barely to call a Frenchman a European, so little would his native character be known by it.

I own it may be said there is a difference in the other part of this island between the English and the Welsh; but I think it is hardly in any degree to be compared with the above-mentioned distinction.

You will conclude I am speaking only of such among the people of Scotland who have not had the advantages of fortune and education, for letters and converse with polite strangers will render all mankind equal, so far as their genius and application will admit; some few prejudices, of no very great consequence, excepted.

A crowd of other remarks and observations were just now pressing for admittance, but I have rejected them all, as fit only to anticipate some of the contents of the sheets that are to follow; and therefore I am now at liberty to begin my account of the most northern part of Great Britain, so far as it has fallen within my knowledge.

The Highlands take up more than one-half of Scotland; they extend from Dumbarton, near the mouth of the River Clyde, to the northernmost part of the island, which is above two-hundred miles and their breadth is from fifty to above a hundred; but how to describe them to you, so as to give you any tolerable idea of such a rugged country – to you, I say, who have never been out of the south of England – is, I fear, a task altogether impracticable.

If it had been possible for me to procure a landscape (I should say heathscape or rockscape) of any one tremendous view among the mountains, it would be satisfactory and informing at one single cast of the eye; but language, you know, can only communicate ideas, as it were, by retail; and a description of one part of an object, which is composed of many, defaces or weakens another that went before; whereas painting not only shows the whole entire at one view, but leaves the several parts to be examined separately and at leisure by the eye.

From words we can only receive a notion of such unknown objects as bear some resemblance with others we have seen, but painting can even create ideas of bodies utterly unlike to anything that ever appeared to our sight.

Thus am I entering upon my most difficult task, for the customs and manners of the Highlanders will give me little trouble more than the transcribing; but as I believe I am the first who ever attempted a minute description of any such mountains I cannot but greatly doubt of my success herein; and nothing but your friendship and your request (which to me is a command) could have engaged me to hazard my credit even with you, indulgent as you are, by an undertaking wherein the odds are so much against me. But to begin. The Highlands are, for the greatest part, composed of hills, as it were, piled one upon another, till the complication rises and swells to mountains, of which the heads are frequently above the clouds, and near the summit have vast hollows filled up with snow, which, on the north side, continues all the year long.

From the west coast they rise, as it were, in progression upwards, toward the midland country eastward (for on the east side of the island they are not generally quite so high), and their ridges, for the most part, run west and east, or near those points, as do likewise all the yet discovered beds or seams of minerals they contain, with which, I have good reason to believe, they are well furnished.

This position of the mountains has created arguments for the truth of a universal deluge; as if the waters had formed those vast inequalities, by rushing violently from east to west.

The summits of the highest are mostly destitute of earth; and the huge naked rocks, being just above the heath, produce the disagreeable appearance of a scabbed head, especially when they appear to the view in a conical figure; for as you proceed round them in valleys, on lesser hills, or the sides of other mountains, their form varies according to the situation of the eye that beholds them.

They are clothed with heath interspersed with rocks, and it is very rare to see any spot of grass; for those (few as they are) lie concealed from an outward view, in flats and hollows among the hills. There are, indeed, some mountains that have woods of fir, or small oaks on their declivity, where the root of one tree is almost upon a line with the top of another: these are rarely seen in a journey; what there may be behind, out of all common ways, I do not know; but none of them will pay for felling and removing over rocks, bogs, precipices, and conveyance by rocky rivers, except such as are near the sea coast, and hardly those, as I believe the York Buildings Company will find in the conclusion.

I have already mentioned the spaces of snow near the tops of the mountains: they are great hollows, appearing below as small spots of white (I will suppose of the dimensions of a pretty large table), but they are so diminished to the eye by their vast height and distance, from, perhaps, a mile or more in length, and breadth proportionable. This I know by experience, having ridden over such a patch of snow in the month of June: the surface was smooth, not slippery, and so hard my horse's feet made little or no impression on it; and in one place I rode over a bridge of snow hollowed into a kind of arch. I then made no doubt this passage for the water, at bottom of the deep burn, was opened by the warmth of springs; of which, I suppose, in dry weather, the current was wholly composed.

From the tops of the mountains there descend deep, wide, and winding hollows, ploughed into the sides by the weight and violent rapidity of the waters, which often loosen and bring down stones of an incredible bigness.

Of one of these hollows, only part appears to sight in different places of the descent; the rest is lost to view in meanders among the hills.

When the uppermost waters begin to appear with white streaks in these cavities, the inhabitants who are within view of the height say, 'The Grey Mare's Tail begins to grow', and it serves to them as a monitor of ensuring peril, if at that time they venture far from home; because they might be in danger, by waters, to have all communication cut off between them and shelter or sustenance. And they are very skilful to judge in what course of time the rivers and burns will become impassable.

The dashing and foaming of these cataracts among the rocks make them look exceedingly white, by comparison with the bordering heath; but when the mountains are covered with snow, and that is melting, then those streams of water, compared with the whiteness near them, look of a dirty yellowish colour, from the soil and sulphur mixed with them as they descend. But everything, you know, is this or that by comparison.

I shall soon conclude this description of the outward appearance of the mountains which I am already tired of, as a disagreeable subject, and I believe you are so too: but, for your future ease in that particular, there is not much variety in it, but gloomy spaces, different rocks, heath, and high and low.

To cast one's eye from an eminence toward a group of them, they appear still one above another, fainter and fainter, according to the aerial perspective, and the whole of a dismal gloomy brown drawing upon a dirty purple; and most of all disagreeable when the heath is in bloom.

Those ridges of the mountains that appear next to the ether – by their rugged irregular lines, the heath and black rocks – are rendered extremely harsh to the eye, by appearing close to that diaphanous body, without any medium to soften the opposition; and the clearer the day, the more rude and offensive they are to the sight; yet, in some few places, where any white crags are atop, that harshness is something softened.

But of all the views, I think the most horrid is, to look at the hills from east to west, or vice versa, for then the eye penetrates far among them, and sees more particularly their stupendous bulk, frightful irregularity, and horrid gloom, made yet more sombrous by the shades and faint reflections they communicate one to another.

As a specimen of the height of those mountains, I shall here take notice of one in Lochaber, called Ben Nevis, which, from the level below to that part of the summit only which appears to view, has been several times measured by different artists, and found to be three-quarters of a mile of perpendicular height.

It is reckoned seven Scots miles to that part where it begins to be inaccessible.

Some English officers took it in their fancy to go to the top, but could not attain it for bogs and huge perpendicular rocks; and when they were got as high as they could go, they found a vast change in the quality of the air, saw nothing but the tops of other mountains, and altogether a prospect of one tremendous heath, with here and there some spots of crags and snow.

This wild expedition, in ascending round and round the hills, in finding accessible places, helping one another up the rocks, in disappointments, and their returning to the foot of the mountain, took them up a whole summer's day, from five in the morning. This is according to their own relation. But they were fortunate in an article of the greatest importance to them, i.e. that the mountain happened to be free from clouds while they were in it, which is a thing not very common in that dabbled part of the island, the western hills – I say, if those condensed vapours had passed while they were at any considerable height, and had continued, there would have been no means left for them to find their way down, and they must have perished with cold, wet, and hunger.

In passing to the heart of the Highlands we proceeded from bad to worse, which makes the worst of all the less surprising: but I have often heard it said by my countrymen, that they verily believed, if an inhabitant of the south of England were to be brought blindfold into some narrow, rocky hollow, enclosed with these horrid prospects, and there to have his bandage taken off, he would be ready to die with fear, as thinking it impossible he should ever get out to return to his native country.

Now what do you think of a poetical mountain, smooth and easy of ascent, clothed with a verdant, flowery turf, where shepherds tend their flocks, sitting under the shade of small poplars, etc.? – in short, what do you think of Richmond Hill, where we have passed so many hours together, delighted with the beautiful prospect.

But after this description of these mountains, it is not unlikely you may ask, of what use can be such monstrous excrescences?

To this I should answer, they contain minerals, as I said before; and serve for the breeding and feeding of cattle, wild fowls, and other useful animals, which cost little or nothing in keeping. They break the clouds, and not only replenish the rivers, but collect great quantities of water into lakes and other vast reservoirs, where they are husbanded, as I may say, for the use of mankind in time of drought; and thence, by their gravity, perforate the crannies of rocks and looser strata, and work their way either perpendicularly, horizontally, or obliquely; the two latter, when they meet with solid rock, clay, or some other resisting stratum, till they find their proper passages downward, and in the end form the springs below. And, certainly, it is the deformity of the hills that makes the natives conceive of their naked straths and glens, as of the most beautiful objects in nature.

But as I suppose you are unacquainted with these words, I shall here take occasion to explain them to you.

A 'strath' is a flat space of arable land, lying along the side or sides of some capital river, between the water and the feet of the hills; and keeps its name till the river comes to be confined to a narrow space, by stony moors, rocks, or windings among the mountains.

The 'glen' is a little spot of corn country, by the sides of some small river or rivulet, likewise bounded by hills; this is in general: but there are some spaces that are called glens, from there being flats in deep hollows between the high mountains, although they, are perfectly barren, as Glendhu (or the black glen), Glenalmond, etc.

By the way, this Glenalmond is a hollow so very narrow, and the mountains on each side so steep and high, that the sun is seen therein no more than between two and three hours in the longest day.

Now let us go among the hills, and see if we can find something more agreeable than their outward appearance. And to that end I shall give you the journal of two days' progress; which, I believe, will better answer the purpose than a disjointed account of the inconveniences, hazards, and hardships, that attend a traveller in the heart of the Highlands. But before I begin the particular account of my progress, I shall venture at a general description of one of the mountain spaces, between glen and glen: and when that is done, you may make the comparison with one of our southern rambles, in which, without any previous route, we used to wander from place to place, just so as the beauty of the country invited.

How have we been pleased with the easy ascent of an eminence, which almost imperceptibly brought us to the beautiful prospects seen from its summit! What a delightful variety of fields, and meadows of various tints of green, adorned with trees and bloom-ing hedges; and the whole embellished with woods, groves, waters, flocks, herds, and magnificent seats of the happy (at least seemingly so); and every other rising ground opening a new and lovely landscape!

But in one of these 'monts' (as the Highlanders call them), soon after your entrance upon the first hill, you lose, for good and all, the sight of the plain from whence you parted; and nothing follows but the view of rocks and heath, both beneath and on every side, with high and barren mountains round about.

Thus you creep slowly on, between the hills in rocky ways, sometimes over those eminences, and often on their declivities, continually hoping the next ridge before you will be the summit of the highest, and so often deceived in that hope, as almost to despair of ever reaching the top. And thus you are still rising by long ascents, and again descending by shorter, till you arrive at the highest ground; from whence you go down in much the same manner, reversed, and never have the glen in view that you wish to see, as the end of your present trouble, till you are just upon it. And when you are there, the inconveniences (though not the hazards) are almost as great as in the tedious passage to it

As an introduction to my journal, I must acquaint you that I was advised to take with me some cold provisions, and oats for my horses, there being no place of refreshment till the end of my first day's journey.

2 October 172—

Set out with one servant and a guide; the latter, because no stranger (or even a native, unacquainted with the way) can venture among the hills without a conductor; for if he once go aside, and most especially if snow should fall (which may happen on the very high hills at any season of the year), in that, or any other case, he may wander into a bog to impassable burns or rocks, and every *ne plus ultra* oblige him to change his course, till he wanders from all hopes of ever again seeing the face of a human creature. Or if he should accidentally hit upon the way from whence he strayed, he would not distinguish it from another, there is such a seeming sameness in all the rocky places. Or again, if he should happen to meet with some Highlander, and one that was not unwilling to give him directions, he could not declare his wants, as being a stranger to the language of the country. In short, one might as well think of making a sea voyage without sun, moon, stars, or compass, as pretend to know which way to take, when lost among the hills and mountains.

But to return to my journal from which I have strayed, though not with much danger, it being at first setting out, and my guide with me.

After riding about four miles of pretty good road over heathy moors, hilly, but none high or of steep ascent, I came to a small river, where there was a ferry; for the water was too deep and rapid to pass the ford above. The boat was patched almost every where with rough pieces of boards, and the oars were kept in their places by small bands of twisted sticks.

I could not but inquire its age, seeing it had so many marks of antiquity; and was told by the ferryman it had belonged to his father, and was above sixty years old. This put me in mind of the knife, which was of an extraordinary age, but had, at times, been repaired with many new blades and handles. But in most places of the Highlands, where there is a boat (which is very rare), it is much worse than this, and not large enough to receive a horse; and therefore he is swum at the stern, while somebody holds up his head by a halter or bridle.

The horses swim very well at first setting out; but if the water be wide, in time they generally turn themselves on one of their sides, and patiently suffer themselves to be dragged along.

I remember one of these boats was so very much out of repair, we were forced to stand upon clods of turf to stop the leaks in her bottom, while we passed across the river.

I shall here conclude, in the style of the newswriters – this to be continued in my next.

LETTER XVI

---◆◆◆---

Steep and stony hills—A burn—Wood of fir—Bog—Danger from roots of
trees—Grass rare—Discover a Highlander—A pleasure of the mind—
Crossing a ford—Dangerous pass—Crossing a bog—Precaution—Horse
sinks—Escapes with difficulty—Highland horses accustomed to bogs—
New difficulties—Stony moors—Comforts of discovering a habitation—
Dangerous ford—Best mode of passing—A whimsical expedient—
Highlanders wade the rivers—Dangers to which they are exposed—Frequent
loss of life—Inn—Dangerous stabling—Oats—Dwelling-house—A Highland
toast

FROM the river's side I ascended a steep hill, so full of large
stones, it was impossible to make a trot. This continued up and
down about a mile and half.

At the foot of the hill, tolerable way for a mile, there being no
great quantity of stones among the heath, but very uneven; and, at
the end of it, a small burn descending from between two hills, worn
deep among the rocks, rough, rapid, and steep, and dangerous to
pass. I concluded some rain had fallen behind the hills that were
near me; which I could not see, because it had a much greater fall of
water than any of the like kind I had passed before.

From hence a hill five miles over, chiefly composed of lesser hills;
so stony, that it was impossible to crawl above a mile in an hour.
But I must except a small part of it from this general description; for
there ran across this way (or 'road' as they call it) the end of a wood
of fir trees, the only one I had ever passed.

This, for the most part, was an easy, rising slope of about half a mile. In most places of the surface it was bog about two feet deep, and beneath was uneven rock; in other parts the rock and roots of the trees appeared to view.

The roots sometimes crossed one another, as they ran along a good way upon the face of the rock, and often above the boggy part, by both which my horses' legs were so much entangled, that I thought it impossible to keep them upon their feet. But you would not have been displeased to observe how the roots had run along, and felt, as it were, for the crannies of the rock; and there shot into them, as a hold against the pressure of winds above.

At the end of this hill was a river, or rather rivulet, and near the edge of it a small grassy spot, such as I had not seen in all my way, but the place not inhabited. Here I stopped to bait. My own provisions were laid upon the foot of a rock, and the oats upon a kind of mossy grass, as the cleanest place for the horses' feeding.

While I was taking some refreshment, chance provided me with a more agreeable repast – the pleasure of the mind. I happened to espy a poor Highlander at a great height, upon the declivity of a high hill, and ordered my guide to call him down. The 'trout so' (or come hither) seemed agreeable to him, and he came down with wonderful celerity, considering the roughness of the hill; and asking what was 'my will' (in his language), he was given to understand I wanted him only to eat and drink. This unexpected answer raised such joy in the poor creature, that he could not help showing it by skipping about, and expressing sounds of satisfaction. And when I was retired a little way down the river, to give the men an opportunity of enjoying themselves with less restraint, there was such mirth among the three, as I thought a sufficient recompense for my former fatigue.

But, perhaps, you may question how there could be such merriment, with nothing but water?

I carried with me a quart-bottle of brandy, for my man and the guide; and for myself, I had always in my journeys a pocket pistol, loaded with brandy, mixed with juice of lemon (when they were to be had), which again mingled with water in a wooden cup, was, upon such occasions, my table-drink.

When we had trussed up our baggage, I entered the ford, and passed it not without danger, the bottom being filled with large stones, the current rapid, a steep, rocky descent to the water, and a rising on the further side much worse; for having mounted a little way up the declivity, in turning the corner of a rock I came to an exceedingly steep part before I was aware of it, where I thought my horse would have gone down backwards, much faster than he went up; but I recovered a small flat of the rock, and dismounted.

There was nothing remarkable afterwards, till I came near the top of the hill; where there was a seeming plain, of about a hundred and fifty yards, between me and the summit.

No sooner was I upon the edge of it, but my guide desired me to alight; and then I perceived it was a bog, or peatmoss, as they call it.

I had experience enough of these deceitful surfaces to order that the horses should be led in separate parts, lest, if one broke the turf, the other, treading in his steps, might sink.

The horse I used to ride, having little weight but his own, went on pretty successfully; only now and then breaking the surface a little; but the other, that carried my portmanteau, and being not quite so nimble, was much in danger, till near the further end, and there he sank. But it luckily happened to be in a part where his long legs went to the bottom, which is generally hard gravel, or rock; but he was in almost up to the back.

By this time my own (for distinction) was quite free of the bog, and being frighted, stood very tamely by himself; which he would not have done at another time. In the meanwhile we were forced to wait at a distance, while the other was flouncing and throwing the dirt about him; for there was no means of coming near him to ease him of the heavy burden he had upon his loins, by which he was sometimes in danger to be turned upon his back, when he rose to break the bog before him. But, in about a quarter of an hour, he got out, bedaubed with the slough, shaking with fear, and his head and neck all over in a foam.

This bog was stiff enough at that time to bear the country garrons in any part of it. But it is observed of the English horses, that when they find themselves hampered, they stand still, and tremble till they sink, and then they struggle violently, and work themselves further in; and if the bog be deep, as most of them are, it is next to impossible to get them out, otherwise than by digging them a passage. But the little Highland hobbies, when they find themselves bogged, will lie still till they are relieved. And besides, being bred in the mountains, they have learnt to avoid the weaker parts of the mire; and sometimes our own horses, having put down their heads and smelt to the bog, will refuse to enter upon it.

There is a certain lord in one of the most northern parts, who makes use of the little garrons for the bogs and rough ways, but has a sizeable horse led with him, to carry him through the deep and rapid fords.

As for myself, I was harassed on this slough, by winding about from place to place, to find such tufts as were within my stride or leap, in my heavy boots with high heels; which, by my spring, when the little hillocks were too far asunder, broke the turf, and then I threw myself down toward the next protuberance: but to my guide it seemed nothing; he was light of body, shod with flat brogues, wide in the soles, and accustomed to a particular step, suited to the occasion.

This hill was about three-quarters of a mile over, and had but a short descent on the further side, rough, indeed, but not remarkable in this country. I had now five computed miles to go before I came to my first asylum – that is, five Scots miles, which, as in the north of England, are longer than yours as three is to two; and, if the difficulty of the way were to be taken into account, it might well be called fifteen. This, except about three-quarters of a mile of heathy ground, pretty free from stones and rocks, consisted of stony moors, almost impracticable for a horse with his rider, and likewise of rocky way, where we were obliged to dismount, and sometimes climb, and otherwhile slide down. But what vexed me most of all, they called it a road; and yet I must confess it was preferable to a boggy way. The great difficulty was to wind about with the horses, and find such places as they could possibly be got over.

When we came near the foot of the lowermost hill, I discovered a pretty large glen, which before was not to be seen. I believe it might be about a quarter of a mile wide, enclosed by exceedingly high mountains, with nine dwelling-huts, besides a few others of a lesser size for barns and stables: this they call a town with a pompous name belonging to it; but the comfort of being near the end of my day's journey, heartily tired, was mixed with the allay of a pretty river, that ran between me and my lodging.

Having passed the hill, I entered the river, my horse being almost at once up to his mid-sides; the guide led him by the bridle, as he was sometimes climbing over the loose stones which lay in all positions, and many of them two or three feet diameter; at other times with his nose in the water and mounted up behind. Thus he proceeded with the utmost caution, never removing one foot till he found the others firm, and all the while seeming impatient of the pressure of the torrent, as if he was sensible that, once losing his footing, he should be driven away and dashed against the rocks below.

In other rapid rivers, where I was something acquainted with the fords, by having passed them before, though never so stony, I thought the leader of my horse to be an incumbrance to him; and I have always found, as the rivers while they are passable, are pretty clear, the horse is the surest judge of his own safety. Perhaps some would think it strange I speak in this manner of a creature that we proudly call irrational. There is a certain giddiness attends the violent passage of the water when one is in it, and therefore I always, at entering, resolved to keep my eye steadily fixed on some remarkable stone on the shore of the further side, and my horse's ears, as near as I could, in a line with it, leaving him to choose his steps; for the rider, especially if he casts his eye down the torrent, does not know whether he goes directly forward or not, but fancies he is carried, like the leeway of a ship, sideways along with the stream. If he cannot forbear looking aside, it is best to turn his face toward the coming current.

Another precaution is (and you cannot use too many), to let your legs hang in the water; and, where the stones will permit, to preserve a firmer seat, in case of any sudden slide or stumble.

By what I have been saying you will perceive I still retain the custom of my own country, in not sending my servant before me through these dangerous waters, as is the constant practice of all the natives of Scotland; nor could I prevail with myself to do so, at least unless, like theirs, mine went before me in smooth as well as bad roads. But in that there are several inconveniences: and although a servant may by some be condemned for his servile circumstance of life, I could never bear the thoughts of exposing him to dangers for my own safety and security, lest he should despise me with more justice, and in a greater degree, for the want of a necessary resolution and fortitude.

I shall here mention a whimsical expedient against the danger of these Highland fords.

An officer who was lately quartered at one of the barracks in a very mountainous part of the country, when he travelled, carried with him a long rope; this was to be put round his body, under his arms, and those that attended him were to wade the river, and hold the rope on the other side, that, if any accident should happen to him by depth of water, or the failure of his horse, they might prevent his being carried down the current and drag him ashore.

The instant I had recovered the further side of the river, there appeared, near the water, six Highland men and a woman; these, I suppose had coasted the stream over rocks, and along the sides of steep hills, for I had not seen them before. Seeing they were preparing to wade, I stayed to observe them: first the men and the woman tucked up their petticoats, then they cast themselves into a rank, with the female in the middle, and laid their arms over one another's shoulders; and I saw they had placed the strongest toward the stream, as best able to resist the force of the torrent. In their passage, the large slippery stones, made some of them now and then lose their footing: and, on those occasions, the whole rank changed colour and countenance.

I believe no painter ever remarked such strong impressions of fear and hope on a human face, with so many and sudden successions of those two opposite passions, as I observed among those poor people; but in the Highlands this is no uncommon thing.

Perhaps you will ask, 'How does a single Highlander support himself against so great a force?' He bears himself up against the stream with a stick, which he always carries with him for that purpose.

As I am now at the end of my first day's journey, and have no mind to resume this disagreeable subject in another place, I shall ask leave to mention one danger more attending the Highland fords; and that is, the sudden gushes of waters that sometimes descend from behind the adjacent hills, insomuch that, when the river has not been above a foot deep, the passenger, thinking himself secure, has been overtaken and carried away by the torrent.

Such accidents have happened twice within my knowledge, in two different small rivers, both within seven miles of this town; one to an exciseman and the messenger who was carrying him from hence to Edinburgh, in order to answer some accusations relating to his office; the other to two young fellows of a neighbouring clan – all drowned in the manner above-mentioned. And, from these two instances, we may reasonably conclude that many accidents of the same nature have happened, especially in more mountainous parts, and those hardly ever known but in the narrow neighbourhoods of the unhappy sufferers.

When I came to my inn, I found the stable door too low to receive my large horses, though high enough for the country garrons; so the frame was taken out, and a small part of the roof pulled down for their admittance; for which damage I had a shilling to pay the next morning. My fear was, the hut being weak and small, they would pull it about their ears; for that mischance had happened to a gentleman who bore me company in a former journey, but his horses were not much hurt by the ruins.

When oats were brought I found them so light and so much sprouted, that taking up a handful, others hung to them, in succession, like a cluster of bees; but of such corn it is the custom to give double measure.

My next care was to provide for myself, and to that end I entered the dwelling-house. There my landlady sat, with a parcel of children about her, some quite, and others almost, naked, by a little peat fire, in the middle of the hut; and over the fireplace was a small hole in the roof for a chimney. The floor was common earth, very uneven, and nowhere dry, but near the fire and in the corners, where no foot had carried the muddy dirt from without doors.

The skeleton of the hut was formed of small crooked timber, but the beam for the roof was large out of all proportion. This is to render the weight of the whole more fit to resist the violent flurries of wind that frequently rush into the plains from the openings of the mountains; for the whole fabric was set upon the surface of the ground like a table, stool or other moveable.

Hence comes the Highlander's compliment, or health, in drinking to his friend; for as we say, among familiar acquaintance, 'To your fireside'; he says, much to the same purpose, 'To your roof-tree', alluding to the family's safety from tempests.

The walls were about four feet high, lined with sticks wattled like a hurdle, built on the outside with turf; and thinner slices of the same serve for tiling. This last they call 'divet'.

When the hut has been built some time it is covered with weeds and grass; and, I do assure you, I have seen sheep, that had got up from the foot of an adjoining hill feeding upon the top of the house.

If there happened to be any continuance of dry weather, which is pretty rare, the worms drop out of the divet for want of moisture, insomuch that I have shuddered at the apprehension of their falling into the dish when I have been eating.

LETTER XVII

———◆———

AT a little distance was another hut, where preparations were
making for my reception. It was something less but contained two beds, or boxes to lie in, and was kept as an apartment
for people of distinction – or, which is all one, for such as seem by
their appearance to promise expense. And, indeed, I have often found
but little difference in that article, between one of those huts and the
best inn in England. Nay if I were to reckon the value of what I had
for my own use by the country practice, it would appear to be ten
times dearer: but it is not the maxim of the Highlands alone (as we
know), that those who travel must pay for such as stay at home;
and really the Highland gentlemen themselves are less scrupulous of
expense in these public huts than anywhere else. And their example,
in great measure, authorises impositions upon strangers, who may
complain, but can have no redress.

The landlord not only sits down with you, as in the northern
Lowlands, but, in some little time, asks leave and sometimes not, to

introduce his brother, cousin, or more, who are all to drink your honour's health in whisky; which, though a strong spirit, is to them like water. And this I have often seen them drink out of a scallop shell. And in other journeys, notwithstanding their great familiarity with me, I have several times seen my servant at a loss how to behave, when the Highlander has turned about and very formally drank to him: and when I have baited, and eaten two or three eggs, and nothing else to be had, when I asked the question, 'What is there for eating?' the answer has been, 'Nothing for you, sir; but six pence for your man.'

The host, who is rarely other than a gentleman, is interpreter between you and those who do not speak English; so that you lose nothing of what any one has to say relating to the antiquity of their family, or the heroic actions of their ancestors in war with some other clan.

If the guest be a stranger, not seen before by the man of the house, he takes the first opportunity to inquire of the servant from whence his master came, who he is, whither he is going, and what his business in that country? And if the fellow happens to be surly as thinking the inquiry impertinent, perhaps chiefly from the Highlander's poor appearance, then the master is sure to be subtly sifted (if not asked) for the secret; and, if obtained, it is a help to conversation with his future guests.

Notice at last was brought me that my apartment was ready; but at going out from the first hovel, the other seemed to be all on fire within: for the smoke came pouring out through the ribs and roof all over; but chiefly out at the door, which was not four feet high, so that the whole made the appearance (I have seen) of a fuming dunghill removed and fresh piled up again, and pretty near the same in colour, shape, and size.

By the way the Highlanders say they love the smoke; it keeps them warm. But I retired to my first shelter till the peats were grown red, and the smoke thereby abated.

This fuel is seldom kept dry, for want of convenience; and that is one reason why, in lighting or replenishing the fire, the smokiness continues so long a time – and Moggy's puffing of it with her petticoat, instead of a pair of bellows, is a dilatory way.

I believe you would willing know (being an Englishman) what I had to eat. My fare was a couple of roasted hens (as they call them), very poor, new killed, the skins much broken with plucking; black with smoke, and greased with bad butter.

As I had no great appetite to that dish, I spoke for some hard eggs; made my supper of the yolks, and washed them down with a bottle of good small claret.

My bed had clean sheets and blankets! but, which was best of all (though negative), I found no inconvenience from those troublesome companions with which most other huts abound. But the bare mention of them brings to my remembrance a passage between two officers of the army, the morning after a Highland night's lodging. One was taking off the slowest kind of the two, when the other cried out, 'Z—ds! What are you doing? Let us first secure the dragoons; we can take the foot at leisure.'

But I had like to have forgot a mischance that happened to me the next morning; for rising early, and getting out of my box pretty hastily, I unluckily set my foot in the chamber-pot, a hole in the ground by the bedside, which was made to serve for that use in case of occasion

I shall not trouble you with anything that passed till I mounted on horseback; only, for want of something more proper for breakfast, I took up with a little brandy, water, sugar, and yolks of eggs, beat up together; which I think they call 'old man's milk'.

I was now provided with a new guide, for the skill of my first extended no further than this place: but this could speak no English, which I found afterwards to be an inconvenience.

Second Day. At mounting I received many compliments from my host; but the most earnest was, that common one of wishing me good weather. For, like the seafaring man, my safety depended upon it; especially at that season of the year.

As the plain lay before me, I thought it all fit for culture; but in riding along, I observed a good deal of it was bog, and here and there rock even with the surface: however, my road was smooth; and if I had had company with me, I might have said jestingly, as was usual among us after a rough way, 'Come, let us ride this over again'.

At the end of about a mile, there was a steep ascent, which they call a 'carne' – that is, an exceedingly stony hill, which at some distance seems to have no space at all between stone and stone. I thought I could compare it with no ruggedness so aptly as to suppose it like all the different stones in a mason's yard thrown promiscuously upon one another. This I passed on foot, at the rate of about half a mile in the hour. I do not reckon the time that was lost in backing my horses out of a narrow place withoutside of a rock, where the way ended with a precipice of about twenty feet deep. Into this gap they were led by the mistake or carelessness of my guide. The descent from the top of this carne was short, and thence I ascended another hill not so stony; and at last, by several others (which, though very rough, are not reckoned extraordinary in the Highlands), I came to a precipice of about a hundred yards in length.

The side of the mountain below me was almost perpendicular; and the rest above, which seemed to reach the clouds, was exceedingly steep. The path which the Highlanders and their little horses had worn was scarcely two feet wide, but pretty smooth; and below was a lake whereinto vast pieces of rock had fallen, which I suppose had made, in some measure, the steepness of the precipice; and the water that appeared between some of them seemed to be under my stirrup. I really believe the path where I was is twice as high from the lake as the cross of St Paul's is from Ludgate Hill; and I thought I had good reason to think so, because a few huts beneath, on the further side of the water, which is not very wide, appeared to me each of them like a black spot not much bigger than the standish before me.

A certain officer of the army going this way was so terrified with the sight of the abyss that he crept a little higher, fondly imagining he should be safer above, as being further off from the danger, and so to take hold of the heath in his passage. There a panic terror seized him, and he began to lose his forces, finding it impracticable to proceed, and being fearful to quit his hold and slide down, lest in so doing he should overshoot the narrow path; and had not two soldiers come to his assistance, viz. one who was at some little distance before him, and the other behind, in all probability he had gone to the bottom. But I have observed that particular minds are wrought upon by particular dangers, according to their different sets of ideas. I have sometimes travelled in the mountains with officers of the army, and have known one in the middle of a deep and rapid ford cry out he was undone; another was terrified with the fear of his horse's falling in an exceeding rocky way; and perhaps neither of them would be so much shocked at the danger that so greatly affected the other; or, it may be, either of them at standing the fire of a battery of cannon. But for my own part I had passed over two such precipices before, which rendered it something less terrifying; yet, as I have hinted, I chose to ride it, as I did the last of the other two, knowing by the first I was liable fear, and that my horse was not subject either to that disarming passion or giddiness, which in that case I take to be the effect of apprehension.

It is a common thing for the natives to ride their horses over such little precipices; but for myself I never was upon the back of one of them; and, by the account some Highlanders have given me of them, I think I should never choose it in such places as I have been describing.

There is in some of those paths, at the very edge or extremity, a little mossy grass, and those shelties, being never shod, if they are ever so little footsore, they will, to favour their feet, creep to the very brink, which must certainly be very terrible to a stranger.

It will hardly ever be out of my memory, how I was haunted by a kind of poetical sentence, after I was over this precipice, which did not cease till it was supplanted by the new fear of my horse's falling among the rocks in my way from it. It was this:

There hov'ring eagles wait the fatal trip.

By the way, this bird is frequently seen among the mountains, and, I may say, severely felt sometimes, by the inhabitants, in the loss of their lambs, kids, and even calves and colts.

I had now gone about six miles, and had not above two, as I understood afterwards, to the place of baiting. In my way, which I shall only say was very rough and hilly, I met a Highland chieftain with fourteen attendants, whose offices about his person I shall hereafter describe, at least the greatest part of them. When we came, as the sailor says, almost broadside and broadside, he eyed me as if he would look my hat off; but, as he was at home, and I a stranger in the country, I thought he might have made the first overture of civility, and therefore I took little notice of him and his ragged followers. On his part he seemed to show a kind of disdain at my being so slenderly attended, with a mixture of anger that I showed him no respect before his vassals; but this might only be my surmise – yet it looked very like it. I supposed he was going to the glen from whence I came, for there was no other hut in all my way, and there he might be satisfied by the landlord who I was, etc.

I shall not trouble you with any more at present, than that I safely arrived at my baiting place; for, as I hinted before, there is such a sameness in the parts of the hills that the description of one rugged way, bog, ford, etc. will serve pretty well to give you a notion of the rest.

Here I desired to know what I could have for dinner, and was told there was some undressed mutton. This I esteemed as a rarity, but, as I did not approve the fingers of either maid or mistress, I ordered my man (who is an excellent cook, so far as a beefsteak or a mutton chop) to broil me a chop or two, while I took a little turn to ease my legs, weary with sitting so long on horseback.

This proved an intolerable affront to my landlady, who raved and stormed, and said, 'What's your master? I have dressed for the Laird of this and the Laird of that, such and such chiefs; and this very day,' says she, 'for the Laird of —,' who, I doubted not, was the person I met on the hill. To be short, she absolutely refused to admit of any such innovation; and so the chops served for my man and the guide, and I had recourse to my former fare hard eggs.

Eggs are seldom wanting at the public huts, though, by the poverty of the poultry, one might wonder how they should have any inclination to produce them.

Here was no wine to be had; but as I carried with me a few lemons in a net, I drank some small punch for refreshment. When my servant was preparing the liquor, my landlord came to me, and asked me seriously if those were apples he was squeezing. And indeed there are as many lemon trees as apple tees in that country, nor have they any kind of fruit in their glens that I know of.

Their huts are mostly built on some rising rocky spot at the foot of a hill, secure from any burn or springs that might descend upon them from the mountains; and, thus situated, they are pretty safe from inundations from above or below, and other ground they cannot spare from their corn. And even upon the skirts of the Highlands, where the laird has indulged two or three trees from his house, I have heard the tenant lament the damage done by the droppings and shade of them, as well as the space taken up by the trunks and roots.

The only fruit the natives have, that I have seen, is the bilberry, which is mostly found near springs, in hollows of the heaths. The taste of them to me is not very agreeable, but they are much esteemed by the inhabitants, who eat them with their milk: yet in the mountain woods, which for the most part, are distant and difficult of access, there are nuts, raspberries, and strawberries; the two last, though but small, are very grateful to the taste; but those woods are so rare (at least it has always appeared so to me) that few of the Highlanders are near enough to partake of the benefit.

I now set out on my last stage, of which I had gone about five miles, in much the same manner as before, when it began to rain below, but it was snow above to a certain depth from the summits of the mountains. In about half an hour afterwards, at the end of near a mile, there arose a most violent tempest. This, in a little time, began to scoop the snow from the mountains, and made such a furious drift, which did not melt as it drove, that I could hardly see my horse's head.

The horses were blown aside from place to place as often as the sudden gusts came on, being unable to resist those violent eddy-winds; and, at the same time, they were nearly blinded with the snow.

Now I expected no less than to perish, was hardly able to keep my saddle, and, for increase of misery, my guide led me out of the way, having entirely lost his landmarks.

When he perceived his error he fell down on his knees, by my horse's side, and in a beseeching posture, with his arms extended and in a howling tone, seemed to ask forgiveness.

I imagined what the matter was (for I could but just see him, and that too by fits), and spoke to him with a soft voice, to signify I was not in anger; and it appeared afterwards that he expected to be shot, as they have a dreadful notion of the English.

Thus finding himself in no danger of my resentment, he addressed himself to the searching about for the way from which he had deviated, and in some little time I heard a cry of joy, and he came and took my horse by the bridle, and never afterwards quitted it till we came to my new lodging, which was about a mile, for it was almost as dark as night. In the mean time I had given directions to my man for keeping close to my horse's heels; and if anything should prevent it, to call to me immediately, that I might not lose him.

As good luck would have it, there was but one small river in the way, and the ford, though deep and winding, had a smooth, sandy bottom, which is very rare in the Highlands.

There was another circumstance favourable to us (I shall not name a third as one, which is our being not far from the village, for we might have perished with cold in the night as well near it as further off), there had not a very great quantity of snow fallen upon the mountains, because the air began a little to clear, though very little, within about a quarter of a mile of the glen, otherwise we might have been buried in some cavity hid from us by the darkness and the snow.

But if this drift, which happened to us upon some one of the wild moors, had continued, and we had had far to go, we might have perished, notwithstanding the knowledge of any guide whatever.

These drifts are, above all other dangers, dreaded by the Highlanders; for my own part, I could not but think of Mr Addison's short description of a whirlwind in the wild, sandy deserts of Numidia.

LETTER XVIII

Whirlwinds—Inn—Burlesque—Curious visitor—Peat smoke—Great fall of
rain—Danger of being shut in by—A Highlander lost in the mountains—
County of Atholl—Part of ancient Caledonia—A tract well cultivated—
Highlanders originally from Ireland—Spenser's *View of Ireland*—National
pride—Stature of the Highlanders—Deformity—Some general assertions
ridiculous—Gasconade—Remedy against fever—Esculapian honour—
Additional remarks—Frequent rain—Shallow and stony soil—Clouds—
Pursuit of a rainbow—Tenerife—Source of rivers—Lakes—Loch Ness—Its
great depth—Cataracts—Lakes on hills—Strathglass—A lake always
frozen—Waterfall—Danger and difficulty of crossing rivers—Whisky
merchants—Agreeable company—Bogs—Hills—Dangers of—Scarcity of
trees—Anecdote—Value of land

EVERY high wind, in many places of the Highlands, is a
whirlwind. The agitated air, pouring into the narrow and high
spaces between the mountains, being confined in its course, and, if I
may use the expression, pushed on by a crowding rear, till it comes
to a bounded hollow, or kind of amphitheatre – I say, the air, in
that violent motion, is there continually repelled by the opposite
hill, and rebounded from others, till it finds a passage, insomuch
that I have seen, in the western Highlands, in such a hollow, some
scattering oaks, with their bark twisted almost as if it had been done
with a lever.

This, I suppose, was effected when they were young, and
consequently the rest of their growth was in that figure: and I myself

have met with such rebuffs on every side, from the whirling of such winds, as are not easy to be described.

When I came to my inn (you will think the word a burlesque), I found it a most wretched hovel, with several pretty large holes in the sides; and, as usual, exceedingly smoky.

My apartment had a partition about four feet high, which separated it from the lodging of the family; and, being entered, I called for straw or heather to stop the gaps. Some straw was brought; but no sooner was it applied than it was pulled away on the outside.

This put me in a very ill humour, thinking some malicious Highlander did it to plague or affront me; and, therefore, I sent my man (who had just housed his horses, and was helping me) to see who it could be; and immediately he returned laughing, and told me it was a poor hungry cow, that was got to the backside of the hut for shelter, and was pulling out the straw for provender.

The smoke being something abated, and the edifice repaired, I began to reflect on the miserable state I had lately been in; and esteemed that very hut, which at another time I should have greatly despised, to be to me as good as a palace; and, like a keen appetite with ordinary fare, I enjoyed it accordingly, not envying even the inhabitants of Buckingham House.

Here I conclude my journal, which I fear you will think as barren and tedious as the ground I went over; but I must ask your patience a little while longer concerning it, as no great reason yet appears to you why I should come to this wretched place, and go no further.

By a change of the wind, there happened to fall a good deal of rain in the night; and I was told by my landlord the hills presaged more of it, that a wide river before me was become impassable, and if I remained longer in the hills at that season of the year, I might be shut in for most part of the winter; for if fresh snow should fall, and lie lower down on the mountains than it did the day before, I could not repass the precipice, and must wait till the lake was frozen so hard as to bear my horses: and even then it was dangerous in those places where the springs bubble up from the bottom, and render the ice thin and incapable to bear any great weight: but that, indeed, those weak spots might be avoided by means of a skilful guide.

As to the narrow path, he said, he was certain that any snow which might have lodged on it from the drift was melted by the rain which had then ceased. To all this he added a piece of news (not very prudently, as I thought), which was, that some time before I passed the precipice, a poor Highlander leading over it his horse laden with 'creels', or small panniers, one of them struck against the upper part of the hill, as he supposed; and whether the man was endeavouring to save his horse, or how it was, he could not tell, but that they both fell and were dashed to pieces among the rocks.

This to me was very affecting, especially as I was to pass the same way in my return.

Thus I was prevented from meeting a number of gentlemen of a clan, who were to have assembled in place assigned for our interview, about a day and a half's journey further in the hills; and on the other side of the river were numbers of Highlanders waiting to conduct me to them. But I was told, before I entered upon this peregrination, that no Highlander would venture upon it at that time of the year; yet I piqued myself upon following the unreasonable directions of such as knew nothing of the matter.

Now I returned with as hasty steps as the way you have seen would permit, having met with no more snow or rain till I got into the lower country; and then there fell a very great 'storm' as they call it – for by the word storm, they only mean snow. And you may believe I then hugged myself, as being got clear of the mountains.

But before I proceed to give you some account of the natives, I shall in justice, say something relating to part of the country of Atholl, which, though Highlands, claims an exception from the preceding general and gloomy descriptions; as may likewise some other places, not far distant from the borders of the Lowlands, which I have not seen.

This country is said to be a part of the ancient Caledonia. The part I am speaking of is a tract of land, or strath which lies along the sides of the Tay, a capital river of the Highlands.

The mountains, though very high, have an easy slope a good way up, and are cultivated in many places, and inhabited by tenants who, like those below, have a different air from other Highlanders in the goodness of their dress and cheerfulness of their countenances.

The strath, or vale, is wide and beautifully adorned with plantations of various sorts of trees: the ways are smooth, and in one part,
you ride in pleasant glades, in another you have an agreeable vista.
Here you pass through cornfields, there you ascend a small height,
from whence you have a pleasing variety of that wild and spacious
river, woods, fields, and neighbouring mountains, which altogether
give a greater pleasure than the most romantic descriptions in
words, heightened by a lively imagination, can possibly do; but the
satisfaction seemed beyond expression, by comparing it in our minds
with the rugged ways and horrid prospects of the more northern
mountains, when we passed southward from them, through this
vale to the low country; but with respect to Atholl in general, I
must own that some parts of it are very rugged and dangerous.

I shall not pretend to give you, as a people, the original of the
Highlanders, having no certain materials for that purpose; and,
indeed, that branch of history, with respect even to commonwealths
and kingdoms, is generally either obscured by time, falsified by
tradition, or rendered fabulous by invention; nor do I think it would
be of any great importance, could I trace them up to their source
with certainty; but I am persuaded they came from Ireland, in regard
their language is a corruption of the Irish tongue.

Spenser, in his, *View of the State of Ireland*, written in the reign
of Queen Elizabeth, sets forth the dress and customs of the Irish;
and, if I remember right, they were, at that time, very near what the
people are now in the Highlands. But this is by the bye, as having
little relation to antiquity; for dress is variable, and customs may be
abolished by authority; but language will baffle the efforts even of a
tyrant.

The Highlanders are exceedingly proud to be thought an unmixed
people, and are apt to upbraid the English with being a composition
of all nations; but, for my own part, I think a little mixture in that
sense would do themselves no manner of harm.

The stature of the better sort, so far as I can make the comparison,
is much the same with the English, or low country Scots, but the
common people are generally small; nor is it likely that, by being
half-starved in the womb, and never afterwards well fed, they should
by that means be rendered larger than other people.

How often have I heard them described in London as almost giants in size! and certainly there are a great many tall men of them in and about that city; but the truth is, when a young fellow of any spirit happens (as Kite says) to be born to be a 'great man', he leaves the country, to put himself into some foreign service (chiefly in the army), but the short ones are not commonly seen in other countries than their own. I have seen a hundred of them together come down to the Lowlands for harvest work, as the Welsh come to England for the same purpose, and but few sizeable men among them; their women are generally very small.

It has been said, likewise, that none of them are deformed by crookedness: it is true, I have not seen many; for, as I observed of the people bordering upon the Highlands, none are spoiled by over care of their shapes. But is it to be supposed that children who are left to themselves, when hardly able to go alone, in such a rugged country, are free from all accidents? Assertions so general are ridiculous. They are also said to be very healthy and free from distempers, notwithstanding the greet hardships they endure. Surely an account of that country from a native is not unlike a Gascon's account of himself. I own they are not very subject to maladies occasioned by luxury, but very liable to fluxes, fevers, agues, coughs, rheumatisms, and other distempers, incident to their way of living; especially upon the approach of winter, of which I am a witness.

By the way, the poorer sort are persuaded that wine, or strong malt drink, is a very good remedy in a fever; and though I never prescribed either of them, I have administered both with as good success as any medicines prescribed by Dr Radcliffe.

Æsculapius, even as a God, could hardly have had a more solemn act of adoration paid him than I had lately from a Highlander, at whose hut I lay in one of my journeys. His wife was then desperately ill of a fever, and I left a bottle of *Château Margoût* behind me to comfort her, if she should recover; for I had then several horses laden with wine and provisions, and a great retinue of Highlanders with me.

The poor man fell down on his knees in this dirty street, and eagerly kissed my hand; telling me, in Irish, I had cured his wife with my good stuff. This caused several jokes from my countrymen who were present, upon the poor fellow's value for his wife; and the doctor himself did not escape their mirth upon that occasion.

Having yesterday, proceeded thus far in my letter, in order to have the less writing this evening, I had a retrospection in the morning to my journal; and could not but be of opinion that some few additions were necessary to give you a clearer notion of the inner part of the country, in regard to the incidents, in that account, being confined to one short progress, which could not include all that is wanting to be known for the purpose intended.

There are few days pass without some rain or snow in the hills, and it seems necessary it should be so (if we may suppose nature ever intended the worst parts as habitations for human creatures), for the soil is so shallow and stony, and in summer the reflection of the sun's heat from the sides of the rocks is so strong, by reason of the narrowness of the vales – to which may be added the violent Winds – that otherwise the little corn they have would be entirely dried and burnt up for want of proper moisture.

The clouds in their passage often sweep along beneath the tops of the high mountains, and, when they happen to be above them, are drawn, as they pass, by attraction, to the summits, in plain and visible streams and streaks, where they are broke, and fall in vast quantities of water. Nay, it is pretty common in the high country for the clouds, or some very dense exhalation, to drive along the part which is there called the foot of the hills, though very high above the level of the sea; and I have seen, more than once, a very fair rainbow described, at not above thirty or forty yards' distance from me, and seeming of much the same diameter, having each foot of the semicircle upon the ground.

An English gentleman, one day, as we stopped to consider this phenomenon, proposed to ride into the rainbow; and though I told him the fruitless consequence, since it was only a vision made by his eye, being at that distance; having the sun directly behind, and before him the thick vapour that was passing along at the foot of the hill; yet (the place being smooth) he set up a gallop, and found his mistake, to my great diversion with him afterwards, upon his confession that he had soon entirely lost it.

I have often heard it told by travellers, as a proof of the height of Tenerife, that the clouds sometimes hide part of that mountain, and at the same time the top of it is seen above them: nothing is more ordinary than this in the Highlands. But I would not, therefore, be thought to insinuate, that these are as high as that; but they may, you see, be brought under the same description.

Thus you find the immediate source of the rivers and lakes in the mountains is the clouds, and not as our rivers, which have their original from subterraneous aqueducts, that rise in springs below: but, among the hills, the waters fall in great cascades and vast cataracts, and pass with prodigious rapidity through large rocky channels, with such a noise as almost deafens the traveller whose way lies along by their sides. And when these torrents rush through glens or wider straths, they often plough up, and sweep away with them, large spots of the soil, leaving nothing behind but rock or gravel, so that the land is never to be recovered. And for this a proportionable abatement is made in the tenant's rent.

The lakes are very differently situated, with respect to high and low. There are those which are vast cavities filled up with water, whereof the surface is but little higher than the level of the sea; but of a surprising depth. As Lake Ness, for the purpose, which has been ignorantly held to be without a bottom: but was sounded by an experienced seaman, when I was present, and appeared to be one hundred and thirty fathoms or two hundred and sixty yards deep.

It seems to be supplied by two small rivers at its head; but the great increase of water is from the rivers, burns, and cascades from the high mountains at which it is bounded at the water's edge. And it has no other visible issue but by the River Ness, which is not large; nor has the lake any perceptible current, being so spacious, as more than a mile in breadth and twenty-one in length. At a place called Foyers, there is a steep hill close to it, of about a quarter of a mile to the top, from whence a river pours into the lake, by three successive wild cataracts, over romantic rocks; whereon, at each fall, it dashes with such violence, that in windy weather the side of the hill is hid from sight for a good way together by the spray, which looks like a thick body of smoke. This fall of water has been compared with the cataracts of the Tiber, by those who have seen them both.

There are other lakes in large hollows, on the tops of exceedingly high hills – I mean, they seem to any one below, who has only heard of them, to be on the utmost height. But this is a deception; for there are other hills behind unseen, from whence they are supplied with the great quantity of water they contain. And it is impossible that the rain which falls within the compass of one of those cavities should not only be the cause of such a profound depth of water, but also supply the drainings that descend from it, and issue out in springs from the sides of the hills.

There are smaller lakes, which are also seated high above the plain, and are stored with trout; though it seems impossible, by the vast steepness of the burns on every visible side, that those fish should have got up thither from rivers or lakes below. This has often moved the question, 'How came they there?' But they may have ascended by small waters, in long windings out of sight behind, and none steep enough to cause a wonder; for I never found there was any notion of their being brought thither for breed. But I had like to have forgot that some will have them to have sprung from the fry carried from other waters, and dropped in those small lakes by water-fowl.

In a part of the Highlands called Strathglass, there is a lake too high by its situation to be much affected by the reflection of warmth from the plain, and too low between the mountains, which almost join together, to admit the rays of the sun; for the only opening to it is on the north side. Here the ice continues all the year round; and though it yields a little on the surface to the warmth of the circum-ambient air by day, in summertime, yet at the return of night it begins to freeze as hard as ever. This I have been assured of, not only by the proprietor himself, but by several others in and near that part of the country.

I have seen, in a rainy day, from a conflux of waters above, on a distant high hill, the side of it covered over with water by an overflowing, for a very great space, as you may have seen the water pour over the brim of a cistern, or rather like its being covered over with a sheet; and upon the peeping out of the sun the reflected rays have dazzled my eyes to such a degree, as if they were directed to them by the focus of a burning-glass.

So much for the lakes.

In one expedition, where I was well attended, as I have said before, there was a river in my way so dangerous that I was set upon the shoulders of four Highlanders, my horse not being to be trusted to in such roughness, depth, and rapidity; and I really thought sometimes we should all have gone together. In the same journey the shoulders of some of them were employed to ease the horses down from rock to rock; and all that long day I could make out but nine miles. This also was called a road.

Toward the end of another progress, in my return to this town, after several hazards from increasing waters, I was at length stopped by a small river that was become impassable. There happened, luckily for me, to be a public hut in this place, for there was no going back again; but there was nothing to drink except the water of the river. This I regretted the more, as I had refused, at one of the barracks, to accept of a bottle of old hock, on account of the carriage, and believing I should reach hither before night. In about three hours after my arrival at this hut, there appeared, on the other side of the water, a parcel of merchants with little horses loaded with roundlets of whisky.

Within sight of the ford was a bridge, as they called it, made for the convenience of this place; it was composed of two small fir trees, not squared at all, laid, one beside the other, across a narrow part of the river, from rock to rock: there were gaps and intervals between those trees, and, beneath, a most tumultuous fall of water. Some of my merchants, bestriding the bridge, edged forwards, and moved the whisky vessels before them; but the others, afterwards, to my surprise, walked over this dangerous passage, and dragged their garrons through the torrent, while the poor little horses were almost drowned with the surge.

I happened to have a few lemons left, and with them I so far qualified the ill taste of the spirit as to make it tolerable; but eatables there were none, except eggs and poor starved fowls, as usual.

The whisky men were my companions, whom it was expected I should treat according to custom, there being no partition to separate them from me; and thus I passed a part of the day and great part of the night in the smoke, and dreading the bed: but my personal hazards, wants, and inconveniences, among the hills, have been so many, that I shall trouble you with no more of them, or very sparingly, if I do at all.

Some of the bogs are of large extent, and many people have been lost in them, especially after much rain in time of snow, as well as in the lesser 'mosses', as they call them, where, in digging of peat, there have been found fir trees of a good magnitude, buried deep, and almost as hard as ebony. This, like the situation of the mountains, is attributed to Noah's Flood, for they conclude the trees have lain there ever since that time, though it may be easily otherwise accounted for. But what seems extraordinary to strangers is, that there are often deep bogs on the declivities of hills, and the higher you go the more you are bogged.

In a part called Glengarry, in my return hither from the west Highlands, I found bog, or a part of one, had been washed down by some violent torrent from the top of a hill into the plain, and the steep slope was almost covered over with the muddy substance that had rested there in its passage downwards. This made a pretty deep bog below, as a gentleman who was with me found from his curiosity to try it, being deceived by the surface, which was dried by the sun and wind, for he forced his horse into it, and sank, which surprised my companion, who I thought, should have known better, being of Ireland.

I have heretofore hinted the danger of being shut in by waters, and thereby debarred from all necessaries of life, but have not yet mentioned the extent of the hills that intervene between one place of shelter and another; and indeed it is impossible to do so in general; for they are sometimes nine or ten Scots miles over, and one of them in particular that I have passed is eighteen, wherein you frequently meet with rivers, and deep, rugged channels in the sides of the mountains, which you must pass, and these last are often the most dangerous of the two; and both, if continued rains should fall, become impassable before you can attain the end, for which a great deal of time is required, by the stoniness and other difficulties of the way. There is, indeed, one alleviation; that as these rivers may, from being shallow, become impracticable for the tallest horse in two or three hours' time, yet will they again be passable, from their velocity, almost as soon, if the rain entirely cease. When the Highlanders speak of these spaces they call them 'monts, without either house or halt'; and never attempt to pass them, if the tops of the mountains presage bad weather; yet in that they are sometimes deceived by a sudden change of wind.

All this way you may go without seeing a tree, or coming within two miles of a shrub; and when you come at last to a small spot of arable land, where the rocky feet of the hills serve for enclosure, what work do they make about the beauties of the place, as though one had never seen a field of oats before!

You know that a polite behaviour is common to the army; but as it is impossible it should be universal, considering the different tempers and other accidents that attend mankind, so we have here a certain captain, who is almost illiterate, perfectly rude, and thinks his courage and strength are sufficient supports to his incivilities.

This officer finding a laird at one of the public huts in the Highlands, and both going the same way, they agreed to bear one another company the rest of the journey. After they had ridden about four miles, the laird turned to him, and said, 'Now all the ground we have hitherto gone over is my own property.' 'By G—!' says the other, 'I have an apple tree in Herefordshire that I would not swap with you for it all.'

But to give you a better idea of the distance between one inhabited spot and another, in a vast extent of country (main and island), I shall acquaint you with what a chief was saying of his quondam estate. He told me, that if he was reinstated, and disposed to sell it, I should have it for the purchase money of three pence an acre.

I did not then take much notice of what he said, it being at a tavern in Edinburgh, and pretty late at night, but, upon this occasion of writing to you, I have made some calculation of it, and find I should have been in danger to have had a very bad bargain. It is said to have been reduced by a survey to a rectangle parallelogram, or oblong square, of sixty miles by forty, which is 2,400 square miles and 1,951,867 square acres. It is called £1,500 a year rent but the collector said he never received £900.

Now the aforesaid number of acres, at 3d per acre, amounts to £24,398 6s 9d and £900 per annum, at twenty-five years' purchase, is but £22,500; the difference is £1,896 6s 9d.

There are other observations that might not be improper, but I shall now defer them, and continue my account of the people, which has likewise been deferred in this letter.

LETTER XIX

Highlands—Distinction between chief and chieftain—Love of chief—Love of clan—Friendship—Plunder—An instance of—Authority of chiefs—Their taxes—Hereditary power—Protect their followers, and lead in battle—Condescension—Arcadian offering—Highland gentleman—His dwelling—Dress—Conversation—English complaisance—Ladies—Personal dislikes and hereditary feuds—Their extent—Reproach—Monuments of battles—They cause others—Chief answerable for his clan—Letters of fire and sword—Battle of Glenshiels— Heroic attachment—Compared with the slave of Caius Gracchus—A romantic story—Natives sleep in wet plaid—A custom from infancy—Distinctions of name—How regulated—Patronymical names—Highlanders not generally indolent—Complaint of a chief—Genealogy—Soldiers—Military pride

THE Highlanders are divided into tribes, or clans, under chiefs, or chieftains, as they are called in the laws of Scotland; and each clan again divided into branches from the main stock, who have chieftains over them. These are subdivided into smaller branches of fifty or sixty men, who deduce their original from their particular chieftains, and rely upon them as their more immediate protectors and defenders. But for better distinction I shall use the word chief for the head of a whole clan, and the principal of a tribe derived from him I shall call a chieftain.

The ordinary Highlanders esteem it the most sublime degree of virtue to love their chief, and pay him a blind obedience, although it be in opposition to the Government, the laws of the kingdom, or even to the law of God. He is their idol; and as they profess to know no king but him (I was going further), so will they say they ought to do whatever he commends without inquiry.

Next to this love of their chief is that of the particular branch from whence they sprang; and, in a third degree, to those of the whole clan or name, whom they will assist, right or wrong, against those of any other tribe with which they are at variance, to whom their enmity, like that of exasperated brothers, is most outrageous.

They likewise owe goodwill to such clans as they esteem to be their particular well-wishers; and lastly, they have an adherence one to another as Highlanders, in opposition to the people of the low country, whom they despise as inferior to them in courage, and believe they have a right to plunder them whenever it is in their power. This last arises from a tradition, that the Lowlands, in old times were the possession of their ancestors.

If the truth of this opinion of theirs stood in need of any evidence, it might, in good measure, be confirmed by what I had from a Highland gentleman of my acquaintance. He told me that a certain chief of a considerable clan, in rummaging lately an old charter-chest, found a letter directed by another chief to his grandfather, who is therein assured of the immediate restitution of his 'lifted' – that is, stolen, cows; for that he (the writer of the letter) had thought they belonged to the Lowland Lairds of Moray, whose goods and effects ought to be a prey to them all.

When I mentioned this tradition, I had only in view the middling and ordinary Highlanders, who are very tenacious of old customs and opinions; and, by the example I have given of a fact that happened almost a century ago, I would be understood that it is very probable such a notion was formerly entertained by some, at least, among those of the highest rank.

The chief exercises an arbitrary authority over his vassals, determines all differences and disputes that happen among them, and levies taxes upon extraordinary occasions, such as the marriage of a daughter, building a house, or some pretence for his support and the honour of the name. And if any one should refuse to contribute to the best of his ability he is sure of severe treatment, and if he persisted in his obstinacy he would be cast out of his tribe by general consent: but instances of this kind have very rarely happened.

This power of the chiefs is not supported by interest, as they are landlords, but as lineally descended from the old patriarchs, or fathers of the families; for they hold the same authority when they have lost their estates, as may appear from several, and particularly one who commands in his clan, though, at the same time, they maintain him, having nothing left of his own.

On the other hand, the chief, even against the laws, is to protect his followers, as they are sometimes called, be they never so criminal. He is their leader in quarrels, must free the necessitous from their arrears of rent, and maintain such who, by accidents, are fallen to total decay.

If, by increase of the tribe, any small farms are wanting for the support of such addition, he splits others into lesser portions, because all must be somehow provided for; and as the meanest among them pretend to be his relations by consanguinity, they insist upon the privilege of taking him by the hand wherever they meet him.

Concerning this last, I once saw a number of very discontented countenances when a certain lord, one of the chiefs, endeavoured to evade this ceremony. It was in presence of an English gentleman in high station, from whom he would willingly have concealed the knowledge of such seeming familiarity with slaves of so wretched appearance, and thinking it, I suppose, as a kind of contradiction to what he had often boasted at other times, viz. his despotic power in his clan.

The unlimited love and obedience of the Highlanders to their chiefs are not confined to the lower order of their followers, but are the same with those who are near them in rank. As for instance – as I was travelling in a very wild part of the country, and approaching the house of one of those gentlemen, who had notice of my coming, he met me at some distance from his dwelling, with his arcadian offering of milk and cream, as usual carried before him by his servants. He afterwards invited me to his hut, which was built like the others, only very long, but without any partition, where the family was at one end, and some cattle at the other. By the way (although the weather was not warm), he was without shoes, stockings, or breeches, in a short coat, with a shirt not much longer, which hung between his thighs, and just hid his nakedness from two daughters, about seventeen or eighteen years old, who sat over against him. After some compliments on either side, and his wishing me 'good weather' we entered into conversation, in which he seemed to be a man of as good sense as he was well-proportioned. In speaking of the country, he told me he knew I wondered how any body would undergo the inconveniences of a Highland life.

You may be sure I was not wanting in an agreeable contradiction, by saying I doubted not that they had their satisfactions and pleasures to countervail any inconveniences they might sustain, though, perhaps, those advantages could not be well known to such as are *en passant.* But he very modestly interrupted me as I was going on, and said he knew that what I said was the effect of complaisance, and could not be the real sentiment of one who knew a good deal of the country: 'But,' says he, 'the truth is, we are insensibly inured to it by degrees; for, when very young, we know no better; being grown up, we are inclined, or persuaded by our near relations, to marry – thence come children, and fondness for them: but above all', says he, 'is the love of our chief, so strongly is it inculcated to us in our infancy; and, if it were not for that, I think the Highlands would be much thinner of people than they now are.' By this, and many other instances, I am fully persuaded, that the Highlanders are at least as fond of the race of their chiefs as a Frenchman is of the House of Bourbon.

Several reasons have just now offered themselves to me, in persuasion to conceal one circumstance of this visit, but your interest with me has prevailed against them all.

The two young ladies, in my saluting them at parting, did me a favour which with you would be thought the utmost invitation; but it is purely innocent with them, and a mark of the highest esteem for their guest. This was no great surprise to me, having received the same compliment several times before in the Highlands, and even from married women, who I may be sure had no further design in it; and like the two above-mentioned young women could never expect to see me again; but I am not singular, for several officers in the army have told me they had received the same courtesy from other females in the hills.

Some of the chiefs have not only personal dislikes and enmity to each other, but there are also hereditary feuds between clan and clan, which have been handed down from one generation to another for several ages.

These quarrels descend to the meanest vassal; and thus, sometimes, an innocent person suffers for crimes committed by his tribe at a vast distance of time before his being began.

When a quarrel begins in words between two Highlanders of different clans, it is esteemed the very height of malice and rancour, and the greatest of all provocations, to reproach one another with the vices or personal defects of their chief, which, for the most part, ends in wounds or death.

Often the monuments of a clan battle, or some particular murder, are the incitements to great mischiefs. The first-mentioned are small heaps of stones, thrown together on the place where every particular man fell in battle; the other is from such a heap first cast upon the spot where the fact was committed, and afterwards by degrees increased to a high pyramid, by those of the clan that was wronged, in still throwing more stones upon it as they pass by. The former I have seen overgrown with moss, upon wide moors, which showed the number of men that were killed in the action. And several of the latter I have observed in my journeys, that could not be less than fourteen or fifteen feet high, with a base proportionable. Thus, if several men of clans at variance, happen to meet in view of one of these memorials, 'tis odds but one party reproaches the other with all the aggravating circumstances that tradition (which is mostly a liar, either in the whole or a part) has added to the original truth; and then some great mischief ensues. But if a single Highlander of the clan that offended, should be met by two or three more of the others, he is sure to be insulted, and receive some cruel treatment from them.

Thus these heaps of stones, as I have heard an old Highlander complain, continue to occasion the revival of animosities that had their beginning perhaps hundreds of years before any of the parties accused were born: and therefore I think they ought, by authority, to be scattered, and effectually defaced. But some of these monuments have been raised in memory of such as have lost their lives in a journey, by snow, rivers, or other accidents; as was the practice of the eastern nations.

By an old Scottish law, the chief was made accountable for any depredations or other violences committed by his clan upon the borders of the Lowlands; and in extraordinary cases he was obliged to give up his son, or some other nearest relation, as a hostage, for the peaceable behaviour of his followers in that respect.

By this law (for I never saw the act), he must surely have had an entire command over them, at least tacitly, or by inference understood. For how unreasonable, not to say unjust, must such a restriction have been to him, if by sanction of the same law he had not had a coercive and judicial authority over those, in whose choice and power it always lay to bring punishment upon him? And if he had such an absolute command over them, was it not to make of every chief a petty prince in his own territory, and his followers a people distinct and separate from all others? For atrocious crimes – such as rebellion, murder, rapes, or opposing the execution of the laws, which is also called rebellion, when, by process, the chief or laird, was condemned in absence, and 'intercommuned', as they call it, or outlawed – the civil power, by law and custom, gave letters of fire and sword against him; and the officer of justice might call for military force to assist in the execution. But, it is certain, some few of the chiefs in former times, were, upon occasions, too powerful to be brought to account by the Government. I have heard many instances of the faithfulness of particular Highlanders to their masters, but shall relate only one, which is to me very well known.

At the Battle of Glenshiels, in the rebellion of the year 1719, a gentleman (George Munroe of Culcairne), for whom I have a great esteem, commanded a company of Highland men, raised out of his father's clan, and entertained at his own expense. There he was dangerously wounded in the thigh, from a party of the rebel Highlanders posted upon the declivity of a mountain, who kept on firing at him after he was down, according to their want of discipline, in spending much fire upon one single officer, which, distributed among the body, might thin the ranks of their enemy.

When, after he fell, and found by their behaviour they were resolved to dispatch him outright, he bid his servant, who was by, get out of the danger, for he might lose his life, but could be of no manner of succour or service to him; and only desired him, that when he returned home, he would let his father and his family know that he had not misbehaved. Hereupon the Highlander burst out into tears and asking him how he thought he could leave him in that condition, and what they would think of him at home, set himself down on his hands and knees over his master, and received several wounds, to shield him from further hurt; till one of the clan, who acted as a sergeant, with a small party, dislodged the enemy, after having taken an oath upon his dirk that he would do it. For my own part, I do not see how this act of fidelity is in any way inferior to the so-celebrated one of Philocratus, slave to Caius Gracchus, who likewise covered his master with his body, when he was found by his enemies in a wood, in such manner that Caius could not be killed by them, till they had first dispatched his domestic.

This man had often waited at table when his master and I dined together, but otherwise is treated more like a friend than a servant.

The Highlanders, in order to persuade belief of their hardiness, have several rhodomontades on that head; for as the French proverb says, '*Tous les Gascons ne sont pas en France*' – 'There are vain boasters in other countries besides Gascony'. It is true, they are liable to great hardships, and they often suffer by them in their health and limbs, as I have often observed in a former letter.

One of these Gasconades is, that the Laird of Keppoch, chieftain of a branch of the McDonalds, in a winter campaign against a neighbouring laird, with whom he was at war about a possession, gave orders for rolling a snowball to lay under his head in the night; whereupon his followers murmured, saying, 'Now we despair of victory, since our leader is become so effeminate he can't sleep without a pillow.' This and many other like stories are romantic; but there is one thing that at first thought might seem very extraordinary, of which I have been credibly assured, that when the Highlanders are constrained to lie among the hills in cold, dry, windy weather, they sometimes soak the plaid in some river or burn; and then holding up a corner of it a little above their heads, they turn themselves round and round, till they are enveloped by the whole mantle. Then they lay themselves down on the heath, upon the leeward side of some hill, where the wet and the warmth of their bodies make a steam like that of a boiling kettle. The wet they say keeps them warm by thickening the stuff, and keeping the wind from penetrating. I must confess I should myself have been apt to question this fact, had I not frequently seen them wet from morning to night; and even at the beginning of the rain, not so much as stir a few yards to shelter, but continue in it, without necessity, till they were, as we say, wet through and through. And that is soon effected by the looseness and sponginess of the plaiding; but the bonnet is frequently taken off, and wrung like a dish-clout, and then put on again. They have been accustomed from their infancy to be often wet, and to take the water like spaniels; and this is become a second nature, and can scarcely be called a hardship to them, insomuch that I used to say, they seemed to be of the duck kind, and to love the water as well. Though I never saw this preparation for sleep in windy weather, yet, setting out early in a morning from one of the huts, I have seen the marks of their lodging, where the ground has been free from rime or snow, which remained all round the spots where they had lain.

The different surnames of the Highlanders in general are but few, in regard they are divided into large families, and hardly any male strangers have intermarried with or settled among them; and with respect to particular tribes, they commonly make that alliance among themselves, who are all of one name, except some few, may have affected to annex themselves to the clan, and those, for the most part, assume the name (without giving up their own).

Thus the surnames, being useless for distinction of persons, are suppressed, and there remain only the Christian names; of which there are everywhere a great number of Duncans, Donalds, Alexanders, Patricks, etc., who, therefore, must be some other way distinguished one from another. This is done by some additional names and descriptions taken from their forefathers; for when their own Christian name, with their father's name end description (which is for the most part the colour of the hair), is not sufficient, they add the grandfather's, and so upwards, till they are perfectly distinguished from all others of the same clan name. As for example, a man whose name is Donald Grant, has for patronymic (as they call it) the name following, viz.

Donald Bane i.e.	White-haired Donald
Mac oil Vane	Son of grey-haired Donald
Vic oil roi	Grandson of red-haired Donald
Vic ean	Great-grandson to John

Thus you see the name of Grant is not used because of all that clan are either so called, or assume that name.

Another thing is, that if this man had descended in a direct line, as eldest, from John, the remotest ancestor, and John had been a chief, he would only be called MacEan, leaving out all the intermediate successions by way of eminence.

These patronymical names, at length, are made use of chiefly in writings, receipts, rentals, etc. and, in ordinary matters, the Highlanders have sometimes other distinctions, which also to some are pretty long.

When numbers of them, composed from different tribes, have been jointly employed in a work, they have had arbitrary and temporary denominations added to their Christian names by their overseers, for the more ready distinction; such as the place they came from, the person who recommended them, some particular vice, or from something remarkable in their persons, etc. by which fictitious names they have also been set down in the books of their employers.

It is a received notion (but nothing can be more unjust) that the ordinary Highlanders are an indolent, lazy people: I know the contrary by troublesome experience – I say troublesome, because in a certain affair wherein I had occasion to employ great numbers of them, and gave them good wages, the solicitations of others for employment were very earnest, and would hardly admit of a denial: they are as willing as other people to mend their way of living; and, when they have gained strength from substantial food, they work as well as others; but why should a people be branded with the name of idlers, in a country where there is generally no profitable business for them to do?

Hence I have concluded, that if any expedient could be found for their employment, to their reasonable advantage, there would be little else wanting to reform the minds of the most savage amongst them. For my own part, I do assure you, that I never had the least reason to complain of the behaviour towards me of any of the ordinary Highlanders, or the Irish; but it wants a great deal that I could truly say as much of the Englishmen and Lowland Scots that were employed in the same business.

One of the chiefs, at his own house, complained to me, but in a friendly manner, as though I had seduced some of his subjects from their allegiance: he had occasion for three or four of those of his clan, whom I employed about a piece of work at home, which they only could do; and, when he was about to pay them for their labour, he offered them six pence a day each (being great wages, even if they had not been his vassals), in consideration he had taken them from other employment; upon which they remonstrated, and said he injured them, in calling them from sixteen pence a day to six pence; and I very well remember he then told me that if any of those people had formerly said as much to their chief, they would have been carried to the next rock and precipitated.

The Highlanders walk nimbly and upright, so that you will never see, among the meanest of them, in the most remote parts, the clumsy, stooping gait of the French *paisans*, or our own country fellows, but, on the contrary, a kind of stateliness in the midst of their poverty; and this I think may be accounted for without much difficulty.

They have a pride in their family, as almost every one is a genealogist: they wear light brogues, or pumps, and are accustomed to skip over rocks and bogs: whereas our country labourers have no such pride, wear heavy, clouted shoes, and are continually dragging their feet out of ploughed land or clays; but those very men, in a short time after they are enlisted into the army, erect their bodies, change their clownish gait, and become smart fellows; and, indeed, the soldiers in general, after being a little accustomed to the toils and difficulties of the country, can, and do, to my knowledge, acquit themselves, in their winter marches and other hardships, as well as the Highlanders. On the other hand, it is observed that the private men of the independent Highland companies are become less hardy than others, from their great pay (as it is to them), the best lodging the country affords, and warm clothing.

I cannot forbear to tell you before I conclude that many of those, private gentlemen have 'gillies', or servants to attend them in quarters, and upon a march to carry their provisions and firelocks; but, as I have happened to touch upon those companies, it may not be amiss to go a little further, for I think I have just room enough for it in this sheet.

There are six of them, viz. three of one hundred men, and three of sixty each, in all, four hundred and eighty men. These are chiefly tenants to the captains; and one of the centurions, or captains of a hundred, is said to strip his other tenants of their best plaids where-with to clothe his soldiers against a review, and to commit many other abuses of his trust. These captains are all of them vying with each other whose company shall best perform the manual exercise; so that four hundred and eighty men, besides the changes made among them, are sufficient to teach that part of the military discipline throughout the whole Highlands.

I am not a prophet nor the son of a prophet, or even second-sighted, yet I foresee that a time may come when the institution of these corps may be thought not to have been the best of policy. I am not unaware it may be said, they are raised in order to facilitate the disarming, and they are useful to prevent the stealing of cattle; but both those reasons are not sufficient to alter my opinion of their continuance.

LETTER XX

———⊰❦⊱———

Gentry—Disposition of natives—Highland town—Manner of life—A
singular practice—Fish—Distresses of the poor—Sufferings of cattle—
Pasturage—Butter and cheese—Poverty—Miserable appearance of cattle—
Drovers—Mode of crossing rivers—Misery of natives in winter—Drifts of
snow—Method of penetrating—Ruin of Swedish army—Horses wild—
Mode of catching—Small, and mostly white—Diverting method of taming—
Corn lands—Implements of husbandry—Articles in wood—Ploughing—
Inquiries—A barbarous custom—Creels—Harvest late—Poor grain—
Women's labour—Ridiculous pride—Anecdote—Odd notion respecting the
moon—Singing—Boast of country—Manners—Singular mowing—Hay—
Enclosures—Rent paid in kind—Mode of tenure—Sheriff's rate—King's tax

THE gentry may be said to be a handsome people, but the
commonalty much otherwise; one would hardly think, by their
faces, they were of the same species, at least of the same country,
which plainly proceeds from their bad food, smoke at home, and
sun, wind, and rain abroad; because the young children have as good
features as any I have seen in other parts of the island.

I have mentioned the sun in this northern climate as partly the
cause of their disguise, for that, as I said before, in summer, the
heat, by reflection from the rocks, is excessive; at the same time, the
cold on the tops of the hills is so vast an extreme as cannot be
conceived by any but those who have felt the difference, and know
the danger of so sudden a transition from one to the other; and this
likewise has its effect upon them.

The ordinary natives are, for the most part, civil when they are kindly used, but most mischievous when much offended, and will hardly ever forgive a provocation, but seek some open or secret revenge, and, generally speaking, the latter of the two.

A Highland town, as before mentioned, is composed of a few huts for dwellings, with barns and stables, and both the latter are of a more diminutive size than the former, all irregularly placed, some one way, some another, and, at any distance, look like so many heaps of dirt; these are built in glens and straths, which are the corn countries, near rivers and rivulets, and also on the sides of lakes, where there is some arable land for the support of the inhabitants: but I am now to speak of the manner in which the lower order of the Highlanders live, and shall begin with the spring of the year.

This is a bad season with them, for then their provision of oatmeal begins to fail, and, for a supply, they bleed their cattle, and boil the blood into cakes, which, together with a little milk and a short allowance of oatmeal, is their food. It is true, there are small trouts, or something like them, in some of the little rivers, which continue in holes among the rocks, which are always full of water, when the stream has quite ceased for want of rain, these might be a help to them in this starving season; but I have had so little notion in all my journeys that they made those fish a part of their diet, that I never once thought of them as such till this moment. It is likely they cannot catch them for want of proper tackle, but I am sure they cannot be without them for want of leisure. What may seem strange is, that they do not introduce roots among them (as potatoes for the purpose); but the land they occupy is so very little, they think they cannot spare any part of it from their corn, and the landlord's demand of rent in kind is another objection. You will perceive I am speaking only of the poor people in the interior parts of the mountains; for near the coast, all around them, there are few confined to such diminutive farms, and the most necessitous of all may share, upon occasion, the benefit of various kinds of shellfish, only for seeking and fetching.

Their cattle are much weakened by want of sufficient food in the preceding winter, and this immoderate bleeding reduces them to so low a plight that in the morning they cannot rise from the ground,

Vol. II.

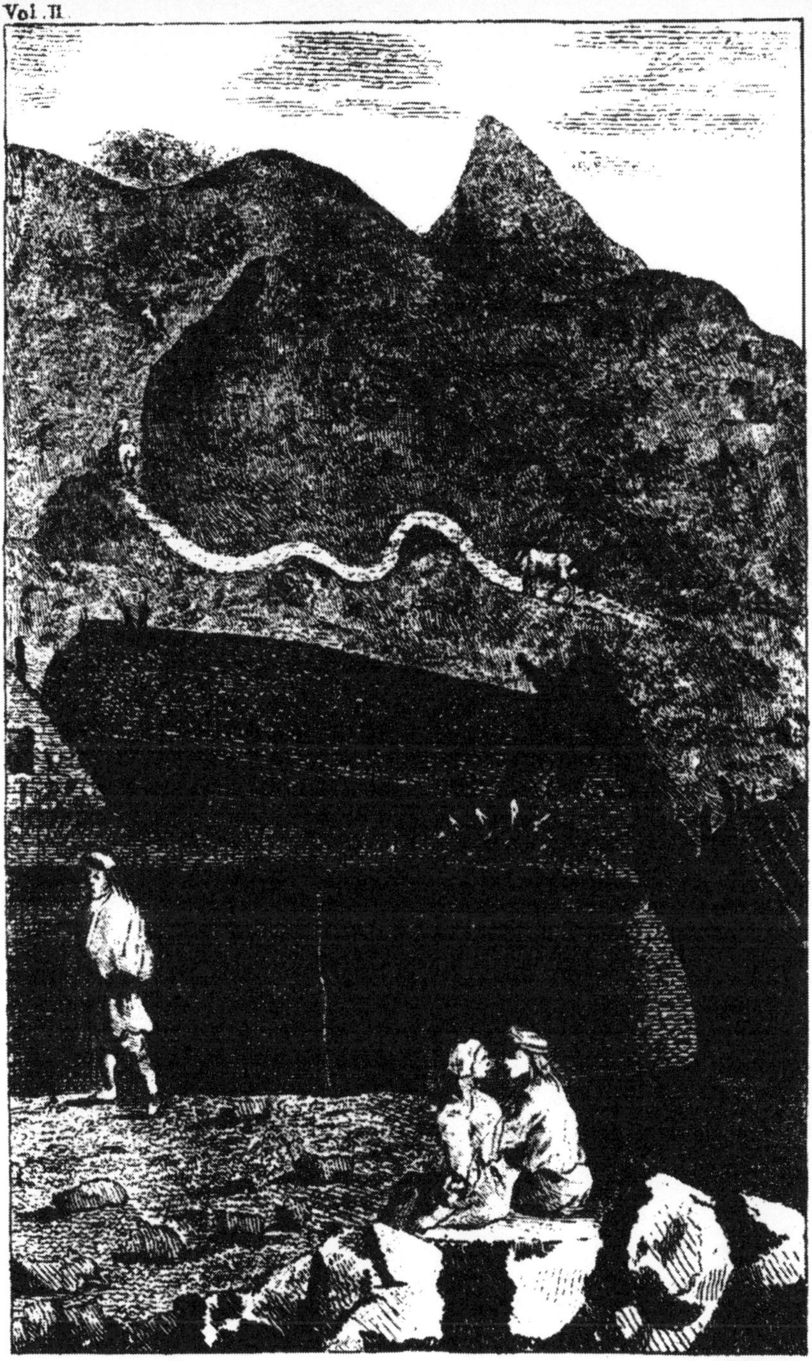

T. Jeffreys sculp.

and several of the inhabitants join together to help up each other's cows, etc.

In summer the people remove to the hills, and dwell in much worse huts than those they leave below; these are near the spots of grazing, and are called 'shealings', scattered from one another as occasion requires. Every one has his particular space of pasture, for which if it be not a part of his farm, he pays, as I shall mention hereafter. Here they make their butter and cheese. By the way, I have seen some of the former with blueish veins, made, as I thought, by the mixture of smoke, not much unlike to Castile soap; but some have said it was a mixture of sheep's milk which gave a part of it that tincture of blue.

When the grazing fails, the Highlanders return to their former habitations, and the cattle to pick up their sustenance among the heath, as before.

At other times the children share the milk with the calves, lambs, and kids; for they milk the dams of them all, which keeps their young so lean that when sold in the low country they are chiefly used, as they tell me, to make soups withal; and when a side of any one of these kinds hangs up in our market the least disagreeable part of the sight is the transparency of the ribs.

About the latter end of August, or the beginning of September, the cattle are brought into good order by their summer feed, and the beef is extremely sweet and succulent, which, I suppose, is owing, in good part, to their being reduced to such poverty in the spring, and made up again with new flesh.

Now, the drovers collect their herds, and drive them to fairs and markets on the borders of the Lowlands, and sometimes to the north of England; and in their passage they pay a certain tribute, proportionable to the number of cattle, to the owner of the territory they pass through, which is in lieu of all reckonings for grazing.

I have several times seen them driving great numbers of cattle along the sides of the mountains at a great distance, but never except once, was near them. This was in a time of rain, by a wide river, where there was a boat to ferry over the drovers. The cows were about fifty in number, and took the water like spaniels; and when they were in, their drivers made a hideous cry to urge them forwards:

this, they told me, they did to keep the foremost of them from turning about; for, in that case, the rest would do the like, and then they would be in danger, especially the weakest of them, to be driven away and drowned by the torrent. I thought it a very odd sight to see so many noses and eyes just above water, and nothing of them more to be seen, for they had no horns, and upon the land they appeared in size and shape like so many large Lincolnshire calves.

I shall speak of the Highland harvest – that is, the autumn, when I come to the article of their husbandry. But nothing is more deplorable than the fate of these people in time of winter. They are in that season often confined to their glens by swollen rivers, snow, or ice in the paths on the sides of the hills, which is accumulated by drippings from the springs above, and so, by little and little, formed into knobs like a stick of sugar-candy, only the parts are not angular like those, but so uneven and slippery no foot can pass.

They have no diversions to amuse them, but sit brooding in the smoke over the fire till their legs and thighs are scorched to an extraordinary degree, and many have sore eyes, and some are quite blind. This long continuance in the smoke makes them almost as black as chimney-sweepers; and when the huts are not water tight, which is often the case, the rain that comes through the roof and mixes with the sootiness of the inside, where all the sticks look like charcoal, falls in drops like ink. But in this circumstance, the Highlanders are not very solicitous about their outward appearance.

To supply the want of candles, when they have occasion for more light than is given by the fire, they provide themselves with a quantity of sticks of fir, the most resinous that can be procured: some of these are lighted and laid upon a stone; and as the light decays they revive it with fresh fuel. But when they happen to be destitute of fire, and none is to be got in the neighbourhood, they produce it by rubbing sticks together; but I do not recollect what kind of wood is fittest for that purpose.

If a drift of snow, from the mountains happens, and the same should be of any continuance, they are thereby rendered completely prisoners. In this case, the snow, being whirled from the mountains and hills, lodges in the plains below, till sometimes it increases to a height almost equal with the tops of their huts; but then it is soon dissolved for a little space round them, which is caused by the warmth of the fire, smoke, family, and cattle within.

Thus are they confined to a very narrow compass; and, in the mean time, if they have any outlying cattle in the hills, they are leaving the heights and returning home: for by the same means that the snow is accumulated in the glen, the hills are cleared of the incumbrance, but the cattle are sometimes intercepted by the depth of snow in the plain, or deep hollows in their way. In such case, when the wind's drift begins to cease, from the wind having a little spent its fury, the people take the following method to open a communication – if the huts are at any distance asunder, one of them begins at the edge of the snow next to his dwelling, and, waving his body from side to side, presses forward and squeezes it from him on either hand; and if it be higher than his head he breaks down that part with his hands. Thus he proceeds till he comes to another hut, and when some of them are got together they go on in the same manner to open a way for the cattle; and in thus doing they relieve one another, when too wet and weary to proceed further, till the whole is completed. Yet, notwithstanding all their endeavours their cattle are sometimes lost.

As this may seem to you a little too extraordinary, and you will believe I never saw it, I shall assure you I had it from a gentleman, who, being nearly related to a chief, has therefore a considerable farm in the inner Highlands, and would not deceive me in a fact that does not recommend his country, of which he is as jealous as any one I have known on this side the Tweed.

A drift of snow like that above described, was said to have been the ruin of the Swedish army, in the last expedition of Charles XII.

Before I proceed to their husbandry, I shall give you some account of an animal necessary to it; that is, their horses, or rather (as they are called) 'garrons'. These horses in miniature run wild among the mountains; some of them till they are eight or ten years old, which renders them exceedingly restive and stubborn. There are various ways of catching them, according to the nature of the spot of country where they chiefly keep their haunts. Sometimes they are haunted by numbers of Highlandmen into a bog; in other places they are driven up a steep hill, where the nearest of the pursuers endeavours to catch them by the hind leg; and I have been told, that sometimes both horse and man have come tumbling down together. In another place they have been hunted from one to another, among the heath and rocks, till they have laid themselves down through weariness and want of breath.

They are so small that a middle-sized man must keep his legs almost in lines parallel to their sides when carried over the stony ways; and it is almost incredible to those who have not seen it, how nimbly they skip with a heavy rider among the rocks and large moorstones, turning zigzag to such places that are passable. I think verily they all follow one another in the same irregular steps, because in those ways there appears some little smoothness, worn by their naked hoofs, which is not anywhere else to be seen. When I have been riding or rather creeping along at the foot of a mountain, I have discovered them by their colour, which is mostly white, and, by their motion, which readily catches the eye, when, at the same time, they were so high above me, they seemed to be no bigger than a lap-dog, and almost hanging over my head. But what has appeared to me very extraordinary is, what when at other times, I have passed near to them, I have perceived them to be (like some of our common beggars in London) in ragged and tattered coats, but full in flesh; and that, even toward the latter end of winter, when I think they could have nothing to feed upon but heath and rotten leaves of trees if any of the latter were to be found. The Highlanders have a tradition that they came originally from Spain, by breeders left there by the Spaniards in former times; and they say, they have been a great number of years dwindling to their present diminutive size. I was one day greatly diverted with the method of taming these wild hobbies.

In passing along a narrow path, on the side of a high hill among the mountains, at length it brought me to a part looking down into a little plain, there I was at once presented with the scene of a Highlandman beating one of these garrons, most unmercifully, with a great stick; and, upon a stricter view, I perceived the man had tied a rope, or something like it, about one of his hind legs, as you may have seen a single hog driven in England; and, indeed, in my situation, he did not seem so big. At the same time the horse was kicking and violently struggling, and sometimes the garron was down and some-times the Highlander, and not seldom both of them together, but still the man kept his hold.

After waiting a considerable time to see the event, though not so well pleased with the precipice I stood upon, I found the garron gave it up; and, being perfectly conquered for that time, patiently suffered himself to be driven to a hut not far from the field of cattle.

I was desirous to ask the Highlander a question or two by the help of my guide, but there were no means for me to get down but by falling; and when I came to a part of the hill where I could descend to the glen, I had but little inclination to go back again, for I never, by choice, made one retrograde step when I was leaving the mountains: but what is pretty strange, though very true (by what charm I know not), I have been well enough pleased to see them again, at my first entrance to them in my returns from England; and this has made my wonder cease that a native should be so fond of such a country.

The soil of the corn lands is in some places so shallow, with rocky ground beneath it, that a plough is of no manner of use. This they dig up with a wooden spade; for almost all their imple-ments of husbandry, which in other countries are made of iron, or partly of that metal, are, in some parts of the Highlands, entirely made of wood – such as the spade, ploughshare, harrow, harness, and bolts; and even locks for doors are made of wood. By the way, these locks are contrived so artfully, by notches made at unequal distances within-side, that it is impossible to open them with anything but the wooden keys that belong to them. But there would be no great difficulty in opening the wall of the hut, as the Highlander did by the portmanteau that he saw lying upon a table, and nobody near it but his companion. 'Out!' says he; 'What fool was this that put a lock upon leather?' and immediately ripped it open with his dirk.

Where the soil is deeper they plough with four of their little horses abreast. The manner this: Being thus ranked they are divided by a small space into pairs, and the driver or rather leader, of the plough, having placed himself before them, holding the two innermost by their heads to keep the couples asunder, he with his face toward the plough, goes backward, observing, through the space between the horses, the way of the plough-share.

When I first saw this awkward method as I then thought it, I rode up to the person who guided the machine, to ask him some questions concerning it: he spoke pretty good English, which made me conclude he was a gentleman; and yet in quality of a proprietor and conductor, might, without dishonour, employ himself in such a work. My first question was, whether that method was common to the Highlands, or peculiar to that part of the country? and, by way of answer, he asked me if they ploughed otherwise anywhere else. Upon my further inquiry why the man went backwards, he stopped and very civilly informed me that there were several small rocks, which I did not see, that had a little part of them just peeping on the surface, and therefore it was necessary his servants should see and avoid them, by guiding the horses accordingly, or otherwise his plough might be spoiled by the rock. The answer was satisfactory and convincing, and I must here take notice that many other of their methods are too well suited to their own circumstances, and those of the country, to be easily amended by such as undertake to deride them.

In the western Highlands they still retain that barbarous custom (which I have not seen anywhere else) of drawing the harrow by the horse's dock, without any manner of harness whatever. And when the tail becomes too short for the purpose, they lengthen it out with twisted sticks. This unnatural practice was formerly forbidden in Ireland by Act of Parliament, as my memory informs me, from accounts I have formerly read of that country for being almost without books I can have little other help wherefrom to make quotations.

When a burden is to be carried on horseback they use two baskets, called 'creels', one on each side of the horse; and if the load be such as cannot be divided, they put it into one of them, and counterbalance it with stones in the other, so that one half of the horse's burden is – I cannot say unnecessary, because I do not see how they could do otherwise in the mountains.

Their harvest is late in the year, and therefore seldom got in dry, as the great rains usually come on about the latter end of August: nor is the corn well preserved afterwards in those miserable hovels they call barns, which are mostly not fit to keep out the bad weather from above; and were it not for the high winds that pass through the openings of the sides in dry weather, it would of necessity be quite spoiled. But as it is, the grain is often grown in the sheaves, as I observed in a former letter.

To the lightness of the oats, one might think they contributed themselves; for if there be one part of their ground that produces worse grain than another, they reserve that, or part of it, for seed, believing it will produce again as well, in quantity and quality, as the best; but, whether in this they are right or wrong, I cannot determine.

Another thing, besides the bad weather, that retards their harvest, is, they make it chiefly the work of the women of the family. Near the Lowlands I have known a field of corn to employ a woman and a girl for a fortnight, which, with proper help, might have been done in two days. And, although the owner might not well afford to employ many hands, yet his own labour would have prevented half the risk of bad weather at that uncertain season.

An English lady, who found herself something decaying in her health, and was advised to go among the hills, and drink goat's milk or whey, told me lately, that seeing a Highlander basking at the foot of a hill in his full dress, while his wife and her mother were hard at work in reaping the oats, she asked the old woman how she could be contented to see her daughter labour in that manner while her husband was only an idle spectator? And to this the woman answered, that her son-in-law was a 'gentleman', and it would be a disparagement to him to do any such work; and that both she and her daughter too were sufficiently honoured by the alliance.

This instance, I own, has something particular in it, as such; but the thing is very common, *à la Palatine*, among the middling sort of people.

Not long ago, a French officer, who was coming hither the hill way, to raise some recruits for the Dutch service, met a Highland man with a good pair of brogues on his feet, and his wife marching bare foot after him. This indignity to the sex raised the Frenchman's anger to such a degree, that he leaped from his horse, and obliged the fellow to take off the shoes, and the woman to put them on.

By this last instance (not to trouble you with others) you may see it is not in their harvest work alone they are something in the Palatine way with respect to their women.

The Highlanders have a notion that the moon, in a clear night, ripens their corn much more than a sunshiny day: for this they plead experience; yet they cannot say by what rule they make the comparison. But by this opinion of theirs, I think they have little knowledge of the nature of those two planets.

In larger farms belonging to gentlemen of the clan, where there are any number of women employed in harvest work, they all keep time together, by several barbarous tones of the voice; and stoop and rise together as regularly as a rank of soldiers when they ground their arms. Sometimes they are incited to their work by the sound of a bagpipe; and by either of these they proceed with great alacrity, it being disgraceful for any one to be out of time with the sickle. They use the same tone, or a piper, when they thicken the newly-woven plaiding, instead of a fulling-mill.

This is done by six or eight women sitting upon the ground, near some river or rivulet, in two opposite ranks, with the wet cloth between them; their coats are tucked up, and with their naked feet they strike one against another's, keeping exact time as above-mentioned. And among numbers of men, employed in any work that requires strength and joint labour (as the launching a large boat, or the like), they must have the piper to regulate their time, as well as whisky to keep up their spirits in the performance; for pay they often have little, or none at all.

Nothing is more common than to hear the Highlanders boast how much their country might be improved, and that it would produce double what it does at present if better husbandry were introduced among them. For my own part, it was always the only amusement I had in the hills, to observe every minute thing in my way: and I do assure you, I do not remember to have seen the least spot that would bear corn uncultivated, not even upon the sides of the hills, where it could be no otherwise broke up than with a spade. And as for manure to supply the salts and enrich the ground, they have hardly any. In summer their cattle are dispersed about the sheelings, and almost all the rest of the year in other parts of the hills; and, therefore, all the dung they can have must be from the trifling quantity made by the cattle while they are in the house. I never knew or heard of any limestone, chalk, or marl, they have in the country; and, if some of their rocks might serve for limestone, in that case their kilns, carriage, and fuel would render it so expensive, it would be the same thing to them as if there were none. Their great dependence is upon the nitre of the snow; and they lament the disappointment if it does not fall early in the season. Yet I have known, in some, a great inclination to improvement; and shall only instance a very small matter, which, perhaps, may be thought too inconsiderable to mention.

Not far from Fort William, I have seen women with a little horse dung brought upon their backs, in creels, or baskets, from that garrison; and, on their knees, spreading it with their hands upon the land, and even breaking the balls, that every part of the little spot might have its due proportion.

These women have several times brought me hay to the fort, which was made from grass cut with a knife by the wayside; and from one I have bought two or three pennyworth; from another, the purchase has been a groat; but sixpennyworth was a most considerable bargain.

At their return from the hay market, they carried away the dung of my stable (which was one end of a dwelling hut) in the manner above-mentioned.

Speaking of grass and hay, it comes to my remembrance, that, in passing through a space between the mountains, not far from Keppoch, in Lochaber, I observed, in the hollow, though too narrow to admit much of the sun, a greater quantity of grass than I remembered to have seen in any such spot in the inner parts of the Highlands; it was in the month of August, when it was grown rank, and flagged pretty much, and therefore I was induced to ask why the owner did not cut it. To this I was answered, it never had been mowed, but was left every year as natural hay for the cattle in winter – that is, to lie upon the ground like litter, and, according to their description, the cows routed for it in the snow, like hogs in a dunghill. But the people have no barns fit to contain a quantity of hay, and it would be impossible to secure it in mows from the tempestuous eddy-winds, which would soon carry it over the mountains: besides, it could not well be made, by reason of rains and want of sun, and therefore they think it best to let it lie as it does, with the roots in the ground.

The advantage of enclosures is a mighty topic with the Highlanders, though they cannot spare for grass one inch of land that will bear corn; if they could, it would be a much more expensive way of grazing their cattle than letting them run as they do in the hills; but enclosures, simply as such, do not better the soil, or, if they might be supposed to be an advantage to it, where is the Highland tenant that can lay out ten shillings for that purpose and what would he be the gainer by it in the end, but to have his rent raised, or his farm divided with some other or, lastly, where are the number of Highlanders that would patiently suffer such an inconvenient innovation? For my part, I think nature has sufficiently enclosed their lands by the feet of the surrounding mountains. Now, after what has been said, where can this improvement be? Yet, it seems, they had rather you should think them ignorant, lazy, or anything else, than entertain a bad opinion of their country. But I have dwelt too long upon this head.

Their rent is chiefly paid in kind – that is to say, great part of it in several species arising from the product of the farm; such, as barley, oatmeal, and what they call 'customs', as sheep, lambs, poultry, butter, etc., and the remainder, if any, is paid in money, or an addition of some one of the before-mentioned species, if money be wanting.

The gentlemen, who are near relations of the chief, hold pretty large farms, if the estate will allow it – perhaps twenty or thirty pounds a year, and they again, generally, parcel them out to under tenants in small portions: hence it comes, that, by such a division of an old farm (part of an upper-tenant's holding), suppose among eight persons, each of them pays an eighth part of everything, even to the fraction of a capon, which cannot in the nature of it be paid in kind, but the value of it is cast in with the rest of the rent, and, notwithstanding the above-mentioned customs are placed in an upper-tenant's rental, yet they properly belong to the chief, for the maintenance of the family in provisions.

Every year, after the harvest, the sheriff of the county, or his deputy, together with a jury of landed men, set a rate upon corn provisions, and the custom of the country regulates the rest. The sheriff's regulation for the year is called the 'feers-price', and serves for a standard whereby to determine everything relating to rents and bargains; so that if the tenant is not provided with all the species he is to pay, then that which is wanting may be converted into money, or something else with certainty.

Before I conclude this letter, I shall take notice of one thing, which, at first, I thought pretty extraordinary, and that is, if any landed man refuses, or fails to pay the king's tax, then, by a warrant from the civil magistrate, a proprotionable number of soldiers are quartered upon him, with sometimes a commissioned officer to command them, all of whom he must maintain till the cess is fully discharged. This is a penalty for his default, even though he had not the means to raise money in all that time: and, let it be ever so long, the tax in the end is still the same. You will not doubt that the men, thus living upon free-quarters, use the best interests with their officers to be sent on such parties.

LETTER XXI

———◆———

Income—Species of rent—A curious rent-roll—Right of landlords—
Poverty of tenants—Laird's income—Fosterage—Description of—
Hanchman—Alarming incident—List of a chief's officers—Pride of chiefs
—A pompous declaration—Customs—The bard—Entertainment of—
A song of—Extravagant admiration—The piper—His service—Stately
step—His gilly, or servant—Question of precedence between a drummer
and a piper—Roes—Red deer—Hounds—Solemn hunting—Description—
Different in different hills—Gamekeeper—Foxes—Wild cats—Birds of
the mountains— Jealousy of clans—Instances of—The dirk—Evils of—
Cruelty—Conduct of chiefs towards each other

YOU will, it is likely, think it strange that many of the Highland
tenants are to maintain a family upon a farm of twelve merks
Scots per annum, which is thirteen shillings and four pence sterling,
with perhaps a cow or two, or a very few sheep or goats; but often
the rent is less and the cattle are wanting.

In some rentals you may see seven or eight columns of various
species of rent, or more, viz. money, barley, oatmeal, sheep, lambs,
butter, cheese, capons, etc.; but every tenant does not pay all these
kinds, though many of them the greatest part. What follows is a
specimen taken out of a Highland rent-roll, and I do assure you it is
genuine, and not the least by many:

	Scots money	English	Butter Stones	lb	oz	Oatmeal Bolls	B	P	Lip	Muttons
Donald mac Oil vic ille challum	£3 10 4	£0 5 10⅛	0	3	2	0	2	1	3	⅛ and 1/16
Murdoch mac illi Christ	£5 17 6	£0 9 9⅛	0	6	4	0	3	3	3	¼ and 1/16
Duncan mac illi Phadrick	£7 0 6	£0 12 3½	0	7	8	1	0	3	0½	¼ and ⅛

I shall here give you a computation of the first article, besides which there are seven more of the same farm and rent, as you may perceive by the fraction of a sheep in the last column:

The money	£0 5 10⅛ Sterling
The butter, three pounds two ounces, at 4d per lb	£0 1 1½
Oatmeal, 2 bushels, 1 peck, 3 lippys and ¼, at 6d per peck	£0 5 9¼ and ½
Sheep, one-eighth and one-sixteenth, at 2s	£0 0 4½
	£0 12 1½ and 1/12

The yearly rent of the farm is

The landlord has, by law, an hypothic, or right of pledge, with respect to the corn for so much as the current year's rent, and may, and often does, by himself or his bailiff, see it reaped to his own use; or, if that is not done, he may seize it in the market or anywhere else: but this last privilege of the landlord does not extend to the crop or rent of any former year.

The poverty of the tenants has rendered it customary for the chief, or laird, to free some of them, every year, from all arrears of rent; this is supposed, upon an average to be about one year in five of the whole estate.

If the tenant is to hire his grazing in the hills, he takes it by 'soumes' – a soume is as much grass as will maintain four sheep; eight sheep are equal to a cow and a half, or forty goats; but I do not remember how much is paid for every soume. The reason of this disproportion between the goats and sheep is, that, after the sheep have eaten the pasture bare, the herbs, as thyme, etc. that are left behind, are of little or no value, except for the browsing of goats.

The laird's income is computed by 'chalders' of victuals, as they are called – a chalder is sixteen bolls of corn, each boll containing about six of our bushels, and therefore, when any one speaks of the yearly value of such a laird's estate, he tells you it is so many chalders; but the measure varies something in different parts of the country.

When a son is born to the chief of a family, there generally arises a contention among the vassals which of them shall have the fostering of the child when it is taken from the nurse; and by this means such differences are sometimes fomented as are hardly ever after thoroughly reconciled. The happy man who succeeds in his suit is ever after called the foster-father, and his children the foster-brothers and sisters, of the young laird. This, they reckon, not only endears them to their chief, and greatly strengthens their interest with him, but gives them a great deal of consideration among their fellow vassals; and the foster-brother having the same education as the young chief, may, besides that, in time become his 'hanchman' or perhaps be promoted to that office under the old patriarch himself, if a vacancy should happen; or otherwise, by their interest, obtain orders and a benefice. This officer, is a sort of secretary, and is to be ready, upon all occasions, to venture his life in defence of his master;

and at drinking bouts he stands behind his seat, at his haunch (from whence his title is derived), and watches the conversation, to see if any one offend his patron.

An English officer, being in company with a certain chieftain and several other Highland gentlemen, near Killichumen, had an argument with the great man; and, both being , well warmed with whisky, at last the dispute grew very hot. A youth who was hanch-man, not understanding a word of English, imagined his chief was insulted, and thereupon drew his pistol from his side, and snapped it at the officer's head; but the pistol misfired, otherwise it is more than probable he might have suffered death from the hand of that little vermin. But it is very disagreeable to an Englishman, over a bottle with the Highlanders, to see every one of them have his 'gilly' – that is, his servant, standing behind him all the while, let what will be the subject of conversation.

When a chief goes a journey in the hills, or makes a formal visit to an equal, he is said to be attended by all, or most part of the officers following, viz.

The Hanchman	Before described
Bard	His poet
Bladier	His spokesman
Gilli-more	Carries his broadsword
Gilli-casflue	Carries him when on foot, over the fords
Gilly-constraine	Leads his horse in rough and dangerous ways
Gilly-trushanarnish	The baggage man
The Piper	Who, being a gentleman, I should have named sooner

And lastly,

The Piper's Gilly	Who carries the bagpipes

There are likewise some gentlemen near of kin who bear him company; and besides a number of the common sort, who have no particular employment, but follow him only to partake of the cheer.

I must own that all these attendants, and the profound respect they pay, must be flattering enough, though the equipage has none of the best appearance. But this state may appear to soothe the pride of the chief to a vast degree, if the declaration of one of them was sincere, who, at dinner, before a good deal of company, English as well as Scots, myself being one of the number, affirmed that if his estate was free from encumbrances, and was none of his own, and he was then put to choose between that and the estate of the Duke of Newcastle, supposing it to be thirty thousand pounds a year (as somebody said it was), he would make choice of the former, with the following belonging to it before the other without it. Now his estate might be about five hundred pounds a year. But this pride is pretty costly; for as his friend is to feed all these attendants, so it comes to his own turn to be at a like, or, perhaps, greater expense when the visit is repaid; for they are generally attended in proportion to the strength of the clan; and by this intercourse they very much hurt one another in their circumstances.

By what has been said, you may know, in part, how necessary the rent called customs is to the family of a Highland chief.

Here I must ask a space for those two sons of Apollo, the bard and the piper.

The bard is skilled in the genealogy of all the Highland families; sometimes preceptor to the young laird; celebrates, in Irish verse, the original of the tribe, the famous warlike actions of the successive heads, and sings his own lyrics as an opiate to the chief when indisposed for sleep – but poets are not equally esteemed and honoured in all countries. I happened to be a witness of the dishonour done to the muse at the house of one of the chiefs, where two of these bards were set at a good distance, at the lower end of a long table, with a parcel of Highlanders of no extraordinary appearance, over a cup of ale. Poor inspiration! They were not asked to drink a glass of wine at our table, though the whole company at it consisted only of the great man, one of his near relations, and myself.

After some little time, the chief ordered one of them to sing me a Highland song. The bard readily obeyed; and with a hoarse voice, and in a tune of few various notes, began, as I was told, one of his own lyrics; and when he had proceeded to the fourth or fifth stanza, I perceived, by the names of several persons, glens, and mountains, which I had known or heard of before, that it was an account of some clan battle. But, in his going on, the chief (who piques himself upon his school-learning), at some particular passage, bid him cease, and cried out to me – 'There's nothing like that in Virgil or Homer!' I bowed, and told him I believed so. This you may believe, was very edifying and delightful.

I have had occasion before to say something of the piper, but not as an officer of the household.

In a morning, while the chief is dressing, he walks backward and forward, close under the window, without doors, playing on his bagpipe, with a most upright attitude and majestic stride.

It is a proverb in Scotland, viz. 'the stately step of a piper'. When required, he plays at meals, and in an evening is to divert the guests with his music, when the chief has company with him: his attendance in a journey, or at a visit I have mentioned before.

His gilly holds the pipe till he begins; and the moment he has done with the instrument, he disdainfully throws it down upon the ground, as being only the passive means of conveying his skill to the ear, and not a proper weight for him to carry or bear at other times. But, for a contrary reason, his gilly snatches it up – which is, that the pipe may not suffer indignity from its neglect.

The captain of one of the Highland companies entertained me some time ago at Stirling, with an account of a dispute that happened in his corps about precedency. This officer, among the rest, had received orders to add a drum to his bagpipe, as a more military instrument; for the pipe was to be retained, because the Highlandmen could hardly be brought to march without it. Now, the contest between the drummer and the piper arose about the post of honour, and at length the contention grew exceedingly hot, which the captain having notice of, he called them both before him, and, in the end, decided the matter in favour of the drum; whereupon the piper remonstrated very warmly. 'Ads wuds, sir,' says he, and shall a little rascal that beats upon a sheep skin, tak the right haund of me, that am a musician?'

There are in the mountains both red deer and roes, but neither of them in very great numbers, that ever I could find. The red deer are large, and keep their haunts in the highest mountains; but the roe is less than our fallow deer, and partakes, in some measure, of the nature of the hare, having no fat about the flesh, and hiding in the clefts of rocks, and other hollows, from the sight of pursuers. These keep chiefly in the woods.

A pack of hounds, like that of Actaeon, in the same metaphorical sense, would soon devour their master. But, supposing they could easily be maintained, they would be of no use, it being impossible for them to hunt over such rocks and rugged steep declivities; or if they could do this, their cry in those open hills would soon fright all the deer out of that part of the country. This was the effect of one single hound, whose voice I have often heard in the dead of the night (as I lay in bed) echoing among the mountains; he was kept by an English gentleman at one of the barracks, and it was loudly complained of by some of the lairds, as being prejudicial to their estates.

When a solemn hunting is resolved on, for the entertainment of relations and friends, the haunt of the deer being known, a number of the vassals are summoned, who readily obey by inclination; and are, besides, obliged by the tenure of their lands, of which one article is, that they shall attend the master at his huntings. This, I think, was part of the ancient vassalage in England.

The chief convenes what numbers he thinks fit, according to the strength of his clan: perhaps three or four hundred. With these he surrounds the hill, and as they advance upwards, the deer flies at the sight of them, first of one side, then of another; and they still, as they mount, get into closer order, till, in the end, he is enclosed by them in a small circle, and there they hack him down with their broadswords. And they generally do it so dexterously, as to preserve the hide entire.

If the chase be in a wood, which is mostly upon the declivity of a rocky hill, the tenants spread themselves as much as they can, in a rank extending upwards; and march, or rather crawl forward, with a hideous yell. Thus they drive everything before them, while the laird and his friends are waiting at the farther end with their guns to shoot the deer. But it is difficult to force the roes out of their cover; insomuch that when they come into the open sight, they sometimes turn back upon the huntsmen, and are taken alive.

What I have been saying on this head is only to give you some taste of the Highland hunting; for the hills, as they are various in their form, require different dispositions of the men that compose the pack. The first of the two paragraphs next above, relates only to such a hill as rises something in the figure of a cone; and the other, you see, is the side of a hill which is clothed with a wood; and this last is more particularly the shelter of the roe. A further detail I think would become tedious.

When the chief would have a deer only for his household, the gamekeeper and one or two more are sent into the hills with guns and oatmeal for their provision, where they often lie, night after night, to wait an opportunity of providing venison for the family. This has been done several times for me, but always without effect.

The foxes and wild cats (or cat-o'-mountain) are both very large in their kind, and always appear to have fed plentifully; they do the Highlanders much more hurt in their poultry, etc. than they yield them profit by their furs; and the eagles do them more mischief than both the others together. It was one of their chief complaints, when they were disarmed, in the year 1725, that they were deprived of the means to destroy those noxious animals, and that a great increase of them must necessarily follow the want of their firearms.

Of the eatable part of the feathered kind peculiar to the mountains is, first, the 'cobberkely', which is sometimes called a wild turkey, but not like it, otherwise than in size. This is very seldom to be met with, being an inhabitant of very high and unfrequented hills, and is therefore esteemed a great rarity for the table. Next is the 'black cock', which resembles, in size and shape, a pheasant, but is black and shining, like a raven; but the hen is not in shape or colour, much unlike to a hen-pheasant: and, lastly, the 'tormican' near about the size of the moorfowl (or grouse), but of a lighter colour, which turns almost white in winter. These, I am told, feed chiefly upon the tender tops of the fir branches, which I am apt to believe, because the taste of them has something tending to turpentine, though not disagreeable. It is said, if you throw a stone so as to fall beyond it, the bird is thereby so much amused or daunted, that it will not rise till you are very near; but I have suspected this to be a sort of conundrum, signifying they are too shy to suffer an approach near enough for that purpose, like what they tell the children about the salt and the bird.

The tribes will not suffer strangers to settle within their precinct, or even those of another clan to enjoy any possession among them; but will soon constrain them to quit their pretensions, by cruelty to their persons, or mischief to their cattle or other property. Of this there happened two flagrant instances, within a few years past.

The first was as follows: Gordon Laird of Glenbucket, had been invested by the D. of G. in some lands in Badenoch, by virtue, I think, of a 'wadsett', or mortgage. These lands lay among the Macphersons; but the tenants of that name refused to pay the rent to the new landlord, or to acknowledge him as such.

This refusal put him upon the means to eject them by law; whereupon the tenants came to a resolution to put an end to his suit and new settlement in the manner following: Five or six of them, young fellows, the sons of gentlemen, entered the door of his hut, and, in fawning words, told him they were sorry any dispute had happened; that they were then resolved to acknowledge him as their immediate landlord, and would regularly pay him their rent; at the same time they begged he would withdraw his process, and they hoped they should be agreeable to him for the future. All this while they were almost imperceptibly drawing nearer and nearer to his bedside, on which he was sitting, in order to prevent his defending himself (as they knew him to be a man of distinguished courage), and then fell suddenly on him, some cutting him with their dirks, and other plunging them into his body. This was perpetrated within sight of the Banack of Ruthven.

I cannot forbear to tell you how this butchery ended, with respect both to him and those treacherous villains. He, with a multitude of wounds upon him, made a shift, in the bustle, to reach down his broadsword from the tester of his bed, which was very low, and with it he drove all the assassins before him; and afterwards, from the duke's abhorrence of so vile a fact, and with the assistance of the troops, they were driven out of the country, and forced to fly to foreign parts.

By the way, the Duke claims the right of chief to the Macphersons, as he is, in fact, of the Gordons.

The other example is of a minister, who had a small farm assigned him; and, upon his entrance to it, some of the clan, in the dead of the night, fired five balls through his hut, which all lodged in his bed, but he, happening to be absent that night, escaped their barbarity, but was forced to quit the country. Of this he made to me an affecting complaint.

This kind of cruelty, I think, arises from their dread of innovations, and the notion they entertain, that they have a kind of hereditary right to their farms; and that none of them are to be dispossessed, unless for some great transgression against their chief, in which case every individual would consent to their expulsion.

Having lately mentioned the dirk, I think it may not be unseasonable here to give you a short description of that dangerous weapon; and the rather, as I may have occasion to speak of it hereafter. The blade is straight, and generally above a foot long; the back near one-eighth of an inch thick; the point goes off like a tuck, and the handle is something like that of a sickle. They pretend they cannot do well without it, as being useful to them in cutting wood, and upon many other occasions; but it is a concealed mischief, hid under the plaid, ready for secret stabbing; and, in a close encounter, there is no defence against it.

I am far from thinking there is anything in the nature of a Highlander, as such, that should make him cruel and remorseless; on the contrary, I cannot but be of opinion that nature in general is originally the same in all mankind, and that the difference between country and country arises from education and example. And from this principle I conclude, that even a Hottentot child, being brought into England before he had any knowledge, might, by a virtuous education and generous example, become as much an Englishman in his heart as any native whatever. But that the Highlanders, for the most part, are cruel, is beyond dispute, though all clans are not alike merciless. In general they have not generosity enough to give quarter to an enemy that falls in their power, nor do they seem to have any remorse at shedding blood without necessity.

This appeared a few years ago, with respect to a party of soldiers, consisting of a sergeant and twelve men, who were sent into Lochaber after some cows that were said to be stolen. The soldiers, with their arms slung, were carelessly marching along by the side of a lake, where only one man could pass in front; and, in this circumstance, fell into an ambuscade of a great number of Highlandmen, vassals of an attainted chief, who was in exile when his clan was accused of the theft.

These were lodged in a hollow on the side of a rocky hill; and though they were themselves out of all danger, or might have descended and disarmed so small a party, yet they chose rather, with their firearms, as it were wantonly to pick them off, almost one by one, till they had destroyed them all, except two, who took to their heels, and waded a small river into the territory of another chief, where they were safe from further pursuit, for the chiefs; like princes upon the continent whose dominions lie contiguous, do not invade each other's boundaries while they are in peace and friendship with one another, but demand redress of wrongs; and whosoever should do otherwise, would commit an offence in which every tribe is interested, besides the lasting feud it might create between the two neighbouring clans.

P.S. One of these soldiers, who, in his flight, had fixed his bayonet, turned about at the edge of the water upon a Highlandman, who, for greater speed, had no other arms than his broadsword, and, at the same time, it is said, the soldier at once sent his bayonet and ball through his body.

LETTER XXII

Military—Cruelty towards—Highland language—Fondness for—Called
Erst—Alphabet—Defective orthography—Highland dress—Full dress
graceful—Common not so—Quarrants—The quelt—Clothing offensive—
Advantages and disadvantages of—Highlanders dislike change—Their
indignation at—Laird's lady travels barefooted—Shyness before the
English—Curious hut—Stockings—A singular vanity—A baronet—
Highland inn—Complaisance—Unwelcome Visitors—Poor children—Those
of a chief—Author's mode of illustration—Living of chiefs—Anecdote—
Affectation of cleanliness—Evil of this vanity—Hospitality—A particular
instance—Houses of chiefs—A burlesque story—Winding hollows

BUT the rancour of some of those people, in another case, was
yet more extraordinary than the instance in my last letter,
as the objects of their malice could not seem, even to the utmost
cowardice, to be in any manner of condition to annoy them. This
was after the Battle of Glenshiels, in the rebellion of 1719, before
mentioned. As the troops were marching from the field of action to
a place of encampment, some of the men who were dangerously
wounded, after their being carried some little way on horseback,
complained they could no longer bear that uneasy carriage, and
begged they might be left behind till some more gentle conveyance
could be provided.

In about three or four hours (the little army being encamped)
parties were sent to them with hurdles, that had been made to serve
as a kind of litter; but, when they arrived, they found to their

astonishment that those poor, miserable creatures had been stabbed with dirks in twenty places of their legs and arms, as well as their bodies, and even those that were dead had been used in the same savage manner. This I have been assured of by several officers who were in the battle, Scots as well as English.

I make no manner of doubt you will take what is to follow to be an odd transition, i.e. from the cruelty of the ordinary Highlanders, to dialect and orthography – although you have met with some others not more consistent; but then you will recollect what I said in my first epistle, that I should not confine myself to method, but give you my account just as the several parts of the subject should occur from my memorandums and memory.

Strange encomiums I have heard from the natives upon the language of their country, although it be but a corruption of the Irish tongue; and, if you could believe some of them, it is so expressive, that it wants only to be better known to become universal. But as for myself, who can only judge of it by the ear, it seems to me to be very harsh in sound, like the Welsh, and altogether as gutteral, which last, you know, is a quality long since banished all the polite languages in Europe.

It likewise seems to me, as if the natives affected to call it Erst, as though it were a language peculiar to their country; but an Irish gentleman who never before was in Scotland, and made with me a Highland tour, was perfectly understood even by the common people; and several of the lairds took me aside to ask me who he was, for that they never heard their language spoken in such purity before. This gentleman told me that he found the dialect to vary as much in different parts of the country as in any two counties of England. There are very few who can write the character, of which the alphabet is as follows:

			Pronounced
a	𝕳	*a*	Ailim
b	*b*	*b*	Beith
c	c	c	Coll
d	*b*	*b*	Duir
e	*e*	e	Eadha

Pronounced

f	𝔉	ꜰ	Fearn
g	𝖅	ꜱ	Gort
h	ℜ	ꜧ	Uath
j i	𝔍 ſ	Ꜳ '	Jogha
l	𝔩	ꞁ	Luis
m	𝔐	ꭑ	Muin
n	𝔑	ꞃ	Nuin
o	𝔒	◦	Oun
p	𝔭	ꝑ	Peithboc
r	𝔯	ꞃ	Ruis
s	𝔰	ꞅ	Suil
t	𝔗	ꞇ	Tinne
u	𝔲	ꭒ	Uir

In writing English, they seem to have no rule of orthography, and they profess they think good spelling of no great use; but if they read English authors, I wonder their memory does not retain the figures, or forms of common words, especially monosyllables but it may, for aught I know, be affectation.

I have frequently received letters from ministers and lay gentlemen, both esteemed for their learning in dead languages, that have been so ill spelt, I thought I might have expected better from an ordinary woman in England. As for one single example, for 'heirs' (of Latin derivation), 'airs' repeated several times in the same letter; and, further, one word was often variously spelt in the same page.

The Highland dress consists of a bonnet made of thrum without a brim, a short coat, a waistcoat, longer by five or six inches, short stockings, and brogues, or pumps without heels. By the way, they cut holes in their brogues, though new made, to let out the water, when they have far to go and rivers to pass: this they do to preserve their feet from galling.

Few besides gentlemen wear the 'trowze' – that is, the breeches and stockings all of one piece, and drawn on together; over this habit they wear a plaid, which is usually three yeards long and two breadths wide, and the whole garb is made of chequered tartan, or plaiding: this, with the sword and pistol, is called a 'full dress', and, to a well-proportioned man, with any tolerable air, it makes an agreeable figure; but this you have seen in London, and it is chiefly their mode of dressing when they are in the Lowlands, or when they make a neighbouring visit, or go anywhere on horseback; but when those among them who travel on foot, and have not attendants to carry them over the waters, they vary it into the quelt, which is a manner I am about to describe.

The common habit of the ordinary Highlanders is far from being acceptable to the eye; with them a small part of the plaid, which is not so large as the former, is set in folds and girt round the waist, to make of it a short petticoat that reaches half way down the thigh, and the rest is brought over the shoulders, and then fastened before, below the neck, often with a fork, and sometimes with a bodkin, or sharpened piece of stick, so that they make pretty nearly the appearance of the poor women in London when they bring their gowns over their heads to shelter them from the rain. In this way of wearing the plaid, they have sometimes nothing else to cover them, and are often barefoot; but some I have seen shod with a kind of pumps, made out of a raw cowhide, with the hair turned outward, which being ill-made, the wearer's foot looked something like those of a roughfooted hen or pigeon: these are called 'quarrants', and are not only offensive to the sight but intolerable to the smell of those who are near them. The stocking rises no higher than the thick of the calf, and from the middle of the thigh to the middle of the leg is a naked space, which being exposed to all weathers, becomes tanned and freckled, and the joint being mostly infected with the country distemper, the whole is very disagreeable, to the eye. This dress is called the 'quelt'; and, for the most part they wear the petticoat so very short, that in a windy day, going up a hill, or stooping, the indecency of it is plainly discovered.

A Highland gentleman told me one day merrily, as we were speaking of a dangerous precipice we had passed over together, that a lady of a noble family had complained to him very seriously, that as she was going over the same place with a gilly, who was upon an upper path leading her horse with a long string, she was so terrified with the sight of the abyss, that, to avoid it, she was forced to look up towards the bare Highlander all the way long.

T. Jefferys sculp

I have observed before, that the plaid serves the ordinary people for a cloak by day and bedding at night: By the latter it imbibes so much perspiration, that no one day can free it from the filthy smell; and even some of better than ordinary appearance, when the plaid falls from the shoulder, or otherwise requires to be readjusted, while you are talking with them, toss it over again, as some people do the knots of their wigs, which conveys the offence in whiffs that are intolerable – of this they seem not to be sensible, for it is often done only to give themselves airs.

Various reasons are given both for and against the Highland dress. It is urged against it, that it distinguishes the natives as a body of people distinct and separate from the rest of the subjects of Great Britain, and thereby is one cause of their narrow adherence among themselves, to the exclusion of all the rest of the kingdom; but the part of the habit chiefly objected to is the plaid (or mantle), which they say, is calculated for the encouragement of an idle life in lying about upon the heath, in the daytime, instead of following some lawful employment; that it serves to cover them in the night when they lie in wait among the mountains, to commit their robberies and depredations; and is composed of such colours as altogether, in the mass, so nearly resemble the heath on which they lie, that it is hardly to be distinguished from it until one is so near them as to be within their power, if they have any evil intention; that it renders them ready at a moment's warning, to join in any rebellion, as they carry continually their tents about them; and lastly, it was thought necessary, in Ireland, to suppress that habit by Act of Parliament, for the above reasons, and no complaint for the want of it now remains among the mountaineers of that country.

On the other hand, it is alleged, the dress is most convenient to those who, with no ill design are obliged to travel from one part to another upon their lawful occasions, viz. that they would not be so free to skip over the rocks and bogs with breeches as they are in the short petticoat; that it would be greatly incommodious to those who are frequently to wade through waters, to wear breeches, which must be taken off upon every such occurrence, or would not only gall the bearer, but render it very unhealthful and dangerous to their limbs, to be constantly wet in that part of the body, especially in winter-time, when they might be frozen; and with respect to the plaid in particular, the distance between one place of shelter and another, is often too great to be reached before night comes on; and, being intercepted by sudden floods, or hindered by other impediments, they are frequently obliged to lie all night in the hills, in which case they must perish, were it not for the covering they carry with them. That even if they should be so fortunate as to reach some hospitable hut, they must lie upon the ground uncovered, there being nothing to be spared from the family for that purpose.

And to conclude, a few shillings will buy this dress for an ordinary Highlander, who, very probably, might hardly ever be in condition to purchase a Lowland suit, though of the coarsest cloth or stuff, fit to keep him warm in that cold climate.

I shall determine nothing in this dispute, but leave you to judge which of these two reasonings is the most cogent.

The whole people are fond and tenacious of the Highland clothing, as you may believe by what is here to follow.

Being, in a wet season, upon one of my peregrinations, accompanied by a Highland gentleman, who was one of the clan through which I was passing, I observed the woman to be in great anger with him about something that I did not understand: at length, I asked him wherein he had offended them? Upon this question he laughed, and told me his great-coat was the cause of their wrath; and that their reproach was, that he could not be contented with the garb of his ancestors, but was degenerated into a Lowlander, and condescended to follow their unmanly fashions.

The wretched appearance of the poor Highland women that come to this town, has been mentioned; and here I shall step out of the way to give you a notable instance of frugality in one of a higher rank.

There is a laird's lady, about a mile from one of the Highland garrisons, who is often seen from the ramparts, on Sunday mornings, coming barefoot to the kirk, with her maid carrying the stockings and shoes after her. She stops at the foot of a certain rock, that serves her for a seat, not far from the hovel they call a church, and there she puts them on; and, in her return to the same place, she prepares to go home barefoot as she came; thus, reversing the old mosaic precept. What English squire was ever blessed with such a housewife!

But this instance, though true to my knowledge, I have thought something extraordinary, because the Highlanders are shy of exposing their condition to strangers, especially the English, and more particularly to a number of officers, to whom they are generally desirous to make their best appearance. But, in my journeys, when they did not expect to be observed by any but their own country people, I have twice surprised the laird and his lady without shoes or stockings, a good way from home, in cold weather. The kirk above mentioned brings to my memory a curiosity of the same kind.

At a place in Badenoch, called Ilan Dou, as I passed by a hut of turf something larger than ordinary, but taking little notice of it, I was called upon by one of the company to stop and observe its figure, which proved to be the form of a cross: this occasioned several jokes from a libertine and a Presbyterian upon the Highland cathedral and the nonjurors, in all which they perfectly agreed.

The ordinary girls wear nothing upon their heads until they are married or have a child, except sometimes a fillet of red or blue coarse cloth, of which they are very proud; but often their hair hangs down over the forehead like that of a wild colt.

If they wear stockings, which is very rare, they lay them in plaits one above another, from the ankle up to the calf, to make their legs appear as near as they can in the form of a cylinder; but I think I have seen something like this among the poor German refugee women and the Moorish men in London. By the way, these girls, if they have no pretensions to family (as many of them have, though in rags), they are vain of being with child by a gentleman; and when he makes love to one of them, she will plead her excuse, in saying he undervalues himself, and that she is a poor girl not worth his trouble, or something to that purpose.

This easy compliance proceeds chiefly from a kind of ambition established by opinion and custom; for as gentility is of all things esteemed the most valuable in the notion of those people, so this kind of commerce renders the poor plebeian girl, in some measure, superior to her former equals.

From thenceforward she becomes proud, and they grow envious of her being singled out from among them, to receive the honour of a gentleman's particular notice: but otherwise they are generally far from being immodest; and as modesty is the capital feminine virtue, in that they may be a reproach to some in higher circumstances, who have lost that decent and endearing quality.

You know I should not venture to talk in this manner at —, where modesty would be decried as impolite and troublesome, and I and my slender party ridiculed and borne down by a vast majority. I shall here give you a sample of the wretchedness of some of them.

In one of my northern journeys, where I travelled in a good deal of company, there was, among the rest, a Scots baronet, who is a captain in the army, and does not seem (at least to me) to affect concealment of his country's disadvantage. This gentleman, at our inn, when none but he and I were together, examined the maidservant about her way of living; and she told him (as he interpreted it to me) that she never was in a bed in her life, or ever took off her clothes while they would hang together: but in this last, I think, she was too general; for I am pretty sure she was forced to pull them off now and then for her own quiet. But I must go a little further.

One half of the hut, by partition, was taken up with the field-bed of the principal person among us, and therefore the man and his wife very courteously offered to sit up and leave their bed to the baronet and me (for the rest of the company were dispersed about in barns); but we could not resolve to accept the favour, for certain reasons, but chose rather to lie upon the benches with our saddles for pillows.

Being in a high part of the country, the night was excessive cold, with some snow upon the mountains, though in August, and the next day was the hottest I think I ever felt in my life.

The violent heat of the sun among the rocks, made my new companions (natives of the hovel) such voracious cannibals that I was obliged to lag behind, and set my servant to take vengeance on them for the plentiful repast they were making at my expense, and without my consent, and by which I was told they were become as red as blood. But I should have let you know, that when the table overnight was spread with such provisions as were carried with us, our chief man would needs have the lady of the house to grace the board; and it fell to my lot to sit next to her till I had loaded her plate, and bid her go and sup with her husband, for I foresaw the consequence of our conjunction.

The young children of the ordinary Highlanders are miserable objects indeed, and are mostly overrun with that distemper which some of the old men are hardly ever freed of from their infancy. I have often seen them come out from the huts early in a cold morning stark naked and squat themselves down (if I might decently use the comparison) like dogs on a dunghill, upon a certain occasion after confinement. And at other times they have but little to defend them from the inclemencies of the weather in so cold a climate: nor are the children of some gentlemen in much better condition, being strangely neglected till they are six or seven years old: this one might know by a saying I have often heard, viz. that 'a gentleman's bairns are to be distinguished by their speaking English'.

I was invited one day to dine with a laird, not very far within the hills; and, observing about the house, an English soldier, whom I had often seen before in this town, I took an opportunity to ask him several questions.

This man was a bird-catcher, and employed by the laird to provide him with small birds, for the exercise of his hawks. Among other things, be told me that for three or four days after his first coming, he had observed in the kitchen (an outhouse hovel) a parcel of dirty children half-naked, whom he took to belong to some poor tenant, till at last he found they were a part of the family; but, although these were so little regarded, the young laird, about the age of fourteen, was going to the university; and the eldest daughter, about sixteen, sat with us at table, clean and genteelly dressed.

But, perhaps, it may seem, that in this and other observations of the like kind, whenever I have met with one particular fact, I would make it thought to be general. I do assure you it is not so: but when I have known anything to be common, I have endeavoured to illustrate it by some particular example. Indeed, there is hardly anything of this sort that I have mentioned, can be so general as to be free from all exception; it is justification enough to me if the matter be generally known to answer my description, or what I have related of it. But I think an apology of this nature to you is needless. It is impossible for me, from my own knowledge, to give you an account of the ordinary way of living of those gentlemen; because, when any of us (the English) are invited to their houses, there is always an appearance of plenty to excess; and it has been often said they will ransack all their tenants rather than we should think meanly of their housekeeping: but I have heard it from many whom they have employed, and perhaps had little regard to their observations as inferior people, that, although they have been attended at dinner by five or six servants, yet, with all that state, they have often dined upon oatmeal varied several ways, pickled herrings, or other such cheap and indifferent diet: but though I could not personally know their ordinary bill of fare, yet I have had occasion to observe they do not live in the cleanest manner, though some of them, when in England, affect the utmost nicety in that particular.

A friend of mine told me, some time ago, that, in his journey hither, he stopped to bait at the Bull Inn, at Stamford, which, I think, is one among the best in England. He soon received a message by the landlord, from two gentlemen in the next room, who were going from these parts to London, proposing they might all dine together: this he readily consented to, as being more agreeable to him than dining alone.

As they sat at table, waiting for dinner, one of them found fault with the tablecloth, and said it was not clean; there was, it seems, a spot or two upon it, which he told them was only the stain of claret, that could not at once be perfectly washed out; then they wiped their knives, forks, and plates with the napkins; and in short, nothing was clean enough for them – and this to a gentleman who is himself extremely nice in everything of that nature. At last, says my friend, vexed at the impertinent farce, as he called it, 'Gentlemen, I am vastly pleased at your dislikes, as I am now upon my journey to Scotland (where I have never yet been), because I must infer I shall there find these things in better condition.' 'Troth,' says one of them, 'ye canno want it.'

I am sorry for such instances, whereby a fop, conscious of the fallacy, exposes his country, and brings a ridicule upon other gentlemen of modesty and good sense, to serve a momentary vanity, if not to give affronts, by such gross impositions.

I know very well what my friend thinks of them now, and, perhaps, by their means, of many others who do not deserve it.

There is one Gasconade of the people hereabouts, which is extraordinary: they are often boasting of the great hospitality of the Highlanders to strangers; for my own part, I do not remember to have received one invitation from them, but when it was with an apparent view to their own interest: on the contrary, I have several times been unasked to eat, though there was nothing to be purchased within many miles of the place. But one particular instance was most inhospitable. Being benighted, soon after it was dark, I made up to the house of one to whom I was well known; and, though I had five or six miles to travel over a dangerous rugged way, wherein there was no other shelter to be expected; yet, upon the trampling of my horses before the house, the lights went out in the twinkling of an eye, and deafness at once seized the whole family.

The latter part of what I have written of this letter relates chiefly to gentlemen who inhabit the hills not far from the borders of the Lowlands, or not very far from the sea, or communication with it by lakes; as, indeed, most part of the houses of the chiefs of clans are in one or other of these situations. These are sometimes built with stone and lime, and though not large, except some few, are pretty commodious, at least with comparison to these that are built in the manner of the huts, of which, if any one has a room above, it is, by way of eminence, called a 'lofted' house; but in the inner part of the mountains there are no stone buildings that I know of, except the barracks; and one may go a hundred miles an-end without seeing any other dwellings than the common huts of turf.

I have, indeed, heard of one that was intended to be built with stone in a remote part of the Highlands, from whence the laird sent a number of Highlanders with horses to fetch a quantity of lime from the Borders; but, in their way home, there happened to fall a good deal of rain, and the lime began to crackle and smoke. The Highlanders not thinking, of all things, water would occasion fire, threw it all into a shallow rivulet, in order to quench it before they proceeded further homeward; and this, they say, put an end to the project. But I take this to be a Lowland sneer upon the Highlanders, though not improbable.

I have mentioned above, among other situations of stone-built houses, some that are near to lakes which have a communication with the sea.

There are, in several parts of the Highlands, winding hollows between the feet of the mountains whereinto the sea flows, of which hollows some are navigable for ships of burden, for ten or twenty miles, together inland: those the natives call 'lochs', or lakes, although they are salt, and have a flux and reflux, and therefore, more properly, should be called arms of the sea. I could not but think this explanation necessary, to distinguish those waters from the standing fresh-water lakes, which I have endeavoured to describe in a former letter.

LETTER XXIII

Marriage—Winding sheet—Setting up in life—Customs at a death—
Dancing—Hired mourners—Funeral piles—Veneration of—Second sight—
An instance of—Witches and goblins—A commercial prophecy—Curious
superstition—Notion on removing dead bodies—Marriage confined to
natives—Inconveniences of this—Inquiry answered—Irregular marriage
of a Highland chief—Its consequences—Reproach of clan—Binding a
bargain—Highland arms—Pledge of peace—Highland firing—Choice of
ground in Battle—Battle of Killiecrankie—Fiery cross—Blackmail—
Uplifting—Lifting cattle—Mode of—Michaelmas moon—Robbers
exchange booty—A Highland woman's notion of honour—Recovery of
stolen cattle— Robbers seldom prosecuted—Chiefs prefer compounding—
This crime considered a trifling offence—No reflection on the country at
large—Gross ignorance of a criminal—Personal robberies rare—Trifling
robberies more frequent—A laird's dishonesty—Unwelcome travelling
companion—Good effect of personal courage

WHEN a young couple are married, for the first night the
company keep possession of the dwelling-house or hut, and
send the bridegroom and bride to a barn or outhouse, giving them
straw, heath, or fern, for a bed, with blankets for their covering;
and then they make merry, and dance to the piper all the night long.

Soon after the wedding day, the new-married woman sets herself
about spinning her winding-sheet, and a husband that should sell or
pawn it, is esteemed, among all men, one of the most profligate.

At a young Highlander's first setting up for himself, if he be of
any consideration, he goes about among his near relations and

friends; and from one he begs a cow, from another a sheep; a third gives him seed to sow his land, and so on, till he has procured for himself a tolerable stock for a beginner. This they call 'thigging'.

After the death of anyone, not in the lowest circumstances, the friends and acquaintance of the deceased assemble to keep the near relations company the first night; and they dance, as if it were at a wedding, till the next morning, though all the time the corpse lies before them in the same room. If the deceased be a woman, the widower leads up the first dance; if a man the widow. But this Highland custom I knew to my disturbance, within less than a quarter of a mile of Edinburgh, before I had been among the mountains. It was upon, the death of a smith, next, door to my lodgings, who was a Highlander.

The upper-class hire women to moan and lament at the funeral of their nearest relations. These women cover their heads with a small piece of cloth, mostly green, and every now and then break out into a hideous howl and 'Ho-bo-bo-bo-booo', as I have often heard is done in some parts of Ireland.

This part of the ceremony is called 'coronoch', and, generally speaking, is the cause of much drunkenness, attended with its concomitants, mischievous encounters and bloody broils; for all that have arms in their possession, accoutre themselves with them upon those occasions.

I have made mention of their funeral piles in a former letter; but I had once occasion to take particular notice of a heap of stones, near the middle of a small piece of arable land. The plough was carefully guided as near to it as possible; and the pile, being like others I had seen upon the moors, I asked, by an interpreter, whether there was a rock beneath it; but being answered in the negative, I further inquired the reasons why they lost so much ground, and did not remove the heap. To this I had for answer, it was a burial place, and they deemed it a kind of sacrilege to remove a single stone; and that the children from their infancy, were taught the same veneration for it. Thus a parcel of loose stones are more religiously preserved among them than, with us, the costly monuments in Westminster Abbey; and thence I could not but conclude that the inclination to preserve the remains and memory of the dead is greater with those people than it is among us. The Highlanders, even here in this town, cannot forego the practice of the hills, in raising heaps of stones over such as have lost their lives by some misfortune; for in Oliver's Fort, no sooner was the body of an officer removed from the place where he fell in a duel, than they set about the raising such a heap of stones upon the spot where he had lain. So much for mountain monuments.

Those who are said to have the 'second sight' deal chiefly in deaths, and it is often said to be a gift peculiar to some families – that is, the cheat has, with some, been handed down from father to son; yet I must confess they seldom fail to be right when they reveal their predictions, for they take the surest method to prophetise, which is to divulge the oracle after the fact. Of this I had once an opportunity to convince a Highland gentleman, from whom I thought might have been expected more reason and less prejudice, than to be gulled by such impostors.

The matter was this: a poor Highlander was drowned in wading a ford, and his body afterwards put into a small barn; not many days after, the laird endeavouring to pass the same water, which was hard by his own house, his horse gave way, and he was likewise drowned, and carried into the same hut. Soon after, a story began to pass for current, that such a one, the second-sighted, foretold, when the body of the poor man lay exposed to view, that it would not be long before a greater man than he should lie in the same place. This was all that was pretended, and that too was afterwards found to be an invention, arising from the circumstance of two persons at a little distance of time, being drowned in the same ford, and both their bodies carried to one hovel, which, indeed, stood singly, near the place where they were both stopped by the rocks.

Witches and goblins are likewise pretty common among the Highlanders, and they have several old prophecies handed down to them by tradition; among which, this is one, that the time shall come when they shall measure out the cloth of London with a long pole.

As the little manufacture they had was cloth, so, at the time when this pretended prophecy was broached, they esteemed that the only riches, and did not know of the treasure of Lombard Street; like the country boy, that fed poorly and worked hard, who said, if he were a gentleman, he would eat fat bacon, and swing, all day long upon Gaffer Such a one's 'yate'.

A certain laird, whom I have mentioned several times before, though not by name, is frequently heard to affirm, that, at the instant he was born, a number of swords, that hung up in the hall of the Mansion House, leaped of themselves out of the scabbards, in token, I suppose, that he was to be a mighty man in arms; and this vain romance seems to be believed by the lower order of his followers; and I believe there are many that laugh at it in secret, who dare not publicly declare their disbelief. But, because the miracle has hitherto only portended the command of his clan and an independent company, he has endeavoured to supply the defeat of the presage by his own epitaph, altogether as romantic, in his own kirk, which he still lives to read, whenever he pleases to gratify his vanity with the sight of it.

They have an odd notion relating to dead bodies that are to be transported over rivers, lakes, or arms of the sea: before it is put on board they appraise and ascertain the value of the boat or vessel, believing, if that be neglected, some accident will happen to endanger the lives of those who are embarked in it; but, upon recollection, I think some of our seamen entertain this idle fancy in some measure; for, I have heard, they do not care for a voyage with a corpse on board, as though it would be the occasion of tempestuous weather; and, lastly (for I shall not trouble you longer with things of this kind, which are without number), the Highlanders are of opinion, that it is in the power of certain enchantresses to prevent the act of procreation; but I am rather inclined to believe it was originally a male artifice among them to serve as an excuse in case of imbecility.

The marriages of the chiefs and chieftains are, for the most part, confined to the circuit of the Highlands; and they generally endeavour to strengthen their clan by what they call powerful alliances: but I must not be understood to include any of the prime nobility of Scotland, of whom there are some chiefs of clans: their dignity places them quite out of the reach of anything I have said, or have to say, in relation to the heads of Highland families, who reside constantly with them, and govern them in person. As to the lower class of gentry and the ordinary people, they generally marry in the clan whereto they appertain.

All this may be political enough, i.e. the chief to have regard to the Highlands in general, and his followers to their own particular tribe or family, in order to preserve themselves a distinct people; but this continues them in a narrow way of thinking with respect to the rest of mankind and also prevents that addition to the circumstances of the whole, or part of the Highlands, which might be made by marriages of women of fortune in the Lowlands. This, in time, might have a good effect, by producing a union, instead of that coldness, to say no more, which subsists, at present, between the natives of those two parts of Scotland, as if they bore no relation one to another, considered as men and subjects of the same kingdom, and even the same part of it. Yet I must here (and by the by) take notice of one thing, wherein they perfectly agree, which experience has taught me to know perfectly well; and that is, to grudge and envy those of the south part of the island any profitable employment among them, although they themselves are well received and equally encouraged and employed with the natives in that part of the kingdom; and I think further, they have sometimes more than their share, if they must needs keep up such a partial and invidious distinction.

But to return to the marriages of the Highlanders – perhaps, after what has been said of the country, it may be asked, what Lowland woman would care to lead a life attended with so many in-conveniences? Doubtless there are those who would be as fond of sharing the clannish state and power with a husband, as some others are of a name, when they sell themselves for a title; for each of these kinds of vanity is very flattering: besides, there are many of the Lowland women who seem to have a great liking to the Highland men, which they cannot forbear to insinuate in their ordinary conversation. But such marriages are very rare; and I know but one instance of them, which, I must confess, will not much recommend the union of which I have been speaking; but then it is but one, and cannot be the cause of any general inference.

A certain chieftain took to wife the daughter of an Edinburgh goldsmith; but this Lowland match was the cause of much discontent in the tribe, as being not only a diminution of the honour of the house, but, in their opinion, an ill precedent besides; and nothing was more common among the people of that branch of the clan, than to ask among themselves, 'Were there not smiths enough in the clan that had daughters? How comes our chief then to have married the daughter of a Lowland smith?', making no distinction between an Edinburgh goldsmith and a Highland blacksmith. They thought it was a disgrace, of which every one partook, that he should match himself with a tradesman's daughter, a Lowland woman, and no way derived from the tribe.

This proved in the end to be a fatal marriage; but as it is uncertain, and therefore would be unjust for me to determine, in a matter whereof I have not a perfect knowledge, I cannot conclude which of the two, the husband or the wife, was the occasion of the sad catastrophe. I shall only say what I know, viz. that an old rough Highlander, of sixty at least, was imprisoned at one of the barracks, while I was there, for accepting favours from the lady. She was to be sent to Edinburgh to answer the accusation; and, while she was preparing to go, and the messenger waiting without doors, to conduct her thither – she died.

The clan whereto the above mentioned tribe belongs, is the only one I have heard of which is without a chief – that is, being divided into families under several chieftains, without any particular patriarch of the whole name: and this is a great reproach, as may appear from an affair that fell out at my table in the Highlands, between one of that name and a Cameron. The provocation given by the latter was, 'Name your chief'. The return to it at once was, 'You are a fool'. They went out the next morning; but, having early notice of it, I sent a small party of soldiers after them, which, in all probability, prevented some barbarous mischief that might have ensued; for the chiefless Highlander, who is himself a petty chieftain, was going to the place appointed with a small-sword and pistol, whereas the Cameron (an old man) took with him only his broadsword, according to agreement.

When all was over, and I had at least seemingly reconciled them, I was told the words (of which I seem to think but slightly), were to one of that clan the greatest of all provocations.

In a bargain between two Highlanders, each of them wets the ball of his thumb with his mouth, and then joining them together, it is esteemed a very binding act; but in more solemn engagements, they take an oath in a manner which I shall describe in some succeeding letter.

When any one of them is armed at all points, he is loaded with a target, a firelock, a heavy broadsword, a pistol, stock and lock of iron, a dirk; and, besides all these, some of them carry a sort of knife, which they call a '*skeenochles*', from its being concealed in the sleeve near the armpit.

This last is more peculiar to the robbers, who have done mischief with it, when they were thought to have been effectually disarmed.

To see a Highlander thus furnished out might put one in mind of Merry Andrew, when he comes from behind the curtain, in a warlike manner, to dispute the doctor's right to his stage. He is then, in his own individual person, a whole company of foot, being loaded with one of every species of the arms and trophies of a regiment, viz. a pike, halbert, firelock, sword, bayonet, colours, and drum.

Sometimes, when a company of them have previously resolved and agreed to be peaceable and friendly over their whisky, they have drawn their dirks and stuck them all into the cheese-table before them as who should say, 'Nothing but peace at this meeting – no private stabbing tonight'. But, in promiscuous companies, at great assemblies, such as fairs, burials, etc., where much drunkenness prevails, there scarcely ever fails to be great riots and much mischief done among them.

To shoot at a mark, they lay themselves all along behind some stone or hillock on which they rest their piece, and are a long while taking their aim; by which means they can destroy any one unseen, on whom they would wreak their malice or revenge.

When in sight of the enemy, they endeavour to possess themselves of the higher ground, as knowing they give their fire more effectually by their situation one above another, being without discipline; and also that they afterwards descend on the enemy with greater force, having in some measure, put it out of their power to recede in the first onset.

After their first fire (I need not have said their first, for they rarely stand a second), they throw, away their firearms and plaids which encumber them, and make their attack with their swords; but if repulsed, they seldom or never rally, but return to their habitations. If they happen to engage in a plain, when they expect the enemy's fire, they throw themselves down on the ground. They had ever a dread of the cavalry, and did not care to engage them, though but few in number.

I chanced to be in company one time with an old Highlander, as I passed over the plain of Killiecrankie where the battle was fought between King William's troops, commanded by General Mackay, and the rebel Highlanders under the Earl Viscount of Dundee.

When he came to the great stone that is raised about the middle of the flat, upon the spot where Dundee fell, we stopped; and there he described to me, in his manner, the order and end of the battle, of which I shall now give you the substance only, for be was long in telling his story.

He told me that Mackay extended his line, which was only two deep, the whole length of the plain; designing, as he supposed, to surround the Highlanders, if they should descend from the side of an opposite hill, where they were posted. That after the first firing, the rebels came down, six or seven deep, to attack the king's troops; and their rear pushing on their front, they by their weight charged through and through these feeble files; and, having broke them, made with their broadswords a most cruel carnage; and many others who expected no quarter, in order to escape the Highland fury, threw themselves into that rapid river (the Tay), and were drowned. But he said there was an English regiment who kept themselves entire (the only one that was there), whom the Highlanders did not care to attack: and, after the slaughter was over and the enemy retired, that single corps marched from the field in good order. He further told me, there were some few horse badly mounted, who, by the strength of the Highland files were pushed into the river, which was close in their rear.

On any sudden alarm and danger or distress to the chief, he gives notice of it throughout his own clan, and to such others as are in alliance with him. This is done by sending a signal, which they call the 'fiery cross', being two sticks tied together transversely, and burnt at the ends; with this, he sends directions in writing, to signify the place of rendezvous. And when the principal person of any place has received this token, he dismisses the messenger, and sends it forward to another; and so on, till all have received the intelligence. Upon the receipt of this signal, all that are near immediately leave habitations, and repair to the place appointed, with their arms, and oatmeal for their provision. This they mingle with the water of the next river or burn they come to when hunger calls for a supply; and often, for want of a proper vessel, sup the raw mixture out of the palms of their hands.

They have been used to impose a tax upon the inhabitants of the low country, near the, borders of the Highlands, called 'blackmail' (or rent), and levy it upon them by force; and sometimes upon the weaker clans among themselves. But as it was made equally criminal, by several Acts of Parliament, to comply with this taxation and to extort it, the people, to avoid the penalty, came to agreement with the robbers, or some of their correspondents in the Lowlands, to protect their houses and cattle. And, as long as this payment was punctually made, the depredations ceased, or otherwise the collector of this imposition was by contract obliged to make good the loss, which he seldom failed to do.

These collectors gave regular receipts, as for safeguard money; and those who refused to pay it, were sure to be plundered, except they kept a continual guard of their own, well armed, which would have been a yet more expensive way of securing their property. And, notwithstanding the guard of the independent Highland companies, which were raised chiefly to prevent thefts and impositions of this nature, yet I have been certainly informed, that this blackmail, or evasive safeguard money, has been very lately paid in a disarmed part of the northern Highlands; and, I make no doubt, in other places besides, though it has not yet come to my knowledge.

The gathering-in of rents is called 'uplifting' them, and the stealing of cows they call 'lifting', a softening word for theft; as if it were only collecting their dues. This I have often heard; but it has so often occurred to me, that we have the word shoplifting in the sense of stealing, which I take to be an old English compound word. But, as to the etymology of it, I leave that to those who are fond of such unprofitable disquisitions, though I think this is pretty evident.

When a design is formed for this purpose, they go out in parties from ten to thirty men, and traverse large tracts of mountains, till they arrive at the place where they intend to commit their depredations; and that they choose to do as distant as they can from their own dwellings. The principal time for this wicked practice is the Michaelmas moon, when the cattle are in condition fit for markets, held on the borders of the Lowlands. They drive the stolen cows in the night-time, and by day they lie concealed with them in byplaces among the mountains, where hardly any others come; or in woods, if any such are to be found in their way.

I must here ask leave to digress a little, and take notice, that I have several times used the word cows for a drove of cattle. This is according to the Highland style; for they say 'drove of cows' when there are bulls and oxen among them, as we say 'flock of geese'; though there be in it many ganders.

And having just now mentioned the time of lifting, it revived in my memory a malicious saying of the Lowlanders, viz. that the Highland lairds tell out their daughters' 'tochers' by the light of the Michaelmas moon. But to return:

Sometimes one band of these robbers has agreed with another to exchange the stolen cattle; and, in this case, they used to commit their robberies nearer home; and by appointing a place of rendezvous, those that lifted in the north-east (for the purpose) have exchanged with others toward the west, and each have sold them not many miles from home, which was commonly at a very great distance from the place where they were stolen. Nay, further, as I have been well informed, in making this contract of exchange, they have, by correspondence, long before they went out, described to each other the colour and marks of the cows destined to be stolen and exchanged.

I remember a story concerning a Highland woman, who, begging a charity of a Lowland laird's lady, was asked several questions; and, among the rest, how many husbands she had had? To which she answered, three. And being further questioned, if her husbands had been kind to her, she said the two first were honest men, and very careful of their family, for they both 'died for the law' – that is, were hanged for theft. 'Well, but as to the last?' 'Hout!' says she, 'a fulthy peast! He dy'd at hame, lik an auld dug, on a puckle o' strae.'

Those that have lost their cattle sometimes pursue them by the track, and recover them from the thieves. Or if in the pursuit they are 'hounded' (as they phrase it) into the bounds of any other chief, whose followers were not concerned in the robbery, and the track is there lost, he is obliged by law to trace them out of his territory, or make them good to the owner.

By the way, the heath, or heather, being pressed by the foot, retains the impression or at least some remains of it, for a long while, before it rises again effectually; and besides, you know, there are other visible marks left behind by the cattle. But even a single Highlander has been found by the track of his foot, when he took to hills out of the common ways, for his greater safety in his flight, as thinking he could not so well be discovered from hill to hill, every now and then, as he often might be in the road (as they call it) between the mountains.

If the pursuers overtake the robbers, and find them inferior in number, and happen to seize any of them, they are seldom prosecuted, there being but few who are in circumstances fit to support the expense of a prosecution; or, if they were, they would be liable to have their houses burnt, their cattle hocked, and their lives put in danger, from some of the clan to which the banditti belonged.

But, with the richer sort, the chief, or chieftain, generally makes a composition, when it comes to be well known the thieves belonged to his tribe, which he willingly pays, to save the lives of some of his clan; and this is repaid him by a contribution among the robbers, who never refuse to do their utmost to save those of their fraternity. But it has been said this payment has been sometimes made in cows, stolen from the opposite side of the country, or paid out of the produce of them when sold at the market.

It is certain some of the Highlanders think of this kind of depredation as our deer-stealers do of their park and forest enterprises – that is, to be a small crime, or none at all. And, as the latter would think it a scandalous reproach to be charged with robbing a hen-roost, so the Highlander thinks it less shameful to steal a hundred cows than one single sheep; for a sheep stealer is infamous even among them.

If I am mistaken in that part of my account of the lifting of cattle, which is beyond my own knowledge, you may lay the blame to those gentlemen who gave me the information.

But there is no more wonder that men of honesty and probity should disclose, with abhorrence, the evil practices of the vile part of their countrymen, than that I should confess to them we have, among us, a number of villains that cannot plead the least shadow of an excuse for their thievings and highway robberies, unless they could make a pretence of their idleness and luxury.

When I first came into these parts, a Highland gentleman, in order to give me a notion of the ignorance of some of the ordinary Highlanders, and their contempt of the Lowland laws (as they call them), gave me an account, as we were walking together, of the behaviour of a common Highlandman at his trial before the lords of justiciary in the low country. By the way, the appearance of those gentlemen upon the bench is not unlike that of our judges in England.

I shall repeat the fellow's words, as near as I can, by writing in the same broken accent as my Highland friend used in mimicking the criminal.

This man was accused of stealing, with others, his accomplices, a good number of cattle; and, while his indictment was in reading, setting forth that he, as a common thief, had lain in wait, etc., the Highlander lost all patience, and interrupting, cried out, 'Common Tief! Common Tief! Steal ane cow, twa cow, dat be common tief: Lift hundred cow, dat be shentilman's trovers.' After the court was again silent, and some little progress had been made in the particulars of the accusation, he again cried out, 'Ah, hone! Dat such fine shentilmans should sit dere wid der fine cowns on, to mak a parshel o' lees on a peur honesht mon.'

But in conclusion, when he was told what was to be his fate he roared out most outrageously, and, fiercely pointing at the judges, he cried out, 'Ah, for a proadsword an a tirk, to rid de hoose o' tose foul peastes!'

Personal robberies are seldom heard of among them: for my own part, I have several times with a single servant, passed the mountain way from hence to Edinburgh, with four or five hundred guineas in my portmanteau, without any apprehension of robbers by the way, or danger in my lodgings by night, though in my sleep, any one, with ease, might have thrust a sword, from the outside, through the wall of the hut and my body together. I wish we could say as much of our own country, civilized as it is said to be, though one cannot be safe in going from London to Highgate.

Indeed, in trifling matters, as a knife, or some such thing, which they have occasion for, and think it will cause no very strict inquiry, they are some of them, apt to pilfer; while a silver, spoon or a watch might lie in safety because they have no means to dispose of either, and to make use of them would soon discover their theft. But I cannot approve the Lowland saying, viz., 'Show me a Highlander, and I will show you a thief'.

Yet, after all, I cannot forbear doing justice upon a certain laird, whose lady keeps a change far in the Highlands, west of town.

This gentleman, one day, opportunity tempting, took a fancy to the lock of an officer's pistol; another time he fell in love (like many other men) with a fair but deceitful outside, in taking the boss of a bridle, silvered over, to be all of that valuable metal. It is true, I never lost any thing at his hut; but the proverb made me watchful – I need not repeat it.

But let this account of him be of no consequence; for I do assure you, I never knew any one of his rank do anything like it in all the Highlands.

And, for my part, I do not remember that ever I lost anything among them but a pair of new doeskin gloves; and at another time a horse-cloth made of plaiding which was taken away while my horses were swimming across a river; and that was sent me the next day to Fort William, to which place I was going when it was taken from the rest of my baggage, as it lay upon the ground. I say nothing in this place of another robbery, because I know the motive to it was purely revenge.

I thought I had done with this part of my subject; but there is just now come to my remembrance a passage between an ordinary Highlandman and an officer on half-pay, who lives in this town and is himself of Highland extraction.

He told me, a long while ago, that, on a certain time, he was going on foot, and unattended, upon a visit to a laird, about seven or eight miles among the hills; and, being clad in a new glossy summer suit (instead of his Highland dress, which he usually wore upon such occasions), there overtook him in his way an ordinary fellow, who forced himself upon him as a companion.

When they had gone together about a mile, his new fellow traveller said to him, 'Troth, ye ha getten bra clais'; of which the officer took little notice; but, some time after, the fellow began to look sour, and to snort, as they do when they are angry: 'Ah, 'tis ponny geer! What an I sho'd take 'em free ye noo?' Upon this the officer drew a pistol from his breast, and said, 'What do you think of this?'

But at the sight of the pistol, the fellow fell on his knees, and squalled out, 'Ah, hone! Ah, hone! She was but shokin.'

It is true, this dialogue passed in Irish, but this is the language in which I was told the story.

But I have known several instances of common Highlanders, who finding themselves like to be worsted, having crouched and howled like a beaten spaniel, so suddenly has their insolence been turned into fawning. But, you know, we have both of us seen, in our own country, a change in higher life not less unmanly.

You may see, by this additional article, that I can conceal nothing from you, even though it may seem, in some measure, to call in question what I had been saying before.

LETTER XXIV

———— ◆◆◆ ————

Tascal money—Oath taken on a drawn dirk—Varieties of—Specimens of
Highland oaths—Clans which were notorious for robbers—Gypsies—Their
unwelcome visits—Intrusions—Highlanders think little of some oaths—
Remarkable instances—Pride of power— Example—Pit and gallows—Bailie
of Regality—Gross instance of judicial prejudice—Danger of lawless power
—Homage—Despotic power of chiefs—Curious instances—Hired murderers
—Horrid occurrences—Revenge taken on cattle—Execution of criminals—
Hire of an assassin—Inclination of Revenge—A dispute decided—Revenge
of a chieftain—The criminal secured—Attempts at bribery—An offer of
assassination—Highlander's excessive drinking—Their excuse—Dangers
from—Quantity of spirits consumed—Air salubrious—Honey

BESIDES tracking the cows as mentioned in my last letter,
there was another means whereby to recover them; which
was by sending persons into the country suspected, and by them
offering a reward (which they call 'tascal money') to any who
should discover the cattle and those who stole them. This, you
may be sure, was done as secretly as possible. The temptation
sometimes, though seldom, proved too strong to be resisted; and
the cattle being thereby discovered, a restitution, or other satisfaction,
was obtained. But, to put a stop to a practice so detrimental to their
interest and dangerous to their persons, the thievish part of the
Camerons, and others afterwards, by their example, bound
themselves by oath never to receive any such reward, or inform one
against another.

This oath they take upon a drawn dirk, which they kiss in a solemn manner consenting, if ever they prove perjured, to be stabbed with the same weapon, or any other of the like sort.

Hence they think no wickedness so great as the breach of this oath, since they hope for impunity in committing almost every other crime, and are so certainly and severely punished for this transgression.

An instance of their severity in this point happened in December 1723, when one of the said Camerons, suspected of having taken tascal money, was, in the dead of the night, called out of his hut from his wife and children and, under pretence of some new enterprise, allured to some distance, out of hearing, and there murdered: and another, for the same crime, as they call it, was either thrown down some precipice, or otherwise made away with, for he was never heard of afterwards.

Having mentioned above the manner of taking their oath, relating to tascal money, I shall here give you a specimen of a Highland oath upon other occasions; in taking whereof they do not kiss the book, as in England, but hold up their right hand, saying thus, or to this purpose:

'By God himself, and as I shall answer to God at the great day, I shall speak the truth: if I do not, may I never thrive while I live; may I go to Hell and be damned when I die. May my land bear neither grass nor corn: may my wife and bairns never prosper; may my cows, calves, sheep, and lambs, all perish,' etc.

I say to this purpose, for I never heard they had any established form of an oath among them. Besides, you perceive it must necessarily be varied according to the circumstances of the person who swears, at the discretion of him who administers the oath.

When the chief was an encourager of this kind of theft, which I have the charity to believe was uncommon, and the robbers succeeded in their attempt, he received two-thirds of the spoil, or the produce of it; and the remaining third part was divided among the thieves.

The clans that had among them the most of villains addicted to these robberies are said, by the people bordering on the Highlands, to be the Camerons, Mackenzies, the Broadalbinmen, the McGregors, and the McDonalds of Keppock and Glencoe. The chieftain of these last is said, by his near neighbours, to have little besides those depredations for his support; and the chief of the first, whose clan has been particularly stigmatized for those violences, has, as I am very well informed, strictly forbidden any such vile practices, which has not at all recommended him to some of his followers.

Besides these ill-minded people among the clans, there are some stragglers in the hills, who, like our gypsies, have no certain habitation, only they do not stroll about in numbers like them. These go singly, and, though perfectly unknown, do not beg at the door, but, without invitation or formal leave, go into a hut, and sit themselves down by the fire, expecting to be supplied with oatmeal for their present food. When bedtime comes, they wrap themselves up in their plaids, or beg the use of a blanket, if any to be spared, for their covering, and then lay themselves down upon the ground in some corner of the hut. Thus the man and his wife are often deprived of the freedom of their own habitation, and cannot be alone together. But the inhabitants are in little danger of being pilfered by these guests – nor, indeed, do they seem to be apprehensive of it; for not only there is generally little to be stolen, but, if they took some small matter, it would be of no use to the thief for want of a receiver; and, besides, they would be pursued and easily taken. The people say themselves, if it were not for this connivance of theirs, by a kind of customary hospitality, these wanderers would soon be starved, having no money wherewith to purchase sustenance.

But I have heard great complaint of this custom from a Highland farmer of more than ordinary substance, at whose dwelling I happened to see an instance of this intrusion, it being very near to the place where I resided for a time; and he told me he should think himself happy if he was taxed at any kind of reasonable rate, to be freed from this great inconvenience.

Above I have given you a sketch of the Highland oath, and here I shall observe to you how slightly a certain Highlander thought of the Lowland form.

This man was brought as a witness against another in a supposed criminal case: the magistrate tendered him the low country oath, and, seeing the fellow addressing himself confidently to take it, though he greatly suspected, by several circumstances, the man was suborned, changed his method, and offered him the Highland oath, 'No,' says the Highlander, 'I cannot do that, for I will not forswear myself to please anybody!'

This single example might be sufficient to show how necessary it is to swear the common people in the method of their own country; yet, by way of chat, I shall give you another, though it be less different in the fact than in the expression.

At Carlisle Assizes a Highlandman, who had meditated the ruin of another, prosecuted him for horse-stealing, and swore positively to the fact.

This being done, the supposed criminal desired his prosecutor might be sworn in the Highland manner; and, the oath being tendered him accordingly, he refused it, saying, 'Thar is a hantle o' difference betwixt blawing on a buke and dam'ing one's saul.'

But I have heard of several other examples of the same kind, notwithstanding the oath taken in the low country has the same introduction, viz. 'By God, and as I shall answer, etc., but then the land, wife, children and cattle, are not concerned; for there is no imprecation in it either upon them or him that takes the oath.

As most people, when they begin to grow in years, are unwilling to think themselves incapable of their former pleasures, so some of the Highland gentlemen seem to imagine they still retain that exorbitant power which they formerly exercised over the lives of their vassals and followers, even without legal trial and examination. Of this power I have heard several of them vaunt; but it might be ostentation: however, I shall mention one in particular.

I happened to be at the house of a certain chief, when the chieftain of a tribe belonging to another clan came to make a visit; after talking of indifferent matters, I told him I thought some of his people had not behaved toward me, in a particular affair, with that civility I might have expected from the clan. He started; and immediately, with an air of fierceness, clapped his hand on his broadsword, and told me, if I required it, he would send me two or three of their heads.

But I, really thinking he had been in jest, and had acted well (as jesting is not their talent), laughed out, by way of approbation of his capacity for a joke; upon which he assumed if possible, a yet more serious look, and told me peremptorily he was a man of his word; and the chief who sat by made no manner of objection to what he said.

The heritable power of 'pit and gallows', as they call it, which still is exercised by some within their proper districts, is, I think, too much for any particular subject to be entrusted withal. But it is said that any partiality or revenge of the chief, in his own cause, is obviated by the law, which does not allow himself to sit judicially, but obliges him to appoint a substitute as judge in his courts, who is called the Bailie of Regality.

I fear this is but a shadow of safety to the accused, if it may not appear to increase the danger of injustice and oppression; for to the orders and instructions of the chief may be added the private resentment of the bailie, which may make up a double weight against the supposed criminal

I have not, I must own, been accustomed to hear trials in these courts, but have been often told, that one of these bailies, in particular, seldom examines any but with raging words and rancour; and, if the answers made are not to his mind, he contradicts them by blows; and, one time, even to the knocking down of the poor wretch who was examined. Nay, further, I have heard say of him, by a very credible person, that a Highlander of a neighbouring clan, with whom his own had been long at variance, being to be brought before him, he declared upon the accusation, before he had seen the party accused, that the very name should hang him.

I have not mentioned this violent and arbitrary proceeding as though I knew or thought it usual in those courts, but to show how little mankind in general are to be trusted with a lawless power, to which there is no other check or control but good sense and humanity, which are not common enough to restrain every one who is invested with such power, as appears by this example.

The Bailie of Regality, in many cases, takes upon him the same state as the chief himself would do – as for one single instance.

When he travels, in time of snow, the inhabitants of one village must walk before him to make a path to the next; and so on to the end of his progress: and, in a dark night, they light him from one inhabited place to another, which are mostly far distant, by carrying blazing sticks of fir.

Formerly the power assumed by the chief in remote parts was perfectly despotic, of which I shall only mention what was told me by a near relation of a certain attainted lord, whose estate (that was) lies in the northern Highlands; but hold this – this moment, upon recollection, I have resolved to add to it an example of the arbitrary proceeding of one much less powerful than the chief, who nevertheless thought he might dispose of the lives of foreigners at his pleasure. As to the first – the father of the late earl above-mentioned having a great desire to get a fellow apprehended, who was said to have been guilty of many atrocious crimes, set a price upon his head of one hundred and twenty crowns (a species of Scots coin in those days) – I suppose about five pence or six pence, and, of his own authority, gave orders for taking him alive or dead; that the pursuers, thinking it dangerous to themselves to attempt the securing him alive, shot him, and brought his head and one of his hands to the chief; and immediately received the promised reward. The other is as follows:

I remember to have heard, a good while ago, that in the time when Prince George of Denmark was Lord-High-Admiral of England, some Scots gentlemen represented to him, that Scotland could furnish the navy with as good timber for masts and other uses as either Sweden or Norway could do, and at a much more reasonable rate.

This succeeded so far that two surveyors were sent to examine into the allegations of their memorial.

Those gentlemen came first to Edinburgh, where they staid some time to concert the rest of their journey, and to learn from the inhabitants their opinion concerning the execution of their commission, among whom there was one gentleman that had some acquaintance with a certain chieftain in a very remote part of the Highlands, and he gave them a letter to him.

They arrived at the laird's house, declared the cause of their coming, and produced their credentials, which were a warrant and instructions from the prince; but the chieftain, after perusing them, told them he knew nothing of any such person. They then told him he was husband to Queen Anne; and he answered, he knew nothing of either of them; 'But,' says he, 'there came hither, some time ago, such as you from Ireland, as spies upon the country, and we hear they have made their jests upon us among the Irish.'

'Now,' says he, 'you shall have one hour; and if in that time you can give me no better account of yourselves than you have hitherto done, I'll hang you both upon that tree.' Upon which his attendants showed great readiness to execute his orders: and, in this perplexity, he abruptly left them, without seeing the Edinburgh letter; for of that they made but little account, since the authority of the prince, and even the queen, were to him of no consequence: but afterwards, as they were walking backwards and forwards in the garden counting the minutes, one of them resolved to try what the letter might do: this was agreed to by the other, as the last resort; but, in the hurry and confusion they were in, it was not for some time to be found, being worked into a corner of the bearer's usual pocket, and so he passed to another, etc.

Now the hour is expired, and the haughty chieftain enters the garden; and one of them gave him the letter: this he read, and then turning to them, said, 'Why did not you produce this at first? If you had not had it, I should most certainly have hanged you both immediately.'

The scene being thus changed, he took them into his house, gave them refreshment, and told them they might take a survey of his woods the next morning, or when they thought fit.

There is one chief who sticks at nothing to gratify his avarice or revenge.

This oppressor, upon the least offence or provocation, makes no conscience of hiring villains out of another clan, as he has done several times, to execute his diabolical purposes by hocking of cattle, burning of houses, and even to commit murder itself. Out of many enormities, I shall only mention two.

The first was – that being offended, though very unreasonably, with a gentleman, even of his own name and clan, he, by horrid commerce with one who governed another tribe in the absence of his chief, agreed with him for a parcel of assassins to murder his vassal, and bring him, his head, I suppose, as a voucher. The person devoted to death, happened to be absent the night the murderers came to his house, and therefore the villains resolved not to go away empty-handed, but to take his daughter's head in lieu of his own; which the poor creature perceiving, was frighted to such a degree, that she has not recovered her understanding to this day.

The servant-maid they abused with a dirk in a butcherly manner, too shameful to be described: to be short, the neighbours, though at some distance, hearing the cries and shrieks of the females, took the alarm, and the inhuman monsters made their escape.

The other violence related to a gentleman who lives near this town, and was appointed umpire in a litigated affair by the chief and the other party; and, because this laird thought he could not, with any colour of justice, decide in favour of the chief, his cattle, that were not far from his house, were some hocked and the rest of them killed; but the owner of them, as the other, was absent that night, in all probability suspecting (or having some private intelligence of) his danger, and, when this horrid butchery was finished, the ruffians went to his house, and wantonly diverted themselves in telling the servants they had done their master a good piece of service, for they had saved him the expense of a butcher to kill his cattle: and I have been told, that the next morning there were seen a number of calves sucking at the dugs of the dead cows. But two of them were afterwards apprehended and executed.

These men (as is said of Coleman) were allured to secrecy while under condemnation, though sometimes inclined to confess their employer; and thus they continued to depend upon promises till the knot was tied; and then it was too late but all manner of circumstances were too flagrant to admit a doubt concerning the first instigator of their wickedness; yet few of the neighbouring inhabitants dare to trust one another with their sentiments of it.

But here comes the finishing stroke to the first of these execrable pieces of workmanship.

Not long after the vile attempt, he who had furnished the murderers made a demand on the chief of a certain quantity of oatmeal, which was to be the price of the assassination; but, in answer, he was told, if he would send money, it might be had of a merchant with whom he (the chief) had frequent dealings; and as for himself, he had but just enough for his own family till the next crop.

This shuffling refusal occasioned the threats of a lawsuit; but the demander was told, the business had not been effectually performed; and besides, as he knew the consideration, he might commence his process, and declare it in a court as soon as ever he thought fit.

This last circumstance I did not, or perhaps could not, know till lately, when I was in that part of the Highlands from whence the villains were hired.

I must again apologize, and say, I make no doubt you will take this account (as it is intended) to be a piece of historical justice done upon one who is lawless, and deserves much more, and not as a sample of a Highland chief, or the least imputation on any other of those gentlemen.

Yet truth obliges me to confess, that in some parts there remains among the natives a kind of Spanish or Italian inclination to revenge themselves, as it were, by proxy, of those who they think have injured them, or interfered with their interest. This I could not but infer, soon after my coming to the western parts of the Highlands, from the saying of a youth, son of a laird in the neighbourhood.

He was telling me his father's estate had been much embarrassed, but, by a lucky hit, a part of it was redeemed. I was desirous to know by what means, and he proceeded to tell me there were two wadsets upon it, and both of the mortgagees had been in possession, each claiming a right to about half; but one of them being a native, and the other a stranger – that is, not of the clan, the former had taken the latter aside, and told him if he did not immediately quit the country, he would hang him upon the next tree. 'What!' says a Highlander who was born in the east, and went with me into those parts, 'that would be the way to be hanged himself.' 'Out!' says the youth, 'you talk as if you did not know your own country – that would have been done, and nobody knew who did it.' This he spoke with an air as if he had been talking of ordinary business, and was angry with the other for being ignorant of it, who afterwards owned that my presence was the cause of his objection.

Besides what I have recounted in this letter, which might serve as an indication that some, at least, of the ordinary Highlanders are not averse to the price of blood, I shall here take notice of a proposal of that kind which was made to myself.

Having given the preference to a certain clan in a profitable business, it brought upon me the resentment of the chieftain of a small neighbouring tribe, part of a clan at enmity with the former.

This gentleman thought his people had as much right to my favour in that particular as the other: the first instance of his revenge was a robbery committed by one of his tribe, whom I ordered to be 'hounded out', and he was taken. This fellow I resolved to prosecute to the utmost, which brought the chieftain to solicit me in his behalf.

He told me, for introduction, that it was not usual in the hills for gentlemen to carry such matters to extremity, but rather to accept of a composition: and, finding their custom of compounding had no weight with me, he offered a restitution; but I was firmly resolved, *in terrorem*, to punish the thief. Seeing this proposal was likewise ineffectual, he told me the man's wife was one of the prettiest young women in the Highlands, and if I would pardon the husband I should 'have her'.

I told him that was an agreeable bribe, yet it could not prevail over the reasons I had to refer the affair to justice.

Sometime after, a Highlander came privately to me, and, by my own interpreter, told me he heard I had a quarrel with the laird of— and if that was true, he thought he had lived long enough; but not readily apprehending his intention, I asked the meaning of that dubious expression, and was answered, he would kill him for me if I would encourage it. The proposal really surprised me; but soon recovering myself, I ordered him to be told, that I believed he was a trusty honest man, and if I had occasion for such service, I should employ him before any other, but it was the custom in my country, when two gentlemen had a quarrel, to go into the field and decide it between themselves.

At the interpretation of this last part of my speech, he shook his head and said, 'What a foolish custom is that!'

Perhaps this narration, as well as some others that have preceded, may be thought to consist of too many circumstances, and, consequently to be of an unnecessary length; but I hope there are none that do not, by that means, convey the knowledge of some custom or inclination of the people, which otherwise might have been omitted; besides, I am myself, as you know very well, an enemy to long stories.

Some of the Highland gentlemen are immoderate drinkers of whisky – even three or four quarts at a sitting, and, in general, the people that can pay the purchase, drink it without moderation.

Not long ago, four English officers took a fancy to try their strength in this bow of Ulysses, against the like number of the country champions, but the enemy came off victorious; and one of the officers was thrown into a fit of the gout, without hopes; another had a most dangerous fever, a third lost his skin and hair by the surfeit; and the last confessed to me, that when drunkenness and debate ran high he took several opportunities to sham it.

They say, for excuse, the country requires a great deal; but I think they mistake a habit and custom for necessity. They likewise pretend it does not intoxicate in the hills as it would do in the low country; but this I also doubt, by their own practice; for those among them who have any consideration, will hardly care so much as to refresh themselves with it, when they pass near the tops of the mountains: for, in that circumstance, they say it renders them careless, listless of the fatigue, and inclined to sit down, which might invite to sleep, and then they would be in danger to perish with the cold. I have been tempted to think this spirit has in it, by infusion, the seeds of anger, revenge, and murder (this I confess is a little too poetical); but those who drink of it to any degree of excess behave, for the most part, like true barbarians, I think much beyond the effect of other liquors. The collector of the customs at Stornoway, in the Isle of Lewis, told me, that about one hundred and twenty families drink yearly four thousand English gallons of this spirit and brandy together, although many of them are so poor they cannot afford to pay for much of either, which, you know, must increase the quantity drank by the rest; and that they frequently give to children of six or seven years old as much at a time as an ordinary wine glass would hold.

When they choose to qualify it for punch, they sometimes mix it with water and honey, or with milk and honey; at other times the mixture is only the aqua vitae, sugar, and butter; this they burn till the butter and sugar are dissolved.

The air of the Highlands is pure, and consequently healthy; insomuch that I have known such cures done by it as might be thought next to miracles – I mean in distempers of the lungs, as coughs, consumptions, etc.

And as I have mentioned the honey above, I shall here give that its due commendation; I think, then, it is in every respect as good as that of Minorca, so much esteemed, and both, I suppose, are in a great measure produced from the bloom of the heath; for which reason, too, our Hampshire honey is more valued than any from other parts near London, because that county is mostly covered with heath.

As the Lowlanders call their part of the country the land of cakes, so the natives of the hills say they inhabit a land of milk and honey.

P.S. In the low country the cakes are called cookies; and the several species of them, of which there are many, though not much differing in quality one from another, are dignified and distinguished by the names of the reigning toasts, or the good housewife who was the inventor – as for example, Lady Cullen's cookies, etc.

LETTER XXV

———◆———

Mankind alike—English fox-hunter and Highland laird—Their conversation—Western islands—Drying oats—Grinding—The quarn—Customs
in Argyllshire—Meat boiled in the hide, etc.—The 'guid wife' and her
cookery—Anecdote—A laird in the Western Isles—Honours of a musician
—Punishment of presumption—Martin's *Western Islands*—His account of
second sight—Remarks on that work—A motive explained—Conclusion
of this part of the correspondence—Genius of a people—Pleasure of national
speculations

IN a former letter, I ventured to give it you as my opinion, that
mankind in different countries are naturally the same. I shall now
send you a short sketch of what I have observed in the conversation
of an English fox-hunter and that of a Highland laird, supposing
neither of them to have had a liberal and polite education, or to
have been far out of their own countries.

The first of these characters is, I own, too trite to be given you –
but this by way of comparison:

The squire is proud of his estate and affluence of fortune, loud
and positive over his October, impatient of contradiction, or rather
will give no opportunity for it, but whoops and halloos at every
interval of his own talk, as if the company were to supply the absence
of his hounds.

The particular characters of the pack, the various occurrences in
a chase, where Jowler is the eternal hero, make the constant topic of
his discourse, though, perhaps, none others are interested in it; and

his favourites, the trencher-hounds, if they please, may lie undisturbed upon chairs and counterpanes of silk; and, upon the least cry, though not hurt, his pity is excited more for them than if one of his children had broken a limb; and to that pity his anger succeeds, to the terror of the whole family.

The laird is national, vain of the number of his followers and his absolute command over them. In case of contradiction, he is loud and imperious, and even dangerous, being always attended by those who are bound to support his arbitrary sentiments.

The great antiquity of his family, and the heroic actions of his ancestors, in their conquest of enemy clans, is the inexhaustible theme of his conversation; and, being accustomed to dominion, he imagines himself, in his whisky, to be a sovereign prince; and, as I said before, fancies he may dispose of heads at his pleasure.

Thus one of them places his vanity in his fortune, and his pleasure in his hounds; the other's pride is in his lineage, and his delight is command – both arbitrary in their way; and this the excess of liquor discovers in both; so that what little difference there is between them seems to arise from the accident of their birth; and, if the exchange of countries had been made in their infancy, I make no doubt but each might have had the other's place, as they stand separately described in this letter.

On the contrary, in like manner, as we have many country gentlemen, merely such, of great humanity and agreeable (if not general) conversation; so in the Highlands I have met with some lairds, who surprised me with their good sense and polite behaviour, being so far removed from the more civilized part of the world, and considering the wildness of the country, which one would think was sufficient of itself to give a savage turn to a mind the most humane.

The isles to the north-west and to the north of the mainland (if I may so speak of this our island) may not improperly be called Highlands; for they are mountainous, and the natives speak the language, follow the customs, and wear the habit of the Highlanders.

In some of the western islands (as well as in part of the Highlands), the people never rub out a greater quantity of oats than what is just necessary for seed against the following year; the rest they reserve in the sheaves, for their food; and as they have occasion, set fire to some of them, not only to dry the oats, which, for the most part, are wet, but to burn off the husk. Then, by winnowing, they separate, as well as they can, the sooty part from the grain; but as this cannot be done effectually, the 'bannack', or cake they make of it, is very black. Thus they deprive themselves of the use of straw, leaving none to thatch their huts, make their beds, or feed their cattle in the winter season.

They seldom burn and grind a greater quantity of these oats than serves for a day, except on a Saturday; when some will prepare a double portion, that they may have nothing to do on the Sunday following. This oatmeal is called 'graydon meal'.

For grinding the oats, they have a machine they call a 'quarn'. This is composed of two stones; the undermost is about a foot and a half or two feet diameter. It is round, and five or six inches deep in the hollow, like an earthen pan. Within this they place another stone, pretty equal at the edge to that hollow. This last is flat, like a wooden pot-lid, about three or four inches thick, and in the centre of it is a pretty large round hole, which goes quite through, whereby to convey the oats between the stones: there are also two or three holes in different places, near the extreme part of the surface, that go about half-way through the thickness, which is just deep enough to keep a stick in its place, by which, with the hand, they turn it round and round, till they have finished the operation. But in a wild part of Argyllshire, there was no bread of any kind till the discovery of some lead mines, which brought strangers among the inhabitants, who before fed upon the milk of their cows, goats, and sheep.

In summer they used to shake their milk in a vessel, till it was very frothy, which puffed them up, and satisfied them for the present; and their cheese served them instead of bread. The reason why they had no bread was, that there is hardly any arable land for a great space, all round about that part of the country.

I have been assured, that in some of the islands the meaner sort of people still retain the custom of boiling their beef in the hide; or otherwise (being destitute of vessels of metal or earth) they put water into a block of wood, made hollow by the help of the dirk and burning; and then with pretty large stones heated red-hot, and successively quenched in that vessel, they keep the water boiling till they have dressed their food. It is said, likewise, that they roast a fowl in the embers, with the guts and feathers; and when they think it done enough, they strip off the skin, and then think it fit for the table.

A gentleman of my acquaintance told me, that, in coming from Ireland to the western Highlands, he was reduced, by an ague, to the necessity of landing upon the island Macormach; and, arriving at the public change, he observed three-quarters of a cow to lie in a shallow part of the salt water, and the other quarter hanging up against the end of the hut; that, asking the reason of it, he was told they had no salt: and it was their way of preserving their beef.

Sometime after, the woman of the hut (or the 'guid wife') took a side of a calf that had been taken out of the cow, and, holding it by the legs, waved it backward and forward over the fire till part of it was roasted, as she thought, and then tore off one of the limbs, and offered it to him to eat. A tempting dish, especially for a sick stomach!

It is often said, that some of the lairds of those islands take upon them the state of monarchs; and thence their vassals have a great opinion of their power.

Among other stories told of them, there is one pretty well known in the north of Scotland, but whether true, or feigned as a ridicule upon them, I do not know. For notwithstanding the Lowland Scots complain of the English for ridiculing other nations, yet they themselves have a great number of standing jokes upon the Highlanders.

They say a Spanish ship being stranded upon the coast of Barra (a very small island to the south of Lewis), the chief (McNeil) called a council of his followers, which, I think they say were about fifty in number, in order to determine what was to be done with her; that, in the course of the consultation, one of the members proposed if she was laden with wine and brandy, she should be confiscated as an illicit trader upon the coast, but if she was freighted with other merchandise, they should plunder her as a wreck.

Upon this, one of the council, more cautious than the rest, objected that the King of Spain might resent such treatment of his subjects; but the other replied, 'We have nothing to do with that; McNeil and the King of Spain will adjust that matter between themselves.'

As this is a cold country, the people endeavour to vail themselves of the condition of those who live in a more northern climate.

They tell you that some of the lairds in the islands of Shetland, which are far north of the Orkneys, hire a domestic by the half-year, or by the quarter, just as they can agree, whose business it is to put an instrument in order when the laird has an inclination to play upon it, but if he attempts to play a tune himself, he is sure to be discarded.

Of this they give you an instance in a certain laird, who, observing his servant went farther toward an air than he ought to have done by agreement (perhaps vainly imagining he could play better than his master), he had warning to provide himself with another service against the next Martinmas, which was then about two months to come. And, although the man was not suspended, in the mean time, from the exercise of his function (because he was to be paid for the whole time), yet in all that interval no manner of intercession could prevail with the laird to continue him in his service beyond that quarter – no, notwithstanding his own lady strongly solicited him in behalf of the poor unhappy offender; nor could she obtain so much as a certificate in his favour.

Here you will say, all this must be a riddle; and, indeed, so it is. But your friend Sir Alexander, or any other of your Scots acquaintance, can explain it to you much better over a bottle, or walking in St James's Park, than I can do upon paper. They can likewise give you the title of 'the hireling', which I have forgot; and, when all that is done, I dare venture to say, you will conclude there is no occasion for such an officer in any English family. And, for my own part, I really think there is as little need of him anywhere on this side the Tweed within the compass of the ocean.

We had the other day, in our coffee-room, an auction of books, if such trash, and so small a number of them, may go by that name.

One of them I purchased, which I do not remember to have ever heard of before, although it was published so long ago as the year 1703.

It is a *Description of the Western Islands of Scotland*, and came extremely *à propos*, to prevent my saying anything further concerning them.

I have nothing to object against the author's (Mr Martin's) account of those isles, with respect to their situation, mountains, lakes, rivers, caves, etc. For I confess I never was in any one of them, though I have seen several of them from the mainland. But I must observe, that to furnish out his book with much of the wonderful (a quality necessary to all books of travels, and it would be happy if history were less tainted with it), he recounts a great variety of strange customs used by the natives (if ever in use) in days of yore, with many other wonders; among all which the second sight is the superlative.

This, he says, is a faculty, gift, or misfortune (for he mentions it under those three predicaments), whereby all those who are possessed of it, or by it, see the perfect images of absent objects, either human, brute, vegetable, artificial, etc. And if there be fifty other persons in the same place, those sights are invisible to them all: nor even are they seen by any one who has himself, at other times, the second sight, unless the person who has the faculty, at that instant, should touch him with design to communicate it to him.

It is not peculiar to adult persons, but is sometimes given to young children. Women have this supernatural sight, and even horses and cows. It is pity he does not tell us how those two kinds of cattle distinguish between natural and preternatural appearances, so as to be fearless of the one and affrighted at the other, though seemingly the same; and how all this came to be known.

Upon this subject he employs six and thirty pages, i.e., a small part of them in recounting what kind of appearances forebode death, which of them are presages of marriage, etc., as though it were a settled system.

The remaining leaves are taken up in examples of such prophetic apparitions and the certainty of their events.

But I shall trouble you no further with so contemptible a subject; or myself with pointing out the marks of imposture, except to add one remark, which is, that this ridiculous notion has almost excluded another, altogether as weak and frivolous; for he mentions only two or three slight suspicions of witchcraft, but not one fact of that nature throughout his whole book. Yet both this and second sight are sprung from one and the same stock, which I suppose to be very ancient, as they are children of Credulity, who was begotten by Superstition, who was the offspring of Craft – but you must make out the next ancestor yourself, for his name is torn off from the pedigree, but I believe he was the founder of the family.

In looking upwards to what I have been writing, I have paused awhile to consider what it was that could induce me to detain you so long about this trifling matter; and at last I have resolved it into a love of truth, which is naturally communicative, and makes it painful to conceal the impositions of falsehood. But these islands are so remote and unfrequented, they are a very proper subject for invention; and few, I think, would have the curiosity to visit them, in order to disprove any account of them, however romantic.

I can make no other apology for the length of this detail, because I might have gone a much shorter way, by only mentioning the book, and hinting its character; and so leaving it to your choice, whether to take notice of it or reject it.

This letter will bring you the conclusion of our correspondence, so far as it relates to this part of our island; yet if anything should happen hereafter that may be thought qualified to go upon its travels five hundred miles southward, it will be a pleasure to me to give it the necessary despatch.

I have called it 'correspondence', from the remarks I have received from you upon such passages in my letters as gave you the occasion: and I wish my subject would have enabled me to give you opportunities to increase their number.

Writers, you know, for the most part, have not been contented with anything less than the characters and actions of those whom birth or fortune had set up to public view, or the policy or weakness of public councils; the order and event of battles, sieges, and such like, in great measure dressed up in habits cut out by themselves; but the genius of a people has been thought beneath their notice.

This, forsooth, is called supporting the dignity of history. Now, in this case, who shall condescend to give a detail of circumstances generally esteemed to be low, and therefore of little consequence, and at the same time escape the character of a trifler?

But I am unwarily fallen into an apology to you, and not as if I was writing *en confidence* to a friend, but openly to the whole kingdom.

For my own part (who have already lived too long to be dazzled with glittering appearances), I should be as well pleased to see a shepherd of Arcadia, free from poetical fiction, in his rustic behaviour and little economy, or a burgher of ancient Rome in his shop, as to know the character of a consul; for, in either case, it is the comparison of past ages, and foreign countries opposed to our own, that excites my curiosity and gives me satisfaction.

As we are now about to settle our accounts to this time, I shall acknowledge (as every honest man would do) the value of an article which, it is likely, you make little account of, as the Indians are said to have done of their gold when they gave it away for baubles – and that is, the agreeable amusement you have furnished me with, from time to time, concerning such passages as could not, for good reasons, be admitted to the public papers. This to one almost excluded the world may, in some measure, be said to restore him to his native home.

Upon the whole, when all the articles in your favour are brought to account, I think the balance will be on your side; and yet I make no doubt you would cheerfully go on to increase the debt, though I should become a bankrupt, and there did not remain to you the least expectation of payment from, etc.

LETTER XXVI

Concerning the New Roads, etc., 173—

M. Fontenelle—Apology—New roads begun, 1726—Situation on the map
—Roman works—Glenalmond—Ancient funeral pile—Urn claimed by
the Highlanders—Superstition respecting a dead body—Number of
soldiers employed—Their wages—Officers—Breadth of roads—Their
singular appearance—Stony moors—Repetitions excused—Large stones are
set up—Excellence of the roads—Bogs—An adventure in passing—Mosses—
Fords—Declivities—Their roughness—Woods—Steep ascents—Coriarack
Mountain—Road over—Precipices—Frequency of snow—Moray Firth—
A comparison—Loch Ness—Rocks—Highland galley—Loch Oich—Loch
Lochy—Proposed communication—Garrisons—Breaking up rocks—
Anecdote—New houses erected on roads—Pillars—Bridges—Inscription—
Objection to the roads—By the chiefs—By the middling order—Of the
lowest class—Lochart's accusation—Fort Augustus—A proposal—Its
origin—Injustice—Highlands not suited for manufactories—Not inviting—
Healthy air—Its effects on an officer—Mountebank—Rain nine or ten
weeks—Troublesome kind of small fly—Retrospect—Comparisons—
Apology for Latin—Conclusion

IT is now about eight years since I sent you the conclusion of my
rambling account of the Highlands; and, perhaps, you would
not have complained if, in this long interval, you had been perfectly
free of so barren a subject.

Monsieur Fontenelle, I remember, in one of his pastoral dialogues,
makes a shepherd object to another, *'Quoi! Toujours de l' amour?'*
And I think you may as well ask, 'What! Always Highlands?' But in

my situation, without them, I should be in the sorrowful condition of an old woman in her country cottage, by a winter fire, and nobody would hearken to her tales of witches and spirits – that is, to have little or nothing to say. But now I am a perfect volunteer, and cannot plead my former excuses, and really am without any apprehensions of being thought officious in giving you some account of the roads, which, within these few weeks, have been completely finished.

These new roads were begun in the year 1726, and have continued about eleven years in the prosecution; yet, long as it may be thought, if you were to pass over the whole work (for the borders of it would show you what it was), I make no doubt but that number of years would diminish in your imagination to a much shorter tract of time, by comparison with the difficulties that attended the execution.

But, before I proceed to any particular descriptions of them, I shall inform you how they lie, to the end that you may trace them out upon a map of Scotland; and first I shall take them as they are made, to enter the mountains, viz.

One of them begins from Crieff, which is about fourteen miles from Stirling: here the Romans left off their works, of which some parts are visible to this day, particularly the camp at Ardoch, where the vestiges of the fortifications are on a moor so barren, that its whole farm has been safe from culture, or other alteration besides weather and time.

The other road enters the hills at Dimheld, in Atholl, which is about ten miles from Perth.

The first of them, according to my account, though the last in execution, proceeds through Glenalmond (which, for its narrowness, and the height of the mountains, I remember to have mentioned formerly), and thence it goes to Aberfeldy; there it crosses the River Tay by a bridge of freestone, consisting of five spacious arches (by the way, this military bridge is the only passage over that wild and dangerous river), and from thence the road goes on to Dalnachardoch.

The other road from Dunkeld proceeds by the Blairatholl to the said Dalnachardoch.

Here the two roads join in one, and, as a single road, it leads on to Dalwhinny, where it branches out again into two; of which one proceeds towards the north-west, through Garva Moor, and over the Coriarach Mountain to Fort Augustus, at Killichumen, and the other branch goes due north to the barrack of Ruthven, in Badenoch, and thence, by Delmagary, to Inverness. From thence it proceeds something to the southward of the west, across the island, to the aforesaid Fort Augustus, and so on to Fort William, in Lochaber.

The length of all these roads put together is about two hundred and fifty miles.

I have so lately mentioned Glenalmond, in the road from Crieff, northward, that I cannot forbear a digression, though at my first setting out, in relation to a piece of antiquity which happened to be discovered in that vale not many hours before I passed through it in one of my journeys southward.

A small part of the way through this glen having been marked out by two rows of camp colours, placed at a good distance one from another, whereby to describe the line of the intended breadth and regularity of the road by the eye, there happened to lie directly in the way an exceedingly large stone, and, as it had been made a rule from the beginning, to carry on the roads in straight lines, as far as the way would permit, not only to give them a better air, but to shorten the passenger's journey, it was resolved the stone should be removed, if possible, though otherwise the work might have been carried along on either side of it.

The soldiers, by vast labour, with their levers and jacks, or hand-screws, tumbled it over and over till they got it quite out of the way, although it was of such an enormous size that it might be matter of great wonder how it could ever be removed by human strength and art, especially to such who had never seen an operation of that kind: and, upon their digging a little way into that part of the ground where the centre of the base had stood, there was found a small cavity, about two feet square, which was guarded from the outward earth at the bottom, top, and sides, by square flat stones.

This hollow contained some ashes, scraps of bones, and half-burnt ends of stalks of heath; which last we concluded to be a small remnant of a funeral pile. Upon the whole, I think there is no room to doubt but it was the urn of some considerable Roman officer, and the best of the kind that could be provided in their military circumstances;

and that it was so seems plainly to appear from its vicinity to the Roman camp, the engines that must have been employed to remove that vast piece of rock, and the unlikeliness it should, or could, have ever been done by the natives of the country. But certainly the design was to preserve those remains from the injuries of rains and melting snows, and to prevent their being profaned by the sacrilegious hands of those they call Barbarians, for that reproachful name, you know, they gave to the people of almost all nations but their own.

Give me leave to finish this digression, which is grown already longer than I foresaw or intended.

As I returned the same way from the Lowlands, I found the officer, with his party of working soldiers, not far from the stone, and asked him what was become of the urn?

To this he answered, that he had intended to preserve it in the condition I left it, till the commander-in-chief had seen it, as a curiosity, but that it was not in his power so to do; for soon after the discovery was known to the Highlanders, they assembled from distant parts, and having formed themselves into a body, they carefully gathered up the relics, and marched with them, in solemn procession, to a new place of burial, and there discharged their firearms over the grave, as supposing the deceased had been a military officer.

You will believe the recital of all this ceremony led me to ask the reason of such homage done to the ashes of a person supposed to have been dead almost two thousand years. I did so; and the officer, who was himself a native of the hills, told me that they (the Highlanders) firmly believe that if a dead body should be known to lie above ground, or be disinterred by malice or the accidents of torrents of water, etc., and care was not immediately taken to perform to it the proper rites, then there would arise such storms and tempests as would destroy their corn, blow away their huts, and all sorts of other misfortunes would follow till that duty was performed. You may here recollect what I told you so long ago, of the great regard the Highlanders have for the remains of their dead; but this notion is entirely Roman.

But to return to my main purpose. In the summer seasons, five hundred of the soldiers from the barracks, and other quarters about the Highlands, were employed in those works in different stations, by detachments from the regiments and Highland companies.

The private men were allowed six pence a day, over and above their pay as soldiers: a corporal had eight pence, and a sergeant a shilling; but this extra pay was only for working days, which were often interrupted by violent storms of wind and rain, from the heights and hollows of the mountains.

These parties of men were under the command and direction of proper officers, who were all subalterns and received two shillings and six pence per diem, to defray their extraordinary expense in building huts: making necessary provision for their tables from distant parts; unavoidable though unwelcome visits, and other incidents arising from their wild situation.

I should have told you before, that the noncommissioned officers were constant and immediate overseers of the works.

The standard breadth of these roads, as laid down at the first projection, is sixteen feet; but in some parts, where there were no very expensive difficulties, they are wider.

In those places (as I have said before), they are carried on in straight lines till some great necessity has turned them out of the way; the rest, which run along upon the declivities of hills, you know, must have their circuits, risings, and descents accordingly.

To stop and take a general view of the hills before you from an eminence, in some part where the eye penetrates far within the void spaces, the roads would appear to you in a kind of whimsical disorder; and as those parts of them that appear to you are of a very different colour from the heath that chiefly clothes the country, they may, by that contrast, be traced out to a considerable distance.

Now, let us suppose that where you are, the road is visible to you for a short space, and is then broken off to the right by a hollow or winding among the hills; beyond that interruption, the eye catches a small part on the side of another hill, and some again on the ridge of it; in another place, further off, the road appears to run zigzag, in angles, up a steep declivity; in one place, a short horizontal line shows itself below, in another, the marks of the road seem to be almost even with the clouds, etc.

It may be objected, how can you see any part of the flat roof of a building, when you are below? The question would be just; but the edges of the roads on a precipice, and the broken parts of the face of the mountain behind, that has been wrought into to make room for the road – these appear, and discover to them who are below the line of which I have been speaking.

Thus the eye catches one part of the road here, another there, in different lengths and positions; and, according to their distance, they are diminished and rendered fainter and fainter, by the lineal and aerial perspective, till they are entirely lost to sight. And I need not tell you, that, as you pursue your progress, the scene changes to new appearances.

The old ways (for roads I shall not call them) consisted chiefly of stony moors, bogs, rugged, rapid fords, declivity of hills, entangling woods, and giddy precipices. You will say this is a dreadful catalogue to be read to him that is about to take a Highland journey.

I have not mentioned the valleys, for they are few in number, far divided asunder, and generally the roads through them were easily made.

My purpose now is to give you some account of the nature of the perpendicular parts above-mentioned, and the manner how this extraordinary work has been executed; and this I shall do in the order I have ranged them as above.

And first, the stony moors. These are mostly tracts of ground of several miles in length, and often very high, with frequent lesser risings and descents, and having for surface a mixture of stones and heath. The stones are fixed in the earth, being very large and unequal and generally are as deep in the ground as they appear above it; and where there are any spaces between the stones, there is a loose spongy sward, perhaps not above five or six inches deep, and incapable to produce anything but heath, and all beneath it is hard gravel or rock.

I now begin to be apprehensive of your memory, lest it should point out some repetitions of descriptions contained in my former letters; but I have been thus particular, because I know the extent of your journeys, and that with you a morass is called a moor; yet hills that are something of this nature are called moors in the north of England.

Here the workmen first made room to fix their instruments, and then, by strength, and the help of those two mechanic powers, the screw and the lever, they raised out of their ancient beds those massive bodies, and then filling up the cavities with gravel, set them up, mostly endways, along the sides of the road, as directions in time of deep snows, being some of them, as they now stand, eight or nine feet high. They serve, likewise, as memorials of the skill and labour requisite to the performance of so difficult a work.

In some particular spots, where there was a proper space beside the stones, the workmen dug hollows, and, by undermining, dropped them in, where they lie buried so securely, as never more to retard the traveller's journey; but it was thought a moot point, even where it was successful, whether any time or labour was saved by this practice; for those pits, for the most part, required to be made very deep and wide, and it could not be foreseen, without continual boring, whether there might not be rock above the necessary depth, which might be a disappointment after great labour.

The roads on these moors are now as smooth as Constitution Hill, and I have galloped on some of them for miles together in great tranquillity; which was heightened by reflection on my former fatigue, when, for a great part of the way, I had been obliged to quit my horse, it being too dangerous or impracticable to ride, and even hazardous to pass on foot.

The Bogs

There are two species of them, viz. bogs, and those the natives call peat mosses, which yield them their firing; many of the former are very large, and sometimes fill up the whole space between the feet of the mountains. They are mostly not much, if anything, above the level of the sea; but I do not know that any part of the road is carried through them, or think it practicable; yet, as any description of them may be new to you, I shall stop awhile to give you some account of my trotting one of them, which is reckoned about a mile over.

My affairs engaging me to reside for some time among the hills, I resolved and was preparing to make a distant visit; but was told that a hill at the foot of which I lived, was, in the descent from it, exceeding steep and stony; I was therefore prevailed with to have my horses led a roundabout way, and to meet me on the other side.

In lieu of that difficult way, I was to be ferried over a lake, and to traverse the bog above-mentioned, over which a Highlander undertook to conduct me; him I followed close at the heels, because I soon observed he used a step unlike to what he did upon firm ground, and which I could not presently imitate; and also that he chose his way, here and there, as if he knew where was the least danger, although, at the same time, the surface of the part we were going over, seemed to me to be equally indifferent in respect to safety and danger.

Our weight and the spring of motion, in many parts, caused a shaking all round about us, and the compression made the water rise through the sward, which was, in some parts, a kind of short flaggy grass, and in others a sort of mossy heath; but wherever any bushes grew, I knew, by experience of the peat-mosses I had gone over before, that it was not far to the bottom.

This rising of water made me conclude (for my guide was not intelligible to me) that we had nothing but a liquid under us, or, at most, something like a quicksand, and that the sward was only a little toughened by the entwining of the roots, and was supported, like ice, only by water, or something nearly as fluid.

I shall give you no particulars of my visit, further than that the laird treated me in a very handsome and plentiful manner, and, indeed it was his interest so to do; but poor 'Poke Pudding' was so fatigued, and so apprehensive of danger on the bog, that he could not be persuaded to go back again the same way.

The Mosses

Of these I formerly gave you some superficial account; but now that I am about to let you know how the roads were made through them, I shall examine them to the bottom. When I first saw them, I imagined they were formerly made when woods were common in the hills; but since, by several repeated laws, destroyed, to take away that shelter which assisted the Highlanders in their depredations – I say, I have supposed the leaves of trees were driven by winds and lodged in their passage, from time to time, in those cavities till they were filled up. One thing, among others, that induced me to this belief is, that the muddy substance of them is much like the rotted leaves in our woods; but, since that time, l have been told, that, when one of them has been quite exhausted for fuel, it has grown again, and in the course of twenty years, has been as fit to be dug for firing as before. This I can believe, because I have seen many small ones, far from any inhabitants, swelled above the surface of the ground that lies all round about them, and chiefly in the middle, so as to become a protuberance, and therefore by strangers the less suspected, though the deeper and more dangerous.

All beneath the turf is a spongy earth interwoven with a slender, fibrous vegetable, something like the smallest roots of a shrub, and these a little toughen it, and contribute to the making it good fuel; but, when they are quite, or near dug out, the pit is generally almost filled with water. This, I suppose, arises from springs, which may, for aught I know, have been the first occasion of these mosses, which are very deceitful, especially to those who are not accustomed to them, being mostly covered with heath, like the rest of the country, and, in time of rains, become soft, and sometimes impassable on foot.

Now that I have no further occasion for any distinction, I shall call every soft place a bog, except there be occasion sometimes to vary the phrase.

When one of these bogs has crossed the way on a stony moor, there the loose ground has been dug out down to the gravel, or rock, and the hollow filled up in the manner following, viz.

First with a layer of large stones, then a smaller size, to fill up the gaps and raise the causeway higher; and, lastly, two, three, or more feet of gravel, to fill up the interstices of the small stones, and form a smooth and binding surface. This part of the road has a bank on each side, to separate it from a ditch, which is made withoutside to receive the water from the bog, and, if the ground will allow it, to convey it by a trench to a slope, and thereby in some measure drain it.

In a rocky way, where no loose stones were to be found, if a bog intervened, and trees could be had at any portable distance, the road has been made solid by timber and fascines, crowned with gravel, dug out of the side of some hill.

This is durable; for the faggots and trees, lying continually in the moisture of the bog, will, instead of decaying, become extremely hard, as has been observed of trees that have been plunged into those sloughs, and lain there, in all probability, for many ages. This causeway has likewise a bank and a ditch for the purpose above-mentioned.

There is one bog I passed through (literally speaking), which is upon the declivity of a hill; there the mud has been dug away for a proper space, and thrown upon the bog on either side and a passage made at the foot of a hill for the water to run down into a large cavity, insomuch, that, by continual draining, I rode, as it were, in a very shallow rivulet running down the hill upon a rock (which was made smooth by the workmen), with the sides of the bog high above me on both sides, like one of the hollow ways in England.

I must desire you will consider, that the foregoing descriptions, as well as these that are to follow, are, and will be, only specimens of the work; for it would be almost without end to give you all the particulars of so various and extensive a performance.

Fords

No remedy but bridges has been found for the inconveniences and hazards of these rugged and rapid passages; for, when some of them, in the beginning, were cleared from the large, loose stones, the next inundation brought down others in their room, which else would have been stopped by the way, and some of those were of a much larger size than the stones that had been removed.

This was the case (among others) of a small river which, however, was exceedingly dangerous to ford, and for that reason the first bridge was ordered to be built over it; but it gave me a lively idea how short is human foresight, especially in new projects and untried under-takings.

The spring of the arch was founded upon rocks, and it was elevated much above the highest water that had ever been known by the country people; yet, some time after it was finished, there happened a sudden torrent from the mountains, which brought down trees and pieces of rocks; and, by its being placed too near the issue of water from between two hills, though firmly built with stone, it was cropped off, not far beneath the crown of the arch, as if it had neither weight nor solidity.

Declivities

By these I mean the sloping sides of the hills whereon the new roads are made.

The former ways along those slopes were only paths worn by the feet of the Highlanders and their little garrons. They ran along upwards and downwards, one above another, in such a manner as was found most convenient at the first tracing them out: this, I think, I have observed to you formerly.

To these narrow paths the passenger was confined (for there is seldom any choice of the way you would take in the Highlands) by the impassability of the hollows at the feet of the mountains; because those spaces, in some parts, are filled up with deep bogs, or fallen rocks, of which last I have seen many as big as a middling house; and, looking up, have observed others, at an exceeding height, in some measure parted from the main rock, and threatening the crush of some of those below. In other parts there are lakes beneath, and sometimes, where there are none, it was only by these paths you could ascend the hills, still proceeding round the sides of them from one to another.

There the new roads have been carried on in more regular curves than the old paths, and are dug into the hills, which are sloped away above them; and where any rocks have occurred in the performance, they have been bored and blown away with gunpowder.

Above the road are trenches made to receive rains, melting snows, and springs, which last are in many places continually issuing out of the sides of the hills, being draining away from large waters collected in lakes, and other cavities, above in the mountains.

From the above-mentioned trenches are proper channels made to convey the water down the hills; these are secured, by firm pavement, from being gulled by the stream: and in places that required it, there are stone walls built behind the road to prevent the fall of earth or stones from the broken part of the declivity.

Woods

These are not only rare in the way of the new roads, but I have formerly given you some description of the inconvenience and danger of one of them, and therefore I shall only add, in this place, that the trees, for the necessary space, have been cut down and grubbed up; their fibrous roots, that ran about upon the surface, destroyed; the boggy part removed; the rock smoothed, and the crannies firmly filled up; and all this in such manner as to make of it a very commodious road.

Steep Ascents

As the heights, for the most part, are attained, as I have been saying, by going round the sides of the hills from one to another, the exceeding steep ascents are not very common in the ordinary passages; but where they are, the inconvenience and difficulties of them have been removed.

I shall only instance in one, which, indeed, is confessed to be the worst of them all. This is the Coriarack mountain, before mentioned, which rises in the way that leads from Dalwhinny to Fort Augustus. It is above a quarter of a mile of perpendicular height, and was passed by few besides the soldiery when the garrisons were changed, as being the nearest way from one of the barracks to another; and had it not been for the conveniency of that communication, this part of the new roads had never been thought of.

This mountain is so near the perpendicular in some parts, that it was doubtful whether the passenger, after great labour, should get upwards, or return much quicker, than he advanced.

The road over it, not to mention much roughness (which I believe, you have had enough of by this time, and are likely to have more), is carried on upon the south declivity of the hill, by seventeen traverses, like the course of a ship when she is turning to windward, by angles still advancing higher and higher; yet little of it is to be seen below, by reason of flats, hollows, and windings that intercept the sight; and nothing could give you a general view of it, unless one could be supposed to be placed high above the mountain in the air. This is much unlike your hills in the south, that, in some convenient situation of the eye, are seen in one continued smooth slope from the bottom to the top.

Each of the above-mentioned angles is about seventy or eighty yards in length, except in a few places where the hill would not admit of all that extent.

These traverses upward, and the turnings of their extremities, are supported on the outside of the road by stone walls, from ten to fifteen feet in height.

Thus that steep ascent, which was so difficult to be attained, even by the foot passenger, is rendered everywhere more easy for wheel-carriages than Highgate Hill.

On the north side of this mountain, at a place named Snugburgh from its situation, there is a narrow pass between two exceeding high and steep hills. These are joined together by two arches, supported by walls, to take off the sharpness of the short descent, which otherwise could not have been practicable for the lightest wheel-carriage whatever, for it was difficult even for horse or man.

Precipices

I shall say nothing in this place of such of them as are anything tolerable to the mind, in passing them over, though a false step might render them fatal, as there would be no stopping till dashed against the rocks. I shall only mention two that are the most terrible, which I have gone over several times, but always occasionally, not as the shortest way, or by choice, but to avoid extensive bogs, or swelling waters in time of rain, which I thought more dangerous in the other way.

One of these precipices is on the north side of the Moray Firth, where no roads have been made; the other is on a mountain south-ward of this town.

Both these, as I have said above, were useful upon occasion; but the latter is now rendered unnecessary, as the old roundabout way is made smooth, and bridges built over the dangerous waters, and therefore nothing has been done to this precipice; nor, indeed, was it thought practicable to widen the path, by reason of the steepness of the side of the hill that rises above it.

I think the ordinary proverb was never more manifestly verified than it now is, in these two several ways: viz. that 'the farthest way about', etc. Yet, I make no doubt, the generality of the Highlanders will prefer the precipice to the gravel of the road and a greater number of steps.

Not far from this steep place I once baited my horses with oats, carried with me, and laid upon the snow in the month of July; and, indeed, it is there (instead of rain) snow or sleet all the year round.

Thus far I have, chiefly in general terms, described the difficulties that attended the making new roads, and the methods taken to surmount them, which was all I at first intended; but as some of the greatest obstacles, which yet remain undescribed, were met with in the way between this town and Fort William, I shall, previous to any account of them, endeavour to give you some idea of this passage between the mountains, wherein lies no small part of the roads; and this I shall the rather do, because that hollow, for length and figure, is unlike anything of the kind I have seen in other parts of the Highlands; and I hope to accomplish all I have to say of it before I leave this town, being very shortly to make a northern progress among the hills, wherein I shall find none of those conveniences we now have on this side of the Moray Firth.

This opening would be a surprising prospect to such as never have seen a high country, being a mixture of mountains, waters, heath, rocks, precipices, and scattered trees; and that for so long an extent, in which the eye is confined within the space, and, therefore, if I should pretend to give you a full idea of it, I should put myself in the place of one that has had a strange preposterous dream, and, because it has made a strong impression on him, he fondly thinks he can convey it to others in the same likeness as it remains painted on his memory; and, in the end, wonders at the coldness with which it was received.

This chasm begins about four miles west of Inverness, and, running across the island, divides the northern from the southern Highlands.

It is chiefly taken up by lakes, bounded on both sides by high mountains, which almost everywhere (being very steep at the feet) run down exceedingly deep into the water. The first of the lakes, beginning from the east, is Loch Ness, which I have formerly mentioned. It lies in a line along the middle of it, as direct as an artificial canal. This I have observed myself, from a rising ground at the east end, by directing a small telescope to Fort Augustus, at the other extreme.

I have said it is straight by the middle only, because the sides are irregular, being so made by the jutting of the feet of the hills into the water on either side, as well as by the spaces between them; and the various breadths of different parts of the lake.

The depth, the nature of the water, and the remarkable cataracts on the south side, have been occasionally mentioned in former letters; and I think I have told you, it is one-and-twenty Scots miles in length, and from one to near two miles in breadth.

It has hardly any perceptible current, not withstanding it receives a vast conflux of waters from the bordering mountains, by rivers and rivulets that discharge themselves into it. Yet all the water that visibly runs from it in the greatest rains, is limited in its course by the River Ness by which it has its issue into the sea, and that river is not, in some places, above twenty yards wide; and therefore I think the greatest part of the superfluity must be drained away by subterraneous passages.

I have told you long ago, that it never freezes in the calmest and severest frost, and by its depth (being in some parts 360 yards), and by its breadth, and the violent winds that pass through the opening, it often has a swell not much inferior to the ocean.

In several parts on the sides of the lake, you see rocks of a kind of coarse black marble, and I think as hard as the best; these rise to a considerable height, which never, till lately, were trod by human foot; for the old way made a considerable circuit from this lake, and did not come to it but at the west end. In other places are woods upon the steep declivities, which serve to abate the deformity of those parts – I say abate, for the trees being, as I said above, confusedly scattered one above another, they do not hide them. All the rest is heath and rock.

Some time ago there was a vessel, of about five-and-twenty or thirty tons burden, built at the east end of this lake, and called the *Highland Galley*.

She carries six or eight pattereroes, and is employed to transport men, provision, and baggage to Fort Augustus, at the other end of the lake.

The master has an appointment from the government, to navigate this vessel, and to keep her in repair.

When she made her first trip she was mightily adorned with colours, and fired her guns several times, which was a strange sight to the Highlanders, who had never seen the like before – at least, on that inland lake.

For my own part, I was not less amused with the sight of a good number of Highland men and women upon the highest part of a mountain over-against us – I mean the highest that appeared to our view.

These people, I suppose, were brought to the precipice, from some flat behind, by the report of the guns (for even a single voice is understood at an incredible height); and, as they stood, they appeared to the naked eye not to be a foot high in stature; but, by the assistance of a pretty long glass, I could plainly see their surprise and admiration. And I must confess I wondered not much less to see so many people on such a monstrous height, who could not inhabit there in winter, till I reflected it was the time of the year for them to go up to their sheelings. And I was told that they, like us, were not far from a spacious lake, though in that elevated situation.

I need not trouble you with a description of the other two waters and their boundaries, there being but little difference between them and the former; only here the old ways, such as they were, ran along upon the sides of the hills, which were in a great measure rocky precipices, and that these lakes are not quite so wide, and incline a little more to the southward of the west than the other.

The next lake to Loch Ness (which, as I have said is twenty-one miles in length) is Loch Oich; this is four miles long; and Loch Lochy, the last of the three, is nine, in all thirty-four miles, part of the forty-eight, which is the whole length of the opening, and at the end thereof is Fort William, on the west coast, to which the sea flows, as it does likewise to Inverness on the east. Thus the whole extent of ground, between sea and sea, is fourteen miles

Here I must stop a little to acquaint you with a spot of ground which I take to be something remarkable. This I had passed over several times without observing anything extraordinary in it, and, perhaps, should never have taken notice of it, if it had not been pointed out to me by one of the natives.

About the middle of the neck of land that divides the Lakes Oich and Lochy (which is but one mile), not far from the centre or the opening, there descends from the hills, on the south side, a burn, or rivulet, which, as it falls upon the plain, divides into two streams without any visible ridge to part them; and one of them runs through the Lakes Oich and Ness into the east sea, and the other takes the quite contrary course, and passes through Loch Lochy into the western ocean

This, and the short space of land above-mentioned, have given birth to several projects for making a navigable communication across the island, not only to divide effectually the Highlands by the middle, but to save the tedious, costly, and hazardous voyages through St George's Channel, or otherwise round by the isles of Orkney.

This spot, the projectors say, is a level between the two seas, pointed out as it were by the hand of nature, and they pretend the space of land to be cut through is practicable.

But it would be an incredible expense to cut fourteen navigable miles in so rocky a country, and there is yet a stronger objection, which is, that the whole opening lies in so direct a line, and the mountains that bound it are so high, the wind is confined in its passage, as it were, in the nozzle of a pair of bellows; so that, let it blow from what quarter it will without the opening, it never varies much from east or west within.

This would render the navigation so precarious that hardly anybody would venture on it, not to mention the violent flurries of wind that rush upon the lakes by squalls from the spaces between the hills, and also the rocky shores, want of harbour and anchorage; and, perhaps, there might appear other unforeseen inconveniences and dangers, if it were possible the work could be completed.

There are three garrisons in this line, which reaches from east to west, viz. Fort George, at Inverness, Fort Augustus, at Killichumen, and Fort William, in Lochaber, and every one of them pretty equally distant from one another; and the line might be made yet more effectual by redoubts, at proper distances between them, to prevent the sudden joining of numbers ill affected to the government.

Having given you some account of this chasm, I shall, in the next place, say something of the road that lies quite through it, together with some difficulties that attended the work, of which all that part which runs along near the edges of the lakes is on the south side; but, as I have already bestowed so many words upon subjects partly like this, I shall confine myself to very few particulars; and of the rest, which may come under those former descriptions, I need say no more, if I have been intelligible.

I shall begin with that road which goes along above Loch Ness.

This is entirely new, as I have hinted before; and, indeed, I might say the same of every part; but I mean there was no way at all along the edge of this lake till this part of the road was made.

It is, good part of it, made out of rocks; but, among them all, I shall mention but one, which is of a great strength, and, as I have said before, as hard as marble.

There the miners hung by ropes from the precipice over the water (like Shakespeare's gatherers of samphire from Dover Cliffs) to bore the stone, in order to blow away a necessary part from the face of it, and the rest likewise was chiefly done by gunpowder; but, when any part was fit to be left as it was, being flat and smooth, it was brought to a roughness proper for a stay to the feet; and, in this part, and all the rest of the road, where the precipices were like to give horror or uneasiness to such as might pass over them in carriages, though at a good distance from them, they are secured to the lakeside by walls, either left in the working, or built up with stone, to a height proportioned to the occasion.

Now, for the space of twelve miles, it is an even terrace in every part, from whence the lake may be seen from end to end, and from whence the romantic prospect of the rugged mountains would, I dare say, for its novelty, be more entertaining to you than it is to me – I say, it might be agreeable to you, who, not having these hideous productions of nature near you, wantonly procure even bad imitations of them, in little artificial rocks and diminutive cataracts of water. But as some painters travel to Italy, in order to study or copy the most admirable performances of the great masters, for their own instruction, so I would advise your artisans, in that way, to visit this country for their better information.

The next part of this road which I am about to speak of, is that which lies along the side of the hills, arising from the edge of Loch Oich.

The dangers of this part of the old way began at the top of a steep ascent, of about fifty or sixty yards from the little plain that parts this lake and Loch Ness; and, not far from the summit, is a part they call The Maidens Leap, of which they tell a strange romantic story, not worth the remembrance. There the rocks project over the lake, and the path was so rugged and narrow that the Highlanders were obliged, for their safety, to hold by the rocks and shrubs as they passed, with the prospect of death beneath them.

This was not the only dangerous part, but for three miles together, part of the four (which I have said is the length of this lake), it was nowhere safe, and in many places more difficult, and as dangerous, as at the entrance; for the rocks were so steep and uneven, that the passenger was obliged to creep on his hands and knees.

These precipices were so formidable to some that they chose rather to cross the plain above-mentioned, and wade a river on the opposite side of the opening, which by others was thought more hazardous in its kind than the way which their fear excited them to avoid; and when they had passed that water, they had a wide circuit to make among steep and rugged hills, before they could get again into the way they were to go.

The last part of the road along the lakes (as I have divided it into three) runs along on the declivities of Loch Lochy, and reaches the whole length of that lake, which, as I have said before, is nine miles.

This was much of the same nature as the last, exceeding steep, with rocks in several places hanging over the water, and required a great quantity of gunpowder; but, both this and the other two are now as commodious as any other of the roads in the Highlands, which everywhere (bating ups and downs) are equal in goodness to the best in England.

I shall say nothing of the way from the end of this lake to Fort William, any more than I have done of the road from Inverness to Loch Ness, or the spaces between the lakes, because they may be comprehended in the ordinary difficulties already described.

But I might acquaint you with many other obstacles which were thought, at first, to be insurmountable; such as Slock Moach, between Ruthven and Inverness, the rocky pass of Killiekrankie, in Atholl, between Dunkeld and the Blair, etc.

I shall only say, that I have formerly given you some description of the first, but without a name, in the account of an incursion I made to the hills from Inverness; but, both this and the other, which were very bad, are now made easily passable.

The name of Slock Moach is interpreted by the natives, 'a den of hogs', having been, as they say it was formerly, a noted harbour for thieves; who, in numbers, lay in wait within that narrow and deep cavity, to commit their depredations upon cattle and passengers. I suppose this name was given to it when swine were held in abomination among the Highlanders.

The first design of removing a vast fallen piece of a rock was entertained by the country people with great derision, of which I saw one instance myself.

A very old wrinkled Highland woman, upon such an occasion, standing over-against me, when the soldiers were fixing their engines, seemed to sneer at it, and said something to an officer of one of the Highland companies. I imagined she was making a jest of the undertaking, and asked the officer what she said. 'I will tell you her words,' said he:

'What are the fools a-doing? That stone will lie there for ever, for all them.' But when she saw that vast bulk begin to rise, though by slow degrees, she set up a hideous Irish yell, took to her heels, ran up the side of a hill just by, like a young girl, and never looked behind her while she was within our sight. I make no doubt she thought it was magic, and the workmen warlocks.

This, indeed, was the effect of an old woman's ignorance end superstition; but a gentleman, esteemed for his good understanding, when he had seen the experiment of the first rock above Loch Ness, said to the officer that directed the work, 'When first I heard of this undertaking, I was strangely scandalised to think how shamefully you would come off; but now I am convinced there is nothing can stand before you and gunpowder.'

Notwithstanding there may be no remains of my former letters, I believe your memory may help you to reflect what wretched lodging there was in the Highlands when those epistles were written. This evil is now remedied, as far as could be done; and in that road, where there were none but huts of turf for a hundred miles together, there now are houses with chimneys, built with stone and lime, and ten or twelve miles distance one from another; and though they are not large, yet are they well enough adapted to the occasion of travellers, who are seldom many at a time in that country. But I would not be understood that there is any better accommodation than before, besides warm lodging. Another thing is, there are pillars set up at the end of every five miles, mostly upon eminences, which may not only amuse the passenger and lessen the tediousness of the way, but prevent his being deceived in point of time, in rain, snow, drift, or approaching night.

But the last, and I think, the greatest conveniency, is the bridges, which prevent the dangers of the terrible fords.

Of these I shall say but little, because to you they are no novelty. They are forty in number; some of them single arches, of forty or fifty feet diameter, mostly founded upon rocks; others are composed of two; one of three, and one of five, arches. This last is over the Tay, and is the only bridge upon that wild river, as has been said before. It is built with astler-stone, and is 370 feet in length. The middle arch is sixty feet diameter, and it bears the following inscription, made Latin from English, as I have been told, by Dr Friend, Master of Westminster School:

Mirare
Viam hanc Militarem
Ultra Romanos Terminos
M. Passuum CCL. hac illac extensam
Tesquis et Paludibus insultantem
Per Rupes Montesque patefactam

Et indignanti Tavo
Ut cernis instratam
Opus hoc arduum sua solertia
Et decennali Militum Opera
Anno Ær. Christæ 1733, perfecit G. Wade.
Copiarum in Scotia Præfectus.
Ecce quantum valeant
Regia Georgii Secundi Auspicia.

The objections made to these new roads and bridges, by some in the several degrees of condition among the Highlanders, are in part as follow: viz.

I. Those chiefs and other gentlemen complain, that thereby an easy passage is opened into their country for strangers, who, in time, by their suggestions of liberty, will destroy or weaken that attachment of their vassals which it is so necessary for them to support and preserve.

That their fastnesses being laid open, they are deprived of that security from invasion which they formerly enjoyed.

That the bridges, in particular, will render the ordinary people effeminate, and less fit to pass the waters in other places where there are none.

And there is a pecuniary reason concealed, relating to some foreign courts, which to you I need not explain.

II. The middling order say the roads are to them an inconvenience, instead of being useful, as they have turned them out of their old ways; for their horses being never shod, the gravel would soon whet away their hoofs, so as to render them unserviceable: whereas the rocks and moorstones, though together they make a rough way, yet, considered separately, they are generally pretty smooth on the surface where they tread, and the heath is always easy to their feet. To this I have been inconsiderately asked, 'Why then do they not shoe their horses?'

This question is easily put, and costs nothing but a few various sounds. But where is the iron, the forge, the farrier, the people within a reasonable distance to maintain him? And lastly, where is the principal requisite – money?

III. The lowest class, who, many of them, at some times cannot compass a pair of shoes for themselves, they allege, that the gravel is intolerable to their naked feet; and the complaint has extended to their thin brogues.

It is true they do sometimes, for these reasons, go without the road, and ride or walk in very incommodious ways. This has induced some of our countrymen, especially such as have been at Minorca (where roads of this kind have likewise been made), to accuse the Highlanders of Spanish obstinacy, in refusing to make use of so great a conveniency, purely because it is a novelty introduced by the English. But why do the black cattle do the same thing? Certainly for the ease of their feet.

Nor can I believe that either Highlanders or Spaniards are such fools as to deprive themselves of any considerable benefit upon a principle so ridiculous. But I fear it is our own pride that suggests such contemptuous thoughts of strangers. I have seen a great deal of it, and have often thought of Lochart's accusation, in a book that goes under the name of his memoirs, where he says, 'The English despise all nations but their own, for which all the world hates them'; or to that purpose. But whether his observation be just or not, it is in the breast of every one to determine for himself. For my own part, ever since I have known the Highlands, I never doubted but the natives had their share of natural understanding with the rest of mankind.

Notwithstanding I have finished my account of the roads, which was all I at first intended, and although this letter is almost grown into a volume, yet, like other great talkers, I cannot conclude it with satisfaction to myself till I have told my tale quite out.

Fort Augustus, at Killichumen, is not only near the middle of the opening of which I have said so much, but is likewise reckoned to be the most centrical point of the habitable part of the Highlands.

The old barrack was built in the year 1716; I need not tell you upon what occasion. It stands upon a rising ground, at about two or three hundred yards distance from the head of Loch Ness, and the new fort is just upon the border of that water. Before there was any great progress made in building that fortress, it was proposed to make a covered way of communication between both, and that it should be the principal garrison of the Highlands, and the residence of a governor, who was likewise to command the other two in that line, viz. Fort George, at Inverness, and Fort William, in Lochaber, which two last were to be under the command of lieutenant-governors; this was the military scheme. But, besides there was a civil project on foot, which was to build a town after the English manner, and procure for it all the privileges and immunities of a royal borough in Scotland.

These advantages, it was said, would invite inhabitants to settle there, not only from the Lowlands, but even from England, and make it the principal part of the Highlands, by which means the natives would be drawn thither as to the centre; and by accustoming themselves to strangers, grow desirous of a more commodious way of living than their own, and be enabled by traffic to maintain it. And thus (it was said) they would be weaned from their barbarous customs. But surely this scheme was as wild as the Highlanders whom it was proposed to tame by it; yet it was entertained for some months with fondness. But anger blinds and deceives the judgment by the promised sweets of revenge, as avarice does by the pleasing thoughts of gain, though unlawful. And I think I may premise to what I am about to say, that successful revenge is wicked; but an impotent desire of it is not only wicked, but ridiculous. Perhaps you will say I moralize, and you do not yet see the application; but you will hardly believe that this Utopian town had no other foundation than a pique against two or three of the magistrates of Inverness, for whose transgression their town was to be humbled by this contrivance.

I shall wave all considerations of the intent to punish a whole community upon a prejudice taken against two or three of them, and only show you how improbable the success of such an undertaking would have been: and if it had been likely, how distant the prospect of the pleasure proposed by it.

A town of any manner of consideration would take up all, or most part of the country (for so the Highlanders call every arable flat that lies between the mountains); and the place is not above five-and-twenty miles (including the lake) from Inverness, which is a seaport town, and well situated for improvement of foreign trade and home manufactures. But the inner parts of the Highlands will not admit even of manufactories; for the inhabitants are few that can be spared from their farms, which, though they are but small, are absolutely necessary to life; and they are scattered among the hills at great distances, and the habitable spaces are generally not large enough to contain any considerable number of people, or the whole country within reach all round about, sufficient to furnish them with necessary provisions. And lastly, strangers will not be admitted among the clans.

By the way, I have been told the Welsh are not much less averse than the Highlanders to any settlement of strangers among them, though extremely hospitable to visitants, and such as have some temporary business to transact in their country. But to return to my purpose.

As to the corn received by the lairds from their tenants, as rent in kind, and the cattle, when marketable, the first has always been sold by contract to Lowland merchants, and the cattle are driven to such fairs and markets of the low country as are nearest, or otherwise commodious or beneficial to the drovers and their employers. And therefore there is no manner of likelihood that either the one or the other should be brought to any Highland market.

I have told you in a former letter, what kinds and quantities of merchandise were usually brought by the Highlanders, to the fairs at Inverness.

It was a supposition very extraordinary to suppose, that any Lowlanders who could subsist in another place, would shut themselves up in such a prison, without any reasonable prospect of advantage; and I verily believe there is not an Englishman, when he knew the country, but would think of a settlement there with more horror than any Russian would do of banishment to Siberia.

But lastly, if it were possible to suppose there were none of these obstacles, how long a time must have been required to people this new colony, and to render it capable to rival an old established town like Inverness: I need not recite the proverb of the growing grass; it is too obvious.

Yet if the inhabitants of the new settlement proposed, could have lived upon air, I verily believe they would have been fed with better diet than at Montpelier.

Thus am I providing work for myself, but am not so sure it will be entertainment to you; for now I have happened to speak of the healthfulness of the spot, I must tell you whereupon I found my opinion.

The officers and soldiers garrisoned in that barrack, for many successions have found it to be so; and several of them who were fallen into a valetudinary state in other parts, have there recovered their health in a short time. Among other instances, I shall give you only one, which I thought almost a miracle.

A certain officer of the army, when in London, was advised by his physicians to go into the country for better air, as you know is customary with them, when mere shame deters them from taking further fees; and likewise that the patient may be hid under ground, out of the reach of all reflecting observation within the circuit of their practice. But the corps he belonged to being then quartered in the Highlands, he resolved by gentle journeys, to endeavour to reach it, but expected (as he told me) nothing but death by the way; however he came to that place one evening, unknown to me, though I was then in the barrack, and the next morning early I saw upon the parade, a stranger, which is there an unusual sight. He was in a deep consumption, sadly emaciated, and with despair in his counten-ance, surveying the tops of the mountains. I went to him; and after a few words of welcome, etc., his uttermost thoughts became audible in a moment. 'Lord!' says he, 'to what a place am I come? There can nothing but death be expected here.' I own I had conceived a good opinion of that part of the country, and, therefore, as well as in common complaisance, should in course have given him some encouragement: but I do not know how it was; I happened at that instant to be, as it were, inspired with a confidence not ordinary with me, and told him peremptorily and positively the country would cure him; and repeated several times, as if I knew it would be so. How ready is hope with her assistance! Immediately I observed his features to clear up, like the day, when the sun begins to peep over the edge of a cloud.

To be short: he mended daily in his health, grew perfectly well in a little time, obtained leave to return to England, and soon after married a woman with a considerable fortune.

I know so well your opinion of the doctor's skill, that, if I should tell you there was not a physician in the country, you would say it was that very want which made the air so healthy, and was the cause of that wonderful cure.

This poor but wholesome spot reminds me of a quack that mounted a stage in Westminster, but was there very unsuccessful in the sale of his packets. At the end of his harangue he told his mob audience (among whom, being but a boy, myself was one), that he should immediately truss up his baggage and be gone, because he found they had no occasion for physic; 'For,' says he, 'you live in an air so healthy, that where one of you dies, there are twenty that run away.' But to proceed to a conclusion, which I foresee is not far off.

At Fort William, which is not above three or four and twenty miles westward of Fort Augustus, I have heard the people talk as familiarly of a shower (as they call it) of nine or ten weeks, as they would do of anything else that was not out of the ordinary course; but the clouds that are brought oversea by the westerly winds are there attracted and broke by the exceedingly high mountains, and mostly exhausted before they reach the middle of the Highlands at Fort Augustus; and nothing has been more common with us about Inverness, on the east coast, than to ride or walk to recreate ourselves in sunshine, when we could clearly see through the opening, for weeks together, the west side of the island involved in thick clouds. This was often the occasion of a good-natured triumph with us to observe what a pickle our opposite neighbours were in; but I am told the difference in that particular, between the east and western part of England, near the coast, is much the same in proportion to the height of the hills.

I have but one thing more to take notice of in relation to the spot of which I have been so long speaking, and that is, I have been sometimes vexed with a little plague (if I may use the expression), but do not you think I am too grave upon the subject; there are great swarms of little flies which the natives call 'malhoulakins': 'houlack', they tell me, signifies, in the country language, a fly, and 'houlakin' is the diminutive of that name. These are so very small, that, separately, they are but just perceptible and that is all; and, being of a blackish colour, when a number of them settle upon the skin, they make it look as if it was dirty; there they soon bore with their little augers into the pores, and change the face from black to red.

They are only troublesome (I should say intolerable) in summer, when, there is a profound calm; for the least breath or wind immediately disperses them; and the only refuge from them is the house, into which I never knew them to enter. Sometimes, when I have been talking to any one, I have (though with the utmost self-denial) endured their stings to watch his face, and see how long they would suffer him to be quiet; but in three or four seconds, he has slapped his hand upon his face, and in great wrath cursed the little vermin: but I have found the same torment in some other parts of the Highlands where woods were at no great distance.

Here I might say, if it did not something savour of a pun, that I have related to you the most minute circumstances of this long and straight opening of the mountains.

As my former letters relating to this country were the effects of your choice, I could then apologize for them with a tolerable grace; but now that I have obtruded myself upon you, without so much as asking your consent, or giving you the least notice, I have divested myself of that advantage, and therefore shall I take the quite contrary course, and boldly justify myself in what I have done. You know there is no other rule to judge of the quality of many things but by comparison; and this being of their nature, I do affirm with the last confidence (for I have not been here so long for nothing), that the following subjects are inferior to mine either for information or entertainment, viz.

Firstly. The genealogy of a particular family, in which but very few others are interested; and, by the by, for you know I am apt to digress, it must be great good nature and Christian charity to suppose it impossible that any one of the auxiliary sex should step out of the way to the aid of some other in the many successions of five hundred years; and, if that should happen, I would know what relation there then is between him that boasts of his ancestry and the founder of the family; certainly none but the estate; and if that which is the main prop should fail, the high family would soon tumble from its eminence; but this is but very little of that just ridicule that attends this kind of vanity.

We are told that none are gentlemen among the Chinese, but such as have rendered themselves worthy of the title.

Secondly. Tedious collections of the sentiments of great numbers of authors upon subjects that, in all likelihood, had never any being – but this is a parade of reading.

Thirdly. Trifling antiquities, hunted out of their mouldy recesses, which serve to no other purpose but to expose the injudicious searcher.

Fourthly. Tiresome criticisms upon a single word, when it is not of the least consequence whether there is, or ever was, any such sound.

Fifthly. Dissertations upon butterflies, which would take up almost as much time in the reading as the whole life of that insect – *cum multis aliis.*

This small scrap of Latin has escaped me, and I think it is the only 'air' of learning, as they call it, that I have given to any of my letters, from the beginning to this time, and even now I might have expressed the sense of it in homely English with as few words, and a sound as agreeable to the ear: but some are as fond of larding with Latin as a French cook is with bacon, and each of them makes of his performance a kind of linsey-woolsey composition.

As this letter is grown too bulky for the post, it will come to your hands by the favour of a gentleman, Major —, who is to set out for London tomorrow morning upon an affair that requires his expedition.

I can justly recommend him to your acquaintance, as I have already referred him to yours; and I do assure you, that, by his ingenious and cheerful conversation, he has not a little contributed, for a twelvemonth past, to render my exile more tolerable; it is true I might have sent the sheets in parcels, but I have chosen rather to surprise you with them all at once; and I dare say, bating accidents, you will have the last of them sooner by his means than by the ordinary conveyance.